3000 800026 74605
St. Louis Community College

D0205303

BEST RADIO PLAYS OF 1984

Previous Giles Cooper Award volumes

Pearl by John Arden (Special Award 1978)

Best Radio Plays of 1978
Richard Harris: *Is It Something I Said?*
Don Haworth: *Episode on a Thursday Evening*
Jill Hyem: *Remember Me*
Tom Mallin: *Halt! Who Goes There?*
Jennifer Phillips: *Daughters of Men*
Fay Weldon: *Polaris*

Best Radio Plays of 1979
Shirley Gee: *Typhoid Mary*
Carey Harrison: *I Never Killed My German*
Barrie Keeffe: *Heaven Scent*
John Kirkmorris: *Coxcomb*
John Peacock: *Attard in Retirement*
Olwen Wymark: *The Child*

Best Radio Plays of 1980
Stewart Parker: *The Kamikaze Groundstaff Reunion Dinner*
Martyn Read: *Waving to a Train*
Peter Redgrove: *Martyr of the Hives*
William Trevor: *Beyond the Pale*

Best Radio Plays of 1981
Peter Barnes: *The Jumping Mimuses of Byzantium*
Don Haworth: *Talk of Love and War*
Harold Pinter: *Family Voices*
David Pownall: *Beef*
J.P. Rooney: *The Dead Image*
Paul Thain: *The Biggest Sandcastle in the World*

Best Radio Plays of 1982
Rhys Adrian: *Watching the Plays Together*
John Arden: *The Old Man Sleeps Alone*
Harry Barton: *Hoopoe Day*
Donald Chapman: *Invisible Writing*
Tom Stoppard: *The Dog It Was That Died*
William Trevor: *Autumn Sunshine*

Best Radio Plays of 1983
Wally K. Daly: *Time Slip*
Shirley Gee: *Never In My Lifetime*
Gerry Jones: *The Angels They Grow Lonely*
Steve May: *No Exceptions*
Martyn Read: *Scouting for Boys*

BEST RADIO PLAYS OF 1984

The Giles Cooper Award Winners

Stephen Dunstone: Who Is Sylvia?
Robert Ferguson: Transfigured Night
Don Haworth: Daybreak
Caryl Phillips: The Wasted Years
Christopher Russell: Swimmer
Rose Tremain: Temporary Shelter

METHUEN/BBC PUBLICATIONS

First published in Great Britain in 1985 by Methuen London Ltd, 11 New Fetter Lane, London EC4P 4EE and in the USA by Methuen Inc, 733 Third Avenue, New York, NY 10017, and BBC Publications, 35 Marylebone High Street, London W1M 4AA.

Set in IBM 10 point Journal by Tek-Art, Croydon, Surrey
Printed and bound in Great Britain by
Biddles Ltd, Guildford and King's Lynn

British Library Cataloguing in Publication Data

Best radio plays of 1984: the Giles Cooper
Award winners.
1. Radio plays
822'.02'08 PN6120.R2

ISBN 0-413-58430-5

CONTENTS

THE GILES COOPER AWARDS: a note on the selection

Giles Cooper

As one of the most original and inventive radio playwrights of the post-war years, Giles Cooper was the author who came most clearly to mind when the BBC and Methuen were in search of a name when first setting up their jointly sponsored radio drama awards in 1978. Particularly so, as the aim of the awards is precisely to encourage original radio writing by both new and established authors – encouragement in the form of both public acclaim and of publication of their work in book form.

Eligibility

Eligible for the awards was every original radio play first broadcast by the BBC domestic service from December 1983 to December 1984 (almost 500 plays in total). Excluded from consideration were translations, adaptations and dramatised 'features'. In order to ensure that the broad range of radio playwrighting was represented, the judges aimed to select plays which offered a variety of length, subject matter and technique by authors with differing experience of writing for radio.

Selection

The producers-in-charge of the various drama 'slots' were each asked to put forward about five or six plays for the judges' consideration. This resulted in a 'short-list' of some 30 plays from which the final selection was made. The judges were entitled to nominate further plays for consideration provided they were eligible. Selection was made on the strength of the script rather than of the production, since it was felt that the awards were primarily for writing and that production could unduly enhance or detract from the merits of the original script.

Judges

The judges for the 1983 awards were:

Martin Esslin, Professor of Drama, Stanford University, California and ex-head of BBC Radio Drama
Nicholas Hern, Drama Editor, Methuen London
Richard Imison, Script Editor, BBC Radio Drama
Gillian Reynolds, radio critic, *The Daily Telegraph*

PREFACE

During the past year there has been a great deal of talk, in different circles, about the future of broadcasting. There's nothing too unusual about that, of course; periodically, the press, politicians, and the broadcasters themselves – not to mention the all-important listeners and viewers who are their customers – feel it necessary to call for a fresh examination of the phenomenon which in the short space of only sixty years has grown from a technological curiosity for the privileged few into one of the most influential developments of the twentieth century. It has become almost an obligatory ritual to demonstrate that the media which have come so to dominate our lives in the western world are still actually in our control; that the private anxieties to which they give rise may find an effective public expression. It's rather like keeping a large and powerful dog, of which one is basically fond but, occasionally, secretly afraid, and calling it to heel – just to make sure.

This time, however, I believe the debate has been different and deeper, even if not all of those taking part have been aware of it. During 1984 we have not merely been concerned with trends and directions within a well-established pattern of radio and television broadcasting but with fundamental, perhaps revolutionary, developments from which no single activity within broadcasting is likely to emerge unchanged.

On the face of it, the discussion has often appeared to the layman to be on less radical lines, even if the technological advances are mysteriously exciting and the financial implications bewilderingly large. Shall we have DBS and Cable, Teletext and Videorecording? Will it all be in colour, quadraphony and ambisonics? Will it be personal and portable? Before long, shall we feel cheated if programmes have not been individually summoned out of the ether by our own individual dish aerials from a country and channel of our choice? Who shall decide and who shall organise? How much will it all cost and who shall pay for it? Does any of it matter, so long as we can still see *Dallas* and *Dynasty?*

Actually, it matters very much. The unparalleled opportunities which seem currently to face both broadcasters and their public bring with them unparalleled problems. And they are not only financial ones. True, the world's radio and television companies stand like children gazing into the windows of a toyshop of almost unimaginable splendour, while nervously counting the inadequate number of coins in their pockets. True also that in both the public service and the commercial sector there can be an inconvenient divergence between what is affordable and what the public wants. But as those who have been in the business a long time gradually learn to substitute 'video' for television and 'audio' for radio (at least in some instances) so there begin to emerge even greater problems of priority and of definition than those imposed merely by their purses.

It is understandable that most of the debate about serving a broadcasting public turns on the means of transmission rather than the environment for creation because that is to the individual listener and viewer the question that appears to matter most. 'I want what I want, when I want it' as a demand actually seems more reasonable now, when the technology to achieve such an end is with us, or nearly with us, than it used to when that was hardly even conceivable. Moreover, this last year has made it increasingly clear that, in the developed West at least, we are undergoing a revolution that is as much social as technological; one that seems likely to result in ever-increasing numbers of people having ever-increasing amounts of time in their adult lives to devote to leisure pursuits. So, the broadcasters' apparent concentration on the proliferation of services and the extension of broadcasting hours to cater for the needs of different groups at different times seems a justifiable and positive response to society's changing needs.

It would be jumping the gun as yet to take the audio/video argument to its logical conclusion and see in the cassette the answer to perfectly flexible programming. We are still some way from a time when all pre-recorded material might simply be made available in some form to individual listeners and viewers to see and hear at their own leisure; a time when broadcasting itself might have become an old-fashioned concept. But we may already be dangerously close to a time when the editorial implications of a shift in emphasis from the built programmes of the first fifty years of broadcasting to an increasing use of generic services have to be recognised and resolved.

Which brings me to the position of radio drama. And also to a definition of the problems I have been hinting at. For radio drama – in Great Britain at least – in many ways exemplifies an aspect of the broadcasters' responsibility which is every bit as important as high-quality signals and skilful scheduling. The broadcasting organisations are not only purveyors of information and entertainment but they are among the most influential patrons of the writer and artist. It is a role that we forget – or even simply undervalue – at our peril.

In past volumes I have referred to the size and diversity of the market for radio plays. In 1984, the output was as large and varied as ever, with well over 300 original single plays on Radio 4 and Radio 3, out of a massive total of nearly 2000 broadcasts, including series and serials, adaptations, features, readings and poetry emanating from the BBC's Drama Department. In the course of the year nearly 80 playwrights had their work performed, for the first time in any medium – a figure only a little larger than usual but almost certainly due to the very positive response to the Radio Times Play Competition held in the winter of 1982-83.

An average of six new plays every week on radio, sharing air time with classics of the theatre and literature and a whole range of drama in serial form, might seem prodigal if you consider that drama is one of the more expensive ways of using the medium but it is not an example of BBC wastefulness or vainglory. It is both symbol and expression of a continuing commitment to writers and to listeners. In its mixture of entertainment and education, together with a conscious invitation to draw comparisons with existing traditions from other media, the drama output is in the classical mould of public service broadcasting. Expensive only in radio terms, it is highly cost effective; one of the Best Bargain's best bargains.

How well does it succeed in fulfilling the ideals on which it was founded? Can it, in the harsh economic realities of the eighties, and in the face of fierce competition for scarce resources, justify a position of continuing importance in the plans for radio's future? The first question must be asked, and honestly answered, at frequent intervals. The second led me to the argument presented here, for it involves the key role of patron, with all that it implies, for those who contribute to, and those who simply receive, the broadcasting services.

A good patron is a supporter and encourager; one who creates opportunities; an enabler; a guardian saint. In centuries past, these excellent qualities were often selfishly motivated. The artists so supported, and works thereby created, were for the private pleasure of the patron – or to enhance his reputation among his acquaintances. Public patronage has a wider aim. It is to create the conditions in which artists can flourish, for the benefit of all – and thereby to offer a service to the community which the community had not itself dreamed of. Which is not at all the same thing as giving people what they want, but leads – if successfully practised – to a growing range of things which people discover they are prepared to like.

In pursuing these ends, radio drama can, I believe, point to two quite surprising successes. The first lies in the quantity and quality of submitted work, of which even the large number of transmissions quoted above represent only about one tenth. The second is the enormous numbers of people who regularly listen to radio plays – even the difficult ones – despite the tempting range of alternative entertainments now available. The experimental play which may be given wide critical attention in the national press having been seen by a few hundred people (or less) in a fringe theatre is likely to attract at least fifty thousand in radio. Daytime drama on Radio 4, broadcast every day of the week and including three original plays alongside repeats of evening plays such as Saturday Night Theatre or the more demanding Monday Play, was regularly heard in 1984 by about three million.

Within its wide range, radio drama can be a national theatre and a nursery slope; an upholder of traditional values, an explorer of social conscience or an advanced research worker in the dramatic laboratory of the mind. Of these intriguing possibilities, the first two are, I think, quite often achieved with immediate effect for the listener and sometimes a delayed one for the television, film or theatre audience. The third category has grown in importance in radio's output, though caution about the sensibilities of the audience in their domestic surroundings often inhibits the achievement of total realism. That is an important debate which will continue, and doubtless lead to evolution, in the coming year. The last form has always been a rare one, and remains so, though it would be good to see it more often attempted.

As before, the good plays in this volume stand for many more. They have won the acclaim of professionals and will, we hope, inspire others. This year, they are also a piece of tangible evidence in the discussion of the future of broadcasting; a public reminder, perhaps, that public service is many-layered. The plays that did not reach this volume also contributed largely to that service, as did others that did not even reach the air. The point is that they might have done; the opportunity and the encouragement were there. It was worthwhile putting pen to paper once, and it will be so again – to ensure one part of broadcasting in the future.

Richard Imison
(January 1985)

WHO IS SYLVIA?

by Stephen Dunstone

For A.B.D.

Stephen Dunstone was born in Winchester in 1955. He was educated at Winchester College and subsequently at the Universities of Cambridge (where he read German, Danish and Old Norse Literature) and Durham. He taught German for a while, then took a part-time job teaching the flute so that he could devote the rest of his time to writing and music: he is the flautist of the New Cambridge Wind Quintet.

He has written four novels, two of them for children, a number of short stories and two radio plays. The first play, *Who Is Sylvia?* shared first prize in the *Radio Times* Drama Awards for 1983, and has been translated into French, German, Norwegian and Hebrew.

Who Is Sylvia? was first broadcast on BBC Radio 3 on 29 April 1984. The cast was as follows:

ANGELA	Anna Massey
HENRY	Nigel Hawthorne
MICHAEL	Martin Jarvis
SIR ARCHIBALD SOPWITH-PLACKETT	Michael Aldridge
SYLVIA	Frances Jeater

Director: John Tydeman
Running time, as broadcast: 75 minutes 37 seconds.

In the background, just discernible, the closing bars of the 2nd movement of Beethoven's 5th Piano Concerto in E flat, 'The Emperor'.

ANGELA. Henry?

HENRY. Mm?

ANGELA. Oh, Henry, do look.

HENRY. Mm? What?

ANGELA. It'll be any minute now.

HENRY. Of course, yes, forgive me darling, I was thinking of something quite different. Where is it now? Ah yes . . . Yes. (*He looks.*) Are you sure?

ANGELA. Of course I'm sure, darling. Mothers know these things.

Pause while they both study the egg-capsule, or ootheca.

I'm so excited. Aren't you?

HENRY (*with suppressed paternal pride*). Well yes, I must confess I am rather, darling. After all, it's not every day . . .

ANGELA. No . . . (*She sighs.*) A hatching . . . Our very own. It makes me so happy. (*She sighs again. Then, suddenly.*) Ooh, there! Henry! It's starting to split, I'm sure it is!

HENRY. You're right! Darling, I think you're right!

ANGELA. Oh, Henry . . .!

HENRY. Angela . . .

ANGELA. I'm so excited. I wonder how many it'll be.

HENRY. Ken and Doreen had twelve nymphs.

ANGELA. Don't talk to me about Ken and Doreen. I have no desire to hear about them.

HENRY. Darling, simply because they're not our sort of . . .

He is interrupted by ANGELA*'s gasp as the ootheca suddenly splits open. The barely discernible background music slips into the last movement of the concerto.*

ANGELA (*beside herself with joy*). Darling! Oh Darling! I've waited so long . . . Oh Henry, do look, how many can you count? Aren't they adorable? So beautiful, so pale, so translucent. And so . . . innocent. So defenceless without their wings. And so like you . . .! Oh, Henry. I'm sure there are at least twelve, if not more. One, two, three, four – no, no wait, did I count that one? – start again: one, two, three, four, five . . .

HENRY *counts as well. They both count together, but not simultaneously.*

HENRY. One, two, three . . . (*etc.*)

ANGELA. One, two, three . . . (*etc.*)

Neither gets beyond ten, despite several attempts.

Eleven.

HENRY. No, ten I think, darling.

ANGELA. Are you sure?

HENRY. Fairly positive.

ANGELA. There's another one in there!

HENRY Is there? (*After investigation.*) No, I'm afraid it's only embryonic membrane.

ANGELA (*disappointed*). Oh. Still, ten . . .

HENRY. Ten. Ten is a very fine number.

ANGELA. And they are beautiful.

HENRY. It's quality we're talking about.

ANGELA. Not quantity.

HENRY. Exactly.

ANGELA. What I'd do with twelve I don't know.

HENRY. Running around . . .

ANGELA. Getting under our feet.

HENRY. Precisely.

ANGELA. And not able to tell one from another.

HENRY. Quite.

ANGELA. Well. . . . There we are then. Ten fine nymphs! How many boys?

HENRY. How many girls, come to that.

ANGELA. You count the girls, I'll count the boys.

HENRY. All right.

They count, as before, together, but independently.

ANGELA. One . . . two . . . three . . . four . . . five.

HENRY. One . . . two . . . three . . . four . . . five.

ANGELA. Well!

HENRY. As you say.

ANGELA. Fancy that!

HENRY. Perfect.

ANGELA. Just as I've always dreamed it. (*Dreamily.*) Maurice, Sebastian, Paul, Anthony, and . . . Thomas.

HENRY (*equally dreamily*). Sarah, Elizabeth, Rebecca . . .

ANGELA. Angela.

HENRY. Angela? But you're Angela.

ANGELA. Well? Why not?

HENRY. Oh, well, yes why not? Angela . . . and . . . and. . . Sylvia.

ANGELA (*very dreamily*). Sylvia . . .

Music: 'Who is Silvia?' from 'Let Us Garlands Bring' by Gerald Finzi. Opening announcement. Music up then fade.

ANNOUNCER. At the private research laboratory of Sir Archibald Sopwith-Plackett, a year has gone by since the hatching of the nymphs . . .

The office. Silence, but for a large clock ticking. Into this almost-silence: the sound of MICHAEL *whistling amusically under his breath as he checks various sheets of paper at his desk.*

MICHAEL (*musingly, very much to himself*). Hm hm . . . Hmmm . . . Mm. Hm . . . Hmhmmmm. (*He reverts to whistling under his breath; other oral noises made by a man when alone. Noises of* SIR ARCHIBALD SOPWITH-PLACKETT *approaching. The inner door opens, the whistling stops; and as the door closes:*

MICHAEL. Afternoon, Sir Archibald.

PLACKETT. Afternoon Michael. You're in early today. Been here long?

Sounds of outdoor garments being removed. PLACKETT *continues to talk as he puts his lab coat on.*

MICHAEL. Oh, not long. Checked up here and there. Last year's cockroach nymphs have finished their final moult: all of them, those we put in the constant-light and those in the constant-dark tanks as well.

PLACKETT. Good, good. Excellent. We'll be able to start some real work on their circadian rhythms now. That's fine . . . fine. How about the adult male we put under constant-dark at the end of last week?

MICHAEL. It's rather as we thought last night: the graphs show a distinct loss of activity rhythm at last.

PLACKETT. Good. That's fine. I want to do a transplant job on him. If we take one of the new adult males from normal conditions we can transplant its suboesophageal ganglion into old big daddy there, and we should see a revival of rhythm. Good subjects, Periplaneta, good subjects. Tried a fungus beetle once –

MICHAEL. Boletotheros Cornutus?

PLACKETT. That's the fella, used him have you?

MICHAEL. No, just read the Park and Keeper report in *Ecology*.

PLACKETT. Much the same findings. My little bugger kept its rhythm for three and a half months under constant darkness. Three and a half months! Just think what you can do in three and a half months!

MICHAEL. Go round the world one and a third times.

PLACKETT. Quite.

MICHAEL. If you're doing it the hard way.

PLACKETT. Well, yes, goes without saying. Did you do much on rhythms at King's?

MICHAEL. No, I didn't as it happens. It was mostly pest-control research, linked to the sex-attractant pheromones, actually, that we've got down for tomorrow.

PLACKETT. Ah yes. Yes.

MICHAEL. I did do a little on the stick-insect, purely on its locomotor activity rhythm.

PLACKETT. Ah: brain extirpation.

MICHAEL. Yes. We found that brain extirpation, destruction of the anterior brain, extirpation of the suboesophageal ganglion and section of the circumoesophageal ganglion connections all abolished the insect's rhythm.

PLACKETT. Remarkable.

MICHAEL. What was more remarkable was that we couldn't restore the rhythm by the implantation of either brains or ganglia.

PLACKETT. Poor old Carausius Morosus!

MICHAEL. Poor old him indeed. But I'm glad to be on cockroaches.

PLACKETT. Good. Well back to work then.

There is the sound of their passing from office to lab. Then, as the door is closed and they cross the floor:

MICHAEL. Yes. How is Lady Mary this afternoon? Is she any better?

PLACKETT (*thoughtfully*). No . . . no, she's not. You know, I have a . . .

They pause, having reached their objective.

MICHAEL. Yes?

PLACKETT. Well, I have an idea, I hope, that is, I sincerely hope, that she thinks it's worse than it is. Or rather what I mean is: I hope that it's not as bad as she thinks, or fears. And that it's her fears which are making her weak now.

MICHAEL. So it all depends on . . .?

PLACKETT. Exactly. It all depends on the doctor's findings.

MICHAEL. And when are they due?

PLACKETT. Tomorrow? Day after tomorrow?

MICHAEL. I'll keep my fingers tightly crossed.

PLACKETT. Do that. Do that, Michael.

MICHAEL. How's . . . er . . . how's . . . have you heard from . . . er . . .?

PLACKETT. Sylvia?

MICHAEL. Er . . . yes.

PLACKETT. Michael, you are a picture when you're embarrassed.

MICHAEL (*embarrassed*). Oh.

PLACKETT. The delectable Sylvia. You've lusted after my daughter since the day you saw her.

MICHAEL (*still embarrassed – the embarrassment of True Love*). Well, I . . . er . . . think that's . . . er . . .

PLACKETT. But I forgive you, Michael, I forgive you. I can't think of anyone I'd rather have her marry, so you're quite safe. But in answer to your question: no, I haven't heard from her since the beginning of term. And now, both for professional reasons and to save you further embarrassment, we will abstain from idle chatter and embark upon the delicately arduous, the arduously delicate task of suboesophageal ganglion transplantation.

PLACKETT *presses the 'eject' button on a cassette recorder.*

What shall we listen to today?

MICHAEL. Mozart?

PLACKETT. You are a glutton for Mozart.

He searches through cassettes, and selects one.

Mozart. K467?

MICHAEL. Perfect.

PLACKETT. I couldn't agree more.

He presses 'play' and the music begins, then fades.

The music reappears 'pianissimo' at a later stage in the second movement, as if it is now heard considerably muffled through the walls of a large glass laboratory tank, which indeed it is.

ANGELA (*after a while*). It's no good, Henry, you must eat.

HENRY (*a barely audible grunt*). Nng.

ANGELA. Please, Henry . . . For my sake. Oh, Henry . . .

HENRY (*deciding that true depression is fading into truculence*). Hm.

ANGELA (*tentatively relieved*). There Henry, it'll make you feel so much better. A little bit of food. There. I don't know why you've been like this lately. Tell me. Tell me about it.

HENRY. I don't know that you'd understand.

ANGELA. Oh Henry, how can you say that? After the time we've been together!

HENRY. I'm sorry, darling; I don't know that I understand myself. It's just ever since . . . except that it's not ever since, obviously, I mean there was that moment, of course, just after they hatched – I shall never forget, never – when the creature came and . . . took them, just took them, but that was a year ago! And then I remember so well, it was you who was so upset, so bewildered, while I had to be strong, and I was so worried about you. Then we seemed to be contented enough, after all we still had Sebastian –

ANGELA. And Anthony –

HENRY. And Sylvia –

ANGELA. Of course Sylvia. (*He gives a little laugh.*) Strange, but I can hardly think of a time without Sylvia.

HENRY. She's been a tower of strength.

ANGELA. She has, she has . . .

HENRY (*a trace of his depression returning*). But it's been there all the time, underneath.

ANGELA (*firmly*). No, Henry.

HENRY (*oblivious of her*). Underneath it all, a sense of . . . a sense of what? I don't know. A sense of just that: that we don't understand.

ANGELA. Now, Henry, pull yourself –

HENRY. Perhaps it was Ken and Doreen going so suddenly, last week, and Darren.

ANGELA (*offended at the mention*). Henry, please! They may have had their misfortune, but –

HENRY. 'They may have' – no, darling, they have, and they're only cockroaches like the rest of us.

ANGELA. No, Henry, that's where you're wrong. The one thing that has given me strength in all this is the knowledge that we are different. We must beware of false sympathy. If we are to be able to rebuild our lives once more as they used to be, once the crisis is over, then we must uphold the values we know to be true. I won't deny that they lost a lot of their nymphs at the same time as we did, but they were left with four and that's one more than we had, once our Sarah and Elizabeth went, don't forget that. And those two girls of theirs and that nasty-looking boy whose name I forget are so very simple, you can't dispute that. Not an intelligent thought between them.

HENRY (*reluctantly*). No . . .

ANGELA. And Darren! He is simply unpleasant. He is coarse and vulgar. It's a blessing that he's gone. And I shouldn't be surprised (*she lowers her voice*) I shouldn't be surprised if Ken used to . . . beat them.

HENRY. Oh, darling.

ANGELA. Not that that is a cause for sympathy either. They deserved every bit of what they got.

HENRY. But darling, it could scarcely be said to be their fault.

ANGELA (*incredulous*). Not their fault! My dear Henry, they didn't have to behave like young vandals, the boys egging the girls on to do all sorts of . . . unpleasantnesses. They could at least have spoken civilly. At least I would have expected it of the girls.

HENRY. But darling, consider their background.

ANGELA. That's just what I am considering, Henry. Do you remember when we first introduced ourselves? And we had such high hopes? (*She reconstructs.*) 'I'm very pleased to meet you. I'm Angela and this is my husband Henry.' (*She reverts to the present.*) And the way she replied: 'Ooh 'ello Ange!' Ange! She'd not known me ten seconds before she was calling me Ange! (*Again she reconstructs, imitating* DOREEN'*s accent with relish.*) ''ello Ange, I'm Doreen.' *Do*reen. 'And this is Ken – Kenneth.' (*She imitates* KEN.) ''ello, Ange, 'ello 'enry.'

HENRY *is starting to chuckle, despite himself, at the vivacity of* ANGELA'*s performance.*

'Pleased to meet you, Kenneth. Where are you both from?' (*Imitating* DOREEN *again.*) 'Ooh we come only today from a Transport Cafe, nice it were, every so nice, warm, not that this isn't warm, here, nice place you've got yourselves.' 'This isn't our place Doreen, we only arrived yesterday.' 'Oh really, oh well, nice all the same, but as I say the Transport was nice, lavatories we was in, very nice.' Darling! The lavatories. I didn't dare tell her that our ancestors came from the dining-hall of Magdelene College Cambridge!

HENRY. You did tell her, darling.

ANGELA. Did I? Perhaps I did, but it didn't seem to have much effect. And her laugh! Darling, her laugh! How we put up with it for so long! (*More than a year's pent-up desire to imitate* DOREEN*'s laugh is released in a high-pitched, unutterably common cackle.*)

HENRY, *despite his more charitable nature, cannot help laughing. She repeats her performance. Soon they are both hooting and howling with helpless laughter.* SYLVIA *approaches and speaks across their laughter, which subsides.*

SYLVIA. Hello Mum, hello Dad!

She is clearly their daughter, but in her voice can be traced the inevitable result of having mixed with the wrong sort. There is no doubt that ANGELA *and* HENRY *dote. They also treat her rather as a last instar nymph, and not quite as the adult she is.*

ANGELA. Sylvia, darling, have you had a lovely time? Been for a little walk?

SYLVIA. Super thanks. Phew, I'm quite out of breath from running. Jackie and Tracy are –

ANGELA (*with a discernible cooling of affection*). Jackie and Tracy? Sylvia, have you –

SYLVIA. Let me finish, Mum. What I was going to say was –

ANGELA. Sylvia, it is enough that you mentioned them. You obviously have been –

SYLVIA. Oh Mum, be fair!

ANGELA. Please let me speak. I have made it quite plain that –

SYLVIA. Mum, I'm grown up, I can decide for myself.

ANGELA. Grown up or not, there are circumstances which you have yet to understand fully. Your father and I have been through a great deal. As you know, we have every expectation that this is not to be our permanent home, but that we shall go back to where we rightfully belong, and we cannot afford to have you –

SYLVIA. Oh earwigshit, Mum!

ANGELA (*gasps at the uncouth expression*). Sylvia . . .!

SYLVIA. Mum, look –

ANGELA (*sternly*). No, Sylvia, I will not look; I will –

HENRY. For heaven's sake, the pair of you! (*Silence. Then more gently, to* ANGELA.) Darling, let us at least hear what she has to say. Then we can decide.

ANGELA (*frostily*). Very well.

SYLVIA. Well, it's nothing really, I was just saying that Jackie and Tracy are . . . well, they're . . . I mean, I said to them that . . . that you'd said . . . well, I told them that as Ken and Doreen had gone, that, well . . . (*Lamely.*) That we wouldn't mind having them over our side.

There is a horrified silence within the tank. Beyond, the Mozart.

Anyway, Sebastian and Anthony are over there now. Sebastian spends more time than you know over there. He's got a thing about Tracy, too. He fancies her.

Who can say what would have ensued? The family drama is interrupted by the sound of heavy footsteps, gasps from within the tank, the sound of what is rather a large tank being opened, a slight increase in the volume of Mozart, and screams of horror, cries of 'No!' 'The creature!' 'Henry do something!' etc.

ANGELA. Henry!

HENRY. It's all right, darling. He's at the other end.

Distant sounds of panicking cockroaches.

ANGELA. But he might –

HENRY (*more confident than he feels*). No, darling, we're quite safe. I think we should be feeling a little sorry for Jackie and Tracy and . . . whatever that boy's called.

ANGELA (*immensely relieved*). Yes. Yes, Henry, you're quite right. We should be sympa- Henry! Henry! (*Mounting horror.*) Henreeeeee! He's got Sebastian! S E B A S T I A N!!!!! (*She sobs hysterically.*)

The footsteps retire. HENRY *is at a loss for words.*
SYLVIA *starts to sniffle. The only sounds are* SYLVIA'*s sniffling,* ANGELA'*s sobbing and the Mozart. Then the footsteps return, there is a pause as something is deposited in the tank, and the lid is closed, muffling the music. The footsteps, also muffled, retire again. Within the tank the sniffling and the sobbing cease as the three contemplate what has been put inside.*

SYLVIA. Who have they brought?

ANGELA (*dumbfounded*). It's . . . it's . . . No. It can't be. It is!

HENRY. I don't believe it.

SYLVIA. Who are they?

ANGELA. Don't you recognise your own sisters? It's Sarah and Elizabeth returned from the dead. Oh . . . oh . . . ooohh, I think . . . oh . . . ooohh. It's all too much, all of a sudden, everything all at once. . . . I'm . . . I'm going to . . . I'm . . . (*She faints.*)

HENRY. Now look what you've done! Well don't just stand there, girl. Go and say hello to your sisters!

The volume of music gradually fades up to end in a joyful C major cadence.

Sounds of the interior of a restaurant. Nothing brash – this is a superior place. Above this, the sound of MICHAEL *pouring himself a glass of wine. He tries it, and is favourably impressed. Then, as* PLACKETT *arrives:*

MICHAEL. Ah, Sir Archibald.

PLACKETT (*slightly subdued*). Hello, Michael, glad you've got the wine. You've ordered I take it?

MICHAEL. Yes. Shouldn't be long.

PLACKETT (*sits down*). The beef?

MICHAEL. Yes, I thought the beef.

PLACKETT. Good . . . That's fine.

Pause.

MICHAEL. Er . . . how's Lady Mary then? No worse I hope? Not since lunchtime.

PLACKETT (*rather wearily*). No, no not really. But you know, Michael, it's the way she looks at me.

MICHAEL. She doesn't object to our eating out?

PLACKETT. Dammit all, we've got to eat, haven't we? I can't cook, and she's in no position to. Not as if we've got servants nowadays. Only Alice. She brings in a meal for her, but she can't cater for us as well. No, it's not that anyway, she's always been very good about our strange timetable: it's not every husband who's out through the afternoon and most of the night. She's always said 'It is your science that must come first, my dear.' No . . . I mean it's the way she looks at me, not with reproach, but with . . . fear. This evening she said it for the first time, mentioned the word for the first time: 'Archie, tell me, I have got cancer, haven't I?' Cancer. She said it, not I.

MICHAEL. But . . . it's been at the back of both your minds for a while?

PLACKETT. Yes.

Pause.

MICHAEL. Would she rather we abandoned work for a time so that you can be with her?

PLACKETT. I think that would simply make it worse. It would convince her that I knew she was dying and was keeping information from her.

MICHAEL. Yes, I see.

PLACKETT. Ticklish one, isn't it?

MICHAEL. Certainly is.

PLACKETT. Obviously if when the doctor's findings are through we discover that she is, well that she has . . . you know . . . Well then perhaps we should hold our horses for a while on the nightly vigil. (*Brightening determinedly*). But let's not talk about it. What've you got for us here? Vosne-Romanée, eh? Hm.

MICHAEL. I know you prefer a claret –

PLACKETT. Don't mind in the least –

MICHAEL. But I was in Beaune last Easter, as you remember, and I got a crate of Vosne-Romanée from the vineyard. '78 it was though, and it's still rather too young I thought.

PLACKETT. What's this then? Oh, '71. Yes, should be all right by now. Come on then, let's be having some.

MICHAEL *pours for* PLACKETT. *They savour and taste together, expressing simultaneous approval.*

Not bad, not bad. Here's to . . .?

MICHAEL. Lady Mary of course.

PLACKETT. Lady Mary!

They drink. Pause.

PLACKETT. I think we should drink to you and Sylvia too.

MICHAEL (*confused*). Oh . . . er . . . (*He laughs, embarrassed.*)

PLACKETT. You and Sylvia! (*He drinks, smacks his lips etc., and puts the glass down.*) And now, tell me, any developments in the lab since I left?

MICHAEL. No, nothing startling. Those two injected females we put back into normal conditions haven't died yet.

PLACKETT. No. Good . . . good. We got the dose about right then. I'm pleased. It's so difficult to find the exact sub-lethal level. We can do the ultra-violet photography tonight. (*Suddenly worried.*) They're not normal are they, those two?

MICHAEL. Oh heavens no! Slowed right down.

PLACKETT (*relieved*). That's good. Fascinating to see how the heart copes under near paralysis. So that's tonight. And in addition to the usual observations of course there's the eye removal, we mustn't forget that.

MICHAEL. Male or female?

PLACKETT. Doesn't matter. Use a male, then we can dissect a couple of females for their corpora cardiaca tomorrow.

MICHAEL. Right.

PLACKETT. And start the parabiosis tomorrow, of course, as well.

MICHAEL. Yes, I'm a little uneasy about how that's to be done. Even if the one is decapitated and they're both linked into each other's blood system, might they not want to go in opposite directions and pull themselves apart?

PLACKETT. Ah no, Michael, you see we'll use the Harker method and strap the intact insect upside down to the decapitated one.

MICHAEL. Ah, yes. And cut its legs off?

PLACKETT. That's the job. You know it is a constant source of amazement to me how long a cockroach can survive after it's had its head cut off. I wish I'd known that when I was a lad at prep school. We just used to go round stamping on the things in the changing-rooms before breakfast. Of course the really interesting operation will be the day after, when we see what happens if you have two conflicting ganglia in one body. Ah, this looks like the meat. Pity we don't have time for a full-blown meal. William: how nice to see you.

Pause while the waiter serves them. They are known customers. Pleasantries are exchanged: 'How are you keeping sir Archibald?' 'Oh, fit as a fiddle,' etc. etc.

Jolly good. Tuck in then.

Subsequent dialogue is influenced by the fact of their eating and drinking. Civilised pause, which MICHAEL *uses obviously to enjoy his food, but mostly to build up to:*

MICHAEL. Er . . . Sir Archibald?

PLACKETT. Michael.

MICHAEL. It's . . . er . . . Sylvia.

PLACKETT. I should hope it is.

MICHAEL. No, er . . . well it's . . .

PLACKETT (*not conscious of the pun*). Spit it out.

MICHAEL. It's just that . . . (*It comes in a rush.*) Well obviously I don't see her while she's at Cambridge, and I haven't ever told her how I feel, and so I don't know how she feels, and she's younger than me —

PLACKETT (*with his mouth full*). Not much.

MICHAEL. No, but all the same, she is, and she's . . . (*Knowing that he's trotting out the clichés.*) Well, she's learning to fend for herself for the first time, up to a point, and she's in a very stimulating and interesting environment, and she's coming to terms with herself and what she wants to be, and there are bound to be . . . well, there are bound to be –

PLACKETT. Predators.

MICHAEL. What?

PLACKETT. Predators.

MICHAEL. Er . . .

PLACKETT. Men.

MICHAEL. Well . . .

PLACKETT. Yes.

MICHAEL (*glumly*). Yes.

PLACKETT. No.

MICHAEL. No?

PLACKETT. No. She adores you, Michael. Of course she does. She thinks the sun shines out of – she thinks you're marvellous.

MICHAEL (*determined not to be confused this time*). No, I'm sure she doesn't. And there are bound to be . . . well, as you say, predators. She's a fascinating girl, and she's not only fascinating but she's also fascinated: she's interested by so much that she sees, she can't fail to be interested by some irresistible Cambridge undergraduate.

PLACKETT. No, Michael. She's my daughter. Dammit all you forget, I may be an old codger, and pretty old to be her father, but I have known her for twenty years.

MICHAEL. But have you heard from her this term?

PLACKETT. Not yet.

MICHAEL. Well then.

PLACKETT. Dammit, Michael, she was at home six weeks ago.

MICHAEL. Yes, but it wasn't for long. She was off half the time abroad.

PLACKETT. Biology field trip in Spain.

MICHAEL. Things happen on field trips. Anyway, it was Portugal.

PLACKETT. Was it?

MICHAEL. Yes. You see, you don't know what she's doing. You don't know who she might be –

PLACKETT. Michael, my dear fellow, at this very minute you can bet your life she's settled down in the Scientific Periodicals library in Benet Street, and at ten to ten she'll close her books, yawn, say 'Dear oh dear what an exhausting day's work,' and toddle off to her little bed in Clare College. That's where all the clever women go, I'm told, nowadays: Clare.

MICHAEL. It's also where the liberated women go. They have mixed staircases.

PLACKETT. Wouldn't know. Magdalene man myself.

MICHAEL. Yes, I know.

PLACKETT. Fine college.

MICHAEL. I've no doubt.

PLACKETT. Candles in Hall.

MICHAEL. Really.

PLACKETT. Silver cutlery every day.

MICHAEL. Of course.

PLACKETT. Cockroaches swarming about the place every evening.

MICHAEL (*genuinely interested*). Really? Still? Isn't that a bit . . . unhygienic?

PLACKETT. Nothing a Magdalene man can't cope with. Here, have some more wine: help you through the long night hours . . .

MICHAEL. Mm. Perhaps I will . . .

The restaurant noise fades.

In the background, muffled, act one aria 'Non siate ritrosi occhietti vezzosi', from Mozart's Cosi fan tutte. ANGELA *is sobbing mightily,* HENRY *is attempting to console her.*

ANGELA. Boo hoo hoo (*etc.*)

HENRY. There there, darling, don't cry anymore.

ANGELA *continues to sob. Her sobbing is punctuated by speeches, rather than the other way round.*

You can't change anything by crying like this . . . We must learn to see things in perspective.

ANGELA (*he has chosen the wrong word*). 'See'!

HENRY. Speaking figuratively. But at least he was brought back to us. That much we do have. He is alive, darling. Alive.

ANGELA. My precious Anthony . . .

HENRY. He still is your precious Anthony, and mine, and we must be thankful.

ANGELA. But he's blind. (*She wails.*)

HENRY. Oh, darling . . .

ANGELA. I don't know why you're being so cheerful all of a sudden. You were the one who was so depressed this afternoon.

HENRY. Yes darling, but we can't have two of us in a state. I was wrong to let it affect me so before. Our only hope is to be strong. It's not as if it was anything that we did to make him blind; we mustn't reproach ourselves.

ANGELA (*reproaching herself*). We didn't love him enough, we let him wander, we let him go to the Other Side . . .

HENRY. Darling, I'm sure Jackie and Tracy are just as upset as we are –

ANGELA. How can they be?

HENRY. Well, almost as upset.

ANGELA. Yes, they don't quite care enough do they? You couldn't expect them to, with their background.

HENRY. Now darling, that's unfair. You know Sylvia came back and told us how sorry they were –

ANGELA. And how our own daughter could go gadding off to the likes of them at a time like this!

HENRY. Oh darling, be reasonable, she's been a model daughter. She's been tireless. You know she's shown nothing but concern first of all for Sarah and Elizabeth when they turned out to be so retarded, and now for Anthony.

Pause. ANGELA*'s sobbing eases into sniffles, which become only intermittent.*

HENRY. There, darling, there. . . . That's better. That's much better. Try a smile. Come on. You wouldn't want Anthony to see you so upset would you?

ANGELA (*wails again, before* HENRY *realises his gaff*). Ooooohhh! My poor Anthony, he'll never see me again. (*Renewed sobbing.*)

HENRY. No no, darling, that's not what I meant, you know that, I simply meant you wouldn't like Anthony to know you've been crying. Now take a hold of yourself darling, take a hold, you can't go on like this, Angela, neither of us can, it simply won't do, it simply will not do. Angela. We must be firm.

ANGELA *lets herself be consoled once more.*

That's right. Well done. Well done, you're very brave, Angela, very brave, well done. And we must be brave, both of us. And, (*he chooses the word carefully*) think about everything in its true perspective.

ANGELA *gives one last sniff.*

We must think about what we have, and not what we would like to have. Thinking about what we would like to have is all very well in times of plenty when all kinds of adversity are scarce. But such times are rare. No one has any right to happiness; and believing that you do have such a right invariably leads to unhappiness. And bitterness and reproach blind you to – er prevent you . . . realising what causes you may still have for being glad. Nothing happens without a purpose, remember that, even if the purpose is hard to s- to find. Now we must be thankful not only for the small mercies that we have been granted, but also for the ability to . . . perceive that very truth, about purpose. If we had less . . . awareness –

ANGELA. Like Doreen.

HENRY. Well, possibly; I don't wish to make judgements. But if we were less aware, we might fail to . . . notice anything more than the immediate effects of an apparent misfortune. Now as it is, we can . . . understand that the long-term effects might very well give us cause to be glad. For example, the very unfortunate backward state of Sarah and Elizabeth has brought out the greatest depths of compassion in Sylvia, as indeed has Anthony's affliction. And that very affliction might itself lead to Anthony's becoming a far . . . greater cockroach in the long run, spiritually. Think how his perceptions will change! Think of the greater insight he will achieve by contemplation in his new world of darkness, no longer confused by the purely visual. For what is the visual but a clutter of things we see, and not of things we understand! Understanding comes through inward contemplation. That is the way to achieve true nobility of soul. Now my darling, imagine, just imagine that you are without sight . . . Be still . . . be calm, listen . . . listen to the world around you, listen to the way it speaks to your inner self.

They listen. Thanks to cunning editing we are now c. 1½ minutes from the end of the Act One Finale in 'Cosi'.

ANGELA. Oh darling Henry, you're so right. I've been such a silly old thing. You're right. We must not look back. We must always look forward, forever forward with no regrets. (*She sniffs with gladness.*) Oh, Henry. . . .

HENRY. Angela. . . .

Enter SYLVIA, *calling, but appropriately subdued.*

SYLVIA. Hello Mum, hello Dad. Phew, I'm worn out.

ANGELA. Darling, you're wonderful. How's Anthony?

SYLVIA. Oh, bearing up. Keeps asking what time of day it is. I said you'd go to him again soon. Sarah and Elizabeth aren't at all well. They haven't said a thing, but I don't think you must distress yourselves too much: they've never really been with us since they came back and I don't think they have long. . . .

ANGELA *starts to whimper again.*

Oh don't, Mother, you upset me, please.

ANGELA *controls herself.*

There . . . that's right, Mother . . . that's right . . . (*Pause.*) Er . . . Mother . . . well, both of you in fact . . .

ANGELA. Yes dear?

SYLVIA. Well . . . (*She sighs.*) I don't know quite how to put this, but . . .

ANGELA (*anxiously*). Yes?

SYLVIA. Well . . . all it was . . . was I just wanted to say . . . sorry for being such a selfish thing this afternoon. I was very thoughtless. I can be, I know. I love you both very dearly, and I shouldn't have said things to upset you, it was wrong of me, and . . . well that's it really. I'm sorry.

ANGELA (*doing her best to contain her emotion, but failing to suppress a gentle tear and a tremble in her voice*). Oh, Sylvia . . .

SYLVIA (*to conceal her embarrassment*). I'll . . . I'll er . . . I'll get back to Anthony then. Don't be long coming!

As SYLVIA *departs,* ANGELA'*s flood-gates burst and she is overwhelmed with happiness. In the midst of her sobbing can be discerned: 'She called me "Mother" . . . She's so grown up', and from* HENRY *the occasional, hoarsely muttered 'Fine girl, fine girl . . .'*

The sobbing fades. The music fades up to the end of the Act One Finale of 'Cosi'.

Silence. Into this silence: the sound of MICHAEL *whistling amusically under his breath as he checks various sheets of paper at his desk.*

MICHAEL (*musingly, very much to himself*). Mm hm . . . Hmmm. Mm . . . Hm . . . Hmhmmmm. (*He reverts to whistling under his breath; other oral noises made by a man when alone. Then, reading his own notes aloud:*) Temperatures . . . maintained; humidity . . . constant . . . Mhm. General cleanliness . . . excellent. No incidence of cockroach mite 'Rhizoglyphus tarsalis' or 'Pimeliaphilus podapop- podoplo- polopopola- po-podo-pola- podapolapo- podapolalp- podapolopophagus.' Podapolopophagus. Pimeliaphilus podapolopophagus. (*As if nothing could be more natural, as if making a casual comment.*) Pimeliaphilus podapolopophagus. Yes. Oh you mean Pimeliaphilus podapolopophagus? Nasty piece of work, yes, very nasty if you get them in the lab, podapolopophagus, yes, mmm. No no, we haven't got any. No. Podapolopophagus.

He starts to chant it to a catchy rhythm, giving himself a drum accompaniment with his hands on the desk. He is starting to introduce his feet on the sides of the desk and bring syncopations and internal repetitions to the word – which is becoming almost a pop-lyric – when there are noises of PLACKETT *arriving.* MICHAEL *abandons his musicmaking and clears his throat. Enter* PLACKETT *through the inner door.*

Afternoon, Sir Archibald.

PLACKETT (*distinctly weary*). Afternoon, Michael. Sorry I'm late.

MICHAEL. No no no. Not to worry. Everything all right?

PLACKETT *hangs up his coat and hat and begins to don a lab coat.*

PLACKETT. Yes yes. Well, hah, you know. . . . What's the state of play here?

MICHAEL. I haven't started anything new, obviously. General checks, the two injected females have died –

PLACKETT. Too much insecticide after all.

MICHAEL. Yes. And I've taken two other females and a male from normal conditions so that we can use one of the females for the sex-attractant pheromones, then dissect the other female and the male for their corpora cardiaca which we can grind up and inject into the sightless male after the pheromone test. With any luck his rhythm will return.

PLACKETT (*not really with it today*). Mm.

MICHAEL. So we could do either first: the dissection or the simulated mating . . . Yes?

PLACKETT. Er . . . yes, yes, sorry. Sorry, go on.

MICHAEL. Well, what I thought was, we could remove one of the two remaining females from normal and link her in the parabiosis operation to the male we put in constant light at the end of last week . . . and if we do that first, then the dissection, so that the corpora cardiaca are ready ground up, then the pheromone test, and the oesophageal injection last. And what would you suggest we use for the sex-attractant object? Sir Archibald?

PLACKETT. Eh? Sorry? Oh, er . . . don't mind, up to you, paper, match box, don't mind.

Pause.

MICHAEL. Are you sure everything's all right, Sir Archibald?

PLACKETT. Well . . . Yes. No. I don't know. I don't know.

MICHAEL. Lady Mary?

PLACKETT. She looks . . . fatalistic. She could almost get religious.

MICHAEL. Should we . . .?

PLACKETT. No no. Carry on. As I said before, it'll be best if we wait till the doctor's findings are through.

MICHAEL. But they might be today?

PLACKETT. Might have been. Doctor rang up this morning just before lunch to say it'd be tomorrow. Definitely.

MICHAEL. But he couldn't say anymore?

PLACKETT. No . . . (*Pause.*) On we go then. (*A riffling amongst the cassettes.*) I hope you don't mind, Michael, I feel in a rather Mahlerian mood today.

MICHAEL. No, of course I don't mind.

PLACKETT. You can choose tomorrow. Did you remember to bring 'Rheingold', by the way?

MICHAEL. Oh dammit, no, I forgot.

PLACKETT. Never mind. Perhaps just as well. If you can get it for tomorrow evening, I can bring in 'Valkyrie' and 'Siegfried', then if you can get hold of 'Götterdämmerung' we're all set for a few nights of Wagner.

MICHAEL. Fine. Sounds like a good plan.

PLACKETT. Mind you, might have changed my mind by tomorrow evening, might want a touch of the old Masonic Funeral Music.

MICHAEL (*shocked*). Sir Archibald!

PLACKETT. Well, if we can't joke about it what can we do? (*Wearily again.*) No. You're right. You're right. Ah well. (*Cassette recorder on. The opening of Mahler's 5th Symphony.*) Might as well get completely depressed.

Music right up, then fade.

In the background, muffled, the Adagietto from the same symphony.

ANGELA (*somewhat light-headed after the multiple misfortune has befallen them*). I don't care, I don't care, I don't care. No no no. Not a little bit. Not a bit. No. Let them come. Let them come and take me, I don't mind. (*She shouts:*) Do you hear? I don't mind! (*Tailing off into an almost song-like wail.*) I don't m-i-n-d. . . . (*Pause.*) Take me. Come on. Take me. Me. ME! Not them. (*She starts to sob.*) Not my children, not my children . . . (*Pause. Almost a whisper:*) Not my children. . . . (*Pause.*)

HENRY (*gently*). Angela? . . . Angela?

ANGELA *sniffs.*

Angela. We don't know. We can't say. (*Pause.*) We simply don't know. There's been no proof. Not at any stage can we say positively that they killed them. We must beware of hatred. It is hatred that will kill us, that will kill our souls, not the . . . creatures.

ANGELA *is unconvinced.*

(*Hastily.*) And I know, all right, I know, I have to admit that the two girls did die. I know, we saw that, but . . . but they may not have been killed, they may have . . . (*Clutching at straws.*) well the . . . the creatures may have found them somewhere, wandering, sick; and . . . and they decided to return them to us because they knew that they were going to die and they wanted us to be all together before the end, I'm sure that's it!

ANGELA. How could they have found them wandering? They took them away in the first place when they were only six months old. *Pause.*

HENRY. Ah . . . (*Explanatory, deceiving himself:*) well yes, that's it, you see, they did take them, they've taken all the others, gradually one by one –

ANGELA. In twos and threes and fours and –

HENRY. Yes, yes, well all right perhaps not quite one by one, but certainly over the course of the last year, and I'm certain they wouldn't do it like that if they meant them any harm.

ANGELA. Huh.

HENRY. If they'd wanted to they . . . they could have trodden on us, or . . . or . . . they could have done anything. They've always been gentle.

ANGELA (*dully*). They took out Anthony's eyes.

HENRY. Oh nonsense darling! Goodness what nonsense! Whatever gave you that idea? Took out his eyes . . .! Stuff and nonsense!

ANGELA. They took him when he was well, and they brought him back without his eyes, in the dark, and comfortless.

HENRY. Comfortless? Why, how can you say such a thing? There were three of us to comfort him. And you've no indication that they took out his eyes. Why should they bring him back if they did? What for?

ANGELA (*as listless as ever*). So why have they taken him again? And Sylvia . . . Sylvia.

Pause.

HENRY. Ah . . . er . . . Well. It seems to me that . . . er . . . Well it's all quite plain really, what has been happening, from way back last year, which is when it all started of course, as you remember, what has been happening is that . . . er . . . is that . . . (*Inspiration dawns.*) they're taking them somewhere else.

ANGELA. Where?

HENRY (*brilliantly*). Somewhere . . . better. Somewhere where they will be truly happy. Always. After all you have to admit that even before, it wasn't by any means safe, or warm. They've been preparing another place for them where they will be quite safe, and warm, with no one to trouble them. (*He's got it all sorted out. Excitedly*:) And and . . . er . . . and you see what happened was that Sarah and Elizabeth got sick somehow, so they were brought back, because the creatures knew we'd want to see the girls before they died, and the same with Anthony, somehow he got blinded, must have been before he got to the other place, so they brought him back, but when they realised that he wasn't going to die, they thought they'd take him after all, but just so as there was someone to keep an eye . . . er . . . to look after him, they took Sylvia as well! (*Triumphant.*) There!

Pause.

ANGELA. Sylvia . . . I'll never see her again.

HENRY. What? Oh, but darling, you don't understand. They'll come for us too, eventually. They left us till last because after all we are the parents.

ANGELA. They took Ken and Doreen last week and left Jackie and Tracy till today, and that boy . . . whatever his name was.

HENRY. Ah yes. Yes. Well . . . er . . . er that's because it's a different system where they're going, it's probably not so good there so they needed Ken and Doreen to er . . . or probably what it was was that the youngsters were getting out of hand and they had to bring in the parents to sort them out! Unruly lot, not like ours! Simple as that! Oh darling.

A long pause.

ANGELA. Darling Henry. Oh my Henry. You're so good to me. Promise you'll never leave me?

HENRY. I promise. Never.

ANGELA *sighs.*

HENRY. You see it's all going to be all right, isn't it?

ANGELA (*happily*). Mmm.

HENRY. They'll come for us soon, don't you worry, and we won't be frightened, will we?

ANGELA. No.

HENRY. Because they're doing it all for our good.

ANGELA. Yes.

HENRY. They're gentle to us, they don't want to hurt us. They're out there guarding over us, so that we can rest easy. We've no need to fear while they're looking after us; we're in their hands.

Pause.

ANGELA. Oh darling . . .

Music slowly up to the end of the movement, then fade.

Sounds of the interior of a restaurant. Above this, the sound of MICHAEL *pouring himself a glass of wine. He tries it and is even more favourably impressed than before. Then, as* PLACKETT *arrives:*

MICHAEL. Ah, Sir Archibald.

PLACKETT (*very subdued*). Hello Michael.

He sits down heavily. He is reluctant to volunteer information, and MICHAEL *is reluctant to enquire, so there is a pause.*

MICHAEL. Er . . . have some wine?

PLACKETT. Mm. What? Oh, yes, yes . . . thank you.

MICHAEL *pours.*

MICHAEL (*as* PLACKETT *has not appeared to show any interest*). Got one I knew you'd like: Château Figeac. (*Pause.*) '66.

PLACKETT. Mm. What? Oh . . . er Figeac. Yes, yes, thank you. '66, mm. Mm. Yes. Oh well. Yes, cheers then.

He drinks, oblivious of the quality. Pause. They both start to speak at once.

MICHAEL. } When d'you think –
PLACKETT. } How well d'you –

MICHAEL. I'm sorry, Sir Archibald –

PLACKETT. No, no.

MICHAEL. Please go on.

PLACKETT. No, no, Michael, after you.

MICHAEL. Er . . . well, I simply wanted to ask when you thought we should introduce the two remaining cockroaches from normal into constant light.

PLACKETT (*making himself consider it with difficulty*). Er . . . two remaining. Er, yes. Two from normal. Two from normal . . . tonight. Yes, tonight, I should think.

MICHAEL. Ah.

PLACKETT. Yes, yes . . . that should do it.

MICHAEL. The parabiosis pair are in that tank, still, of course.

PLACKETT. No matter.

Pause.

MICHAEL. No. Fine. And the female . . .?

PLACKETT. Which?

MICHAEL. The one we're introducing tonight; she's the one for implantation tomorrow?

PLACKETT. Yes . . . yes.

MICHAEL. Ah. (*Pause.*) Er . . . what did, er . . . did you have, was there, er . . . what was it you were about to say, just now, er . . . Sir Archibald?

PLACKETT. Well I was going to ask you how well you thought you knew Sylvia.

MICHAEL. Oh, nothing about Lady Mary?

PLACKETT. What? Oh no.

MICHAEL. Is she better, then?

PLACKETT. No, no it's . . . no she's not, but er . . . No, it's . . . it's Sylvia.

MICHAEL. She's not, is she, I mean has there been, is she . . . ill?

PLACKETT. What? No, I don't think so. No. I don't know. One would hope not.

Pause.

MICHAEL. But . . .? You wanted to know how well I thought I knew her.

PLACKETT. Yes. Yes, you see . . . Oh dammit all, I might as well tell you. I'm afraid the whole thing's very distressing, Michael. Not at all pleasant. And the worst of it will be that she'll think we don't care, or have disowned her. Perhaps that's what she wants . . .

MICHAEL. But –

PLACKETT. How can one tell? I haven't told Mary, of course, I think the shock would kill her . . .

MICHAEL. But, Sir Arch-

PLACKETT. After all, she's not a girl any more, she can do as she pleases, but to think that we never knew for such a long time . . .

MICHAEL. Sir Archibald!

PLACKETT. Mm?

MICHAEL. Sir Archibald! Please explain!

PLACKETT. What? Oh, yes. Well it was the letter you see. Got it today.

MICHAEL. A letter from Sylvia?

PLACKETT. Yes.

MICHAEL. And what did it say?

PLACKETT. A great deal. Very upsetting. But you see, Michael, she wrote it about six weeks ago, right at the beginning of term, and for some reason we've only just got it, heaven knows why, GPO are normally so good, can't understand why –

MICHAEL. Sir Archibald! What Did It Say?

PLACKETT. What did it say? Why, that she's giving up biology, that she's never really enjoyed it, that she thinks all my research is thoroughly pointless and 'out of touch with the real world', that she's taking up Social and Political Sciences instead, and worst of all, that she's moved out of College and has moved into a house with some fellow called Dave.

Pause.

MICHAEL (*stunned by the one thing that really matters to him*). Dave . . .?

PLACKETT. Nearly six weeks, and we never knew . . .

MICHAEL (*you can almost hear him visualising the forty or so nights she will have spent with Dave*). Moved in with him . . . Does she mean?

PLACKETT. What must she think of us? That we don't care?

MICHAEL. But do you think she's . . .?

PLACKETT. Maybe she's glad, maybe she doesn't want us to care.

MICHAEL (*appalled, or perhaps just envious*). Six weeks . . .

PLACKETT. How on earth could I ever tell Mary?

MICHAEL. Do you think she loves this . . . Dave?

PLACKETT. What? Love? Haven't the first idea.

MICHAEL. But it's . . . well it's . . . awful.

PLACKETT. Such a fine career ahead of her . . .

MICHAEL. Can't we, I mean, isn't there . . . won't she lose her grant or something?

PLACKETT. She doesn't get one.

MICHAEL. Oh. No.

The waiter arrives with their food. They ignore him tonight, but for their polite thanks.

PLACKETT. The thing is, Michael, what do I do? What is there to do? What would you do? I don't know, I simply don't know.

He has not started his food. MICHAEL *has tentatively tucked in.*

After all, one starts to question the whole basis of one's life. We did it all for her, but she doesn't want any part of it. And there's Mary. She's lying there afraid she's dying. I didn't tell Sylvia that for fear of upsetting her, and now I can't tell Mary about Sylvia. What's it all for? Is there someone up there ordaining all this? I've never been a religious man, Michael, but it seems that everything I've striven for is being taken away, piece by piece. Is it sent as a trial? I never told you, there was no need, but we had another daughter, oh a very long time ago, before Sylvia, when we were both still young, but she died as a baby. Mary swore she would never have another. And then Sylvia came along. We cherished her. Gave her everything. We thought she loved us, too. And now . . . this. Mary may have cancer, and Sylvia . . . What's it for, Michael, what's it all for? Oh perhaps I'm too old, too old for it all, too old for all this pointless work. She's right. What is the point of it? Does it answer any of the questions which matter? Perhaps I should try to see it from her point of view . . . Perhaps she feels she can be a great politician . . .

MICHAEL. Social and Political Sciences sounds more like a cop-out to me.

PLACKETT. But you never know, Michael, you never know. And this David –

MICHAEL. Dave.

PLACKETT. Dave, perhaps he's a sensible sort.

MICHAEL. I doubt it.

PLACKETT (*reluctantly agreeing*). No . . . (*Pause.*) You know, Michael, if you don't mind, I don't altogether feel up to eating now.

MICHAEL. It's very good.

PLACKETT (*vaguely*). Yes . . . Will you forgive me if I go home? I think I'd like to be with Mary.

MICHAEL. No, no of course, Sir Archibald. Of course. You go ahead.

PLACKETT. You stay and enjoy your meal, though.

MICHAEL. Ah, yes.

PLACKETT. And I'll see you at the lab later.

MICHAEL. No need if you don't want to.

PLACKETT. Oh yes, I think I should. Do me good. It's just that . . . hmmm.

MICHAEL. Quite so.

They stand.

PLACKETT. Put it on my account of course.

MICHAEL. Oh, er . . . yes, yes, thank you.

PLACKETT. Cheerio then.

MICHAEL. Er, cheerio, Sir Archibald.

PLACKETT *departs.* MICHAEL *sits down again.*

(*To* himself.) Dave . . . huh. (*Which he modifies*:) Doive . . . Doive. Yer. Moi noim's Doive. Uhh. (*Then as himself again.*) Six weeks . . .! Phwor . . .

Restaurant noise fades.

Music, muffled. It is Mahler 5 again – PLACKETT *only has the one depressing tape. This time it is at the first movement, second subject, c.1 minute into the movement. No other sound for a few seconds, then:*

ANGELA. Perhaps . . . perhaps it's being on our own that does it.

HENRY. What's that, my darling?

ANGELA. That makes it all so . . . strange.

HENRY. How, strange?

ANGELA. Well, it's hard to say. A sense of . . . waiting, almost. As if . . . as if . . . Oh, Henry, I'm afraid.

HENRY. Shh, my darling. There's no need.

ANGELA. But Henry, we are alone.

HENRY. Shh.

ANGELA. And what if –

HENRY. No; no darling. No 'what ifs'.

Slight pause.

ANGELA. But –

HENRY. No 'buts'.

Slight pause.

ANGELA. But what if They don't come? What if They don't take us to the others, to Sylvia and Anthony and Sebastian?

HENRY. Hush, my darling. They will. They wouldn't leave us here. What would be the point?

ANGELA. But –

HENRY. We may not know the minds of those in whose care we are held, but we must believe, darling, we must have faith. Without that there is nothing.

Pause. As the original trumpet theme reappears, there are footsteps. The tank is opened, and the music grows slightly louder.

ANGELA. Oh, Henry . . .

HENRY. Shh, darling. Remember what we promised each other? Not to be afraid. We must be still when He takes us. It's hard, I know, but if we have no fear we will come to no harm.

ANGELA. But Henry, suppose He only takes one of us!

HENRY. Have faith, darling. See? He is taking us together.

The music sounds louder as they are transported across the lab, then diminishes as they pass beyond a door to the area which houses the constant-light tanks.

You see, my darling, it is our faith which has kept us together. He is taking us to the others.

ANGELA. But . . . but, Henry, supposing He gets it wrong and He takes us to Ken and Doreen and Jackie and Tracy? And their Darren? Henry, supposing He doesn't know that Sylvia and Anthony are ours, and Sebastian? Henry, He's going to get it wrong, I'm so afraid!

HENRY. Shh, Angela. Don't worry! How could He not know! Could He have been guarding over us for all this long time and not have known? Where is your faith? Be strong!

The music has reverted, funereally, to the second subject. There are sotto voce, tremulous mutterings of 'Oh Henry . . .' then the tank is closed, the music disappears completely, and ANGELA *gasps.*

ANGELA. But Henry! Where are we? What is this place. Oh Henry, Henry . . .

HENRY (*confused*). I don't know, darling, it's . . . it's . . . I . . . I don't know.

ANGELA. Oh, Henry. It's so bright. Why is it so bright?

HENRY. I don't know, Angela. I don't –

ANGELA. It should be dark. Everywhere else is dark, this is so bright, something's wrong, Henry. Where are the others?

HENRY. I don't know, darling, I expect –

ANGELA. Where are they, Henry?

HENRY. I'm sure they're –

ANGELA. It's wrong, Henry, it's all gone wrong, it's gone so terribly wrong. The others aren't here, they're nowhere, it's all a – aaah! Henry, what's that?

HENRY. What's what?

ANGELA. That.

HENRY. Where?

ANGELA. Over there.

HENRY (*gasps also. Stutters*). D-don't be a-afraid, darling, don't be afraid. I'm sure it won't hurt us.

ANGELA (*swallows in terror*). It's huge.

HENRY (*attempting to reassure them both*). Not really, it's not so very big . . .

ANGELA. Oh, but Henry, it's coming this way. It's . . . (*Suddenly amazed.*) It . . . surely it's a cockroach, with something on its back.

HENRY. Why, Angela, I do believe –

ANGELA. It's – (*She gives a little scream.*) Henry! It's got no head. It's walking but it's got no head. Henry! Henry, do something!

HENRY. Keep calm, darling.

ANGELA. But, Henry –

HENRY. Just stay calm and everything'll be –

ANGELA. But what's on its back?

HENRY. It looks –

ANGELA. It's another . . . no it couldn't be, it's got no legs. But it is, and it's upside d- (*She screams as fear of the truth grips her.*) No . . .! No it can't be. No . . . please. Please don't let it be . . .

SYLVIA (*trying to be cheerful, but sounding rather weary, and curiously as if she is upside down, which of course she is*). Hello Mum, hello Dad. Glad you're here. This is Darren I'm on. He's not well.

ANGELA (*her scream echoes and re-echoes around the tank, as does her final cry, gradually fading into silence*). S-Y-L-V-I-A-A-A-A-A . . .

Silence. MICHAEL *checks various sheets of paper at his desk.*

MICHAEL (*to himself*). Yes, yes . . . yep, yep . . . yer . . . yer. . . . Yer, Doive. (*Then, in a high-pitched, nasal parody of himself.*) Hello, Sylvia, it's Michael, I've come to see you. (*Falsetto, as* SYLVIA.) Mikey . . .!! Oh Mikey, I'd like you to meet Dave. (*As himself.*) Hello, Dave! (*As Dave.*) Uhh. Uhh. (*He makes noises of boredom and annoyance.*) Doive. Yer.

Distant sounds of PLACKETT *arriving.*

PLACKETT (*from the office*). Michael?

MICHAEL. In here.

PLACKETT (*coming through*). Ah.

MICHAEL. What news? Any?

PLACKETT (*obviously utterly depressed*). Er . . . no. No, nothing. Not yet. No.

MICHAEL. Ah.

Pause.

PLACKETT. Er . . . everything all right, is it?

MICHAEL. Yes. Er, yes, fine.

Pause.

PLACKETT. Good. (*Pause.*) Er . . . what . . . um, what do we . . . er, what do we have to take care of today, Michael?

MICHAEL. Monitor the two linked in parabiosis. I've checked the graphs already and the activity rhythm's still there, but obviously weaker. Then implant the female cockroach we introduced yesterday with the ganglion from the other female in reverse lighting conditions. I don't suppose she'll last long.

PLACKETT. No. Er . . . look here, Michael, is there any chance you could hold the fort on your own this afternoon?

MICHAEL. Of course.

PLACKETT. Only to tell the truth I'm feeling bloody. Hardly slept. Then woke up to discover that that infernal Alice had given Mary Sylvia's letter. That was the end. (*He sighs at the memory.*) Michael, old son, you've no idea. She wanted me, she was pleading with me, to find her some drugs so that she could end it all. End it all! Oh, Michael. I've given her a sleeping pill, so at least I know she's not about to do something rash while I'm out. But I can't stay away.

MICHAEL. Shall we shut up shop?

PLACKETT. No no, you carry on. Good experience for you. You see, the whole world seems to revolve around Mary and Sylvia. I know Mary won't be able to live unless Sylvia comes home and, well . . . modifies her slightly strange ideas. But she's my daughter. Am I to dictate how she should live? I am broken, Michael. I have no idea what to do. Can anyone dictate how anyone else should live? But Mary's so . . . (*He sighs again.*) She won't live, I'm sure of it. (*Long pause.*) So. If you don't mind . . .

MICHAEL. No, not at all. I'm just very concerned for you all. Couldn't I . . . isn't there anything that I could do for you?

PLACKETT. You just stay on here, Michael, that's more than enough help to me.

MICHAEL. Yes. All right then. Shall I see you . . .?

PLACKETT. Yes. I'll see you for dinner. I'll come along to tell you if there's any news.

MICHAEL. Well I hope there'll be some good news.

PLACKETT. Let's hope so, Michael. Let's hope so. (*Pause.*) Well. Off I go then.

MICHAEL. Yes. Give my, er . . . give my fondest regards to Lady Mary.

PLACKETT. Will do. See you later, Michael.

MICHAEL. See you later, Sir Archibald.

Exit PLACKETT. *When the outer door has closed:*

Mmm. Poor old Lady Mary. (*He gives a long sigh of someone who is sympathetic but doesn't know what to do about it.*) Oh well.

He presses 'play' on the cassette recorder. We hear 'It don't mean a thing if it ain't got that swing' (*George Melly*). *Soon* MICHAEL *is making involuntary noises of enthusiastic participation, culminating in:*

Crazy man, crazy. OK, little lady cockroach, youse a-better beware, coz I'se a-comin. Yessuh, I'se a-coming. . . .

The music gradually fades.

Silence. Then:

SYLVIA (*very wearily*). Do you think They'll bring Mother back?

Pause.

HENRY. I don't know, Sylvia, I don't know. I hope so. Yes, I'm sure They will. They only took her because she was so upset.

SYLVIA. Yes. (*Pause.*) She didn't understand.

Pause.

HENRY. No. (*Pause.*) It was very hard for her. I think she thought (*He lowers his voice.*) I think she thought that Darren had somehow engineered it all.

SYLVIA. It's all right, Dad, he can't hear you.

HENRY. Oh . . . no. No. (*Pause.*) He . . . er . . . he didn't, did he?

SYLVIA. What's that, Dad?

HENRY. Engineer it all?

SYLVIA. Darren? Of course not.

HENRY. No. (*Pause.*) No. (*Pause.*) Who . . . er . . . (*He hesitates before asking the question on which his whole faith depends.*) Er . . . was it . . . it wasn't Them, was it, that cut his head off?

SYLVIA. I don't know, Dad, he couldn't tell me.

HENRY. No. (*Pause.*) I don't expect it was. They wouldn't, I'm sure. Because you're helping him, after all, aren't you? I wonder why They chose you. (*Pause.*) I can't help feeling that you must be very uncomfortable like that, Sylvia, upside down, and with your . . . (*He chokes back a rising tremor in his voice.*) With your legs . . .

SYLVIA. It's very wearying. I expect it's because I'm having to think for Darren too. And I can't tell him to go in a certain direction: I have to will him to.

HENRY (*unable to eliminate all traces of bitterness*). But, Sylvia, They cut off your legs . . .!

SYLVIA. I know, Dad, but it's better like this. I'm comfortable now.

HENRY. But afterwards, when Darren . . . When he . . . Well, if he dies. What then?

Pause.

SYLVIA (*extremely wearily*). I don't know, Dad. There are questions we shouldn't ask. Perhaps we are not meant to know the answers.

HENRY (*hurling his anger at the gods*). But, Sylvia, why?! What was it for?

Pause.

SYLVIA (*almost a whisper*). I don't know.

A long pause.

HENRY (*he has controlled himself*). What is this place, Sylvia, do you know?

SYLVIA (*also making a supreme effort*). No, Dad, no I haven't any idea.

HENRY. I thought They were taking us to the others. This isn't the place. Not the place They were going to take us. (*Pause.*) They will take us, though. We were arrogant and foolish. I thought I knew: I thought They were taking us straight there. But this – this is just a between place. I realise that now. I doubted for a while. One must never doubt. (*Pause.*) Remember that, Sylvia.

Pause.

SYLVIA (*very weakly*). Yes, Dad. (*Pause.*) I'll remember that. (*Pause.*) I'm tired.

Silence.

Restaurant noise.

PLACKETT (*calling cheerfully before* MICHAEL *is halfway across the floor*). Michael! There you are!

MICHAEL (*as he sits down*). How long have you been here? You're embarrassingly cheerful. Good news?

PLACKETT. Splendid. Here, where's your glass? Come on. Touch of this do you good. Had to ask specially. Knew they had it. Château Cantemerle '61.

MICHAEL (*as* PLACKETT *pours*). Your favourite?

PLACKETT. Absolutely.

They savour the aroma of age with an almost unbridled sensual delight.

Thank you. Cheers, then. Happy days.

MICHAEL. I'll drink to that.

They drink.

Mmm . . .! So tell me all. I'm agog.

PLACKETT. All agog are you, old son?

MICHAEL. Certainly am. What's happened?

PLACKETT (*splendidly*). Everything's happened.

MICHAEL. The doctor's been.

PLACKETT. The doctor's been, and gone. And so's the postman. Our dear Alice discovered a letter which had been sitting in her apron pocket since second post! Second post! I could wring her neck.

MICHAEL. Tell me.

PLACKETT. What do you want to hear first?

MICHAEL. Well! I don't mind. Doctor.

PLACKETT. The doctor. The good doctor came, and told us there was nothing to be worried about.

MICHAEL. Just like that?

PLACKETT. Just like that.

MICHAEL. Well!

PLACKETT (*wittily*). She is!

MICHAEL. Very good, very good. So is she quite better, or what?

PLACKETT (*conspiratorially*). Between you and me, old son, our Lady Mary has been suffering heavily from the old psychosomatics.

MICHAEL. So, she's . . . all right?

PLACKETT. Damned weak, of course. But that's her own fault. Nothing a spot of French air won't cure. Thought we'd make a leisurely tour of the old Châteaux in a couple of weeks. Fancy joining us?

MICHAEL. Me? But –

PLACKETT. You see, we'll be taking it slowly, and young people need to have company their own age to chase about with.

MICHAEL. What other –

PLACKETT. And of course Sylvia wouldn't be happy with just the two of us, doddering around –

MICHAEL. Sylvia!

PLACKETT. Well yes, she's got to have someone to look after her. Flighty little thing.

MICHAEL. But . . . I mean . . . what's happened?

PLACKETT. Dear me, Michael, you're very slow on the uptake for a Ph.D. It's all all right. Everything's going to be fine. We had the letter you see!

MICHAEL. From Sylvia?

PLACKETT. Of course, you silly boy, who else?

MICHAEL. What did she say? Tell me!

PLACKETT *takes the letter from his pocket and unfolds it, with great drama.*

PLACKETT. She said . . . 'Dear Mummy and Daddy'. Isn't that charming? Makes her seem so vulnerable. I bet you'd like to have someone write to you like that.

MICHAEL. I haven't got that far in life yet. Go on, get on with it!

PLACKETT. She says . . . 'Oh woe, woe and again woe. Thrice woe'.

MICHAEL. What? No. You're talking rot. What does she really say? Give me the letter!

PLACKETT. Uh uh, Michael, no snatching. She says, quite simply, that she's glad we never responded to that first letter, because it was all a big mistake. From beginning to end. She's been accepted back on the biology course, and she's been given her college room back. Couldn't be better.

MICHAEL. And what about . . . Dave?

PLACKETT (*snorts contemptuously and snaps his fingers*). Gone! So much irrelevance!

MICHAEL (*sighs magnificently*). Wonderful news!

PLACKETT. And. . . . And, me old Michael, there's more.

MICHAEL. Yes?

PLACKETT. Yes.

MICHAEL. Read on!

PLACKETT. Indeed I shall. Though I have to say that what I am about to do is strictly against the wishes of the writer.

MICHAEL. Oh?

PLACKETT. Mm.

MICHAEL. But you'll read it just the same?

PLACKETT. So long as you don't breathe a word to Sylvia.

MICHAEL. No, of course I won't. Of course not. Go on. What does she say?

PLACKETT. She says, and I quote . . . 'By the way,' she says. 'By the way, you needn't mention anything to Michael, but how is he? I was half hoping to get a letter from him. Is he shy? I hope it isn't that he doesn't want to write. He is still with you, isn't he? Make sure he's around for the vac, but don't go dropping any tactless hints, will you?' Hah! As if I would.

MICHAEL *is stunned into speechless joy and manages only gasps and stutters.* PLACKETT *folds the letter away.*

So there we are!

MICHAEL (*recovering slightly*). Yes. Well!

PLACKETT. And that looks like our waiter in the distance. Splendid! You will come to France, then?

MICHAEL. Well, yes!

PLACKETT. Good lad. So as they say over there, (*With the most appalling French accent.*) '*Tout est pour le mieux dans le meilleur des mondes possible*', eh what? Haha, floored you with that one, didn't I?

MICHAEL. You never cease to amaze me, Sir Archibald.

Fade to silence.

Silence. Into the silence:

HENRY. I thought I knew. (*Pause.*) I thought . . . I thought I knew. (*Pause.*) Sylvia? (*Pause.*) She's tired. And this place is so light, always so light. It should be dark. Why isn't it dark? Angela won't come back now. They've taken her. They've taken her away, and They're killing Sylvia. I'm the only one left. Was it for me? Was all this for me? No. While there's life there's hope. Angela's alive, of course she is. She'll come back, and They'll make Sylvia well again. I know They will. (*Dully.*) I know they will. (*Suddenly.*) What have you done? Why have you done this? Why? Wasn't it enough that you took five of our young when they hatched? Did you have to kill Sarah and Elizabeth too, and Sebastian, and Anthony, and Sylvia? (*His anger drops uselessly into the silence. Softly:*) Sylvia. Sylvia? I have been wrong from the beginning: there is no hope. What hope did Sylvia have? She could have . . . she could have had a family of her own. What did she do wrong? Is she being punished? Am I being punished? There was no one to tell us where we went wrong. How could we know? (*A slight pause. He yells:*) WHAT DO YOU WANT OF US . . .?!

Silence.

I had to be strong, for Angela. So I believed; I had faith. Perhaps I was right to have faith. Perhaps the world is good. I thought I knew, but I was wrong: so I still don't know. Have faith. This is not the end, this is just a place for waiting before They take me to the better place. I am not ready for the better place yet. That is why I am here. That is why Sylvia is here. We are all tested in our own ways so that we know our own failings and learn to overcome them. So that we learn to know ourselves. Then we can go on to the better place. Angela will be there too. They will come to take us soon. (*Pause.*) I know They will.

Pause.

SYLVIA (*faintly*). Dad? Dad, is that you?

HENRY. Sylvia, I'm here.

SYLVIA. Don't go, Dad, will you?

HENRY. No, Sylvia, I'm here; I'm here.

Pause.

SYLVIA. I don't want you to go, Dad. (*Pause.*) We'll stay together, won't we?

HENRY. Yes dear, of course we will.

SYLVIA. And it doesn't matter about Darren being with us, does it?

HENRY. No, of course it doesn't matter dear.

SYLVIA. I know . . . I know Mother wouldn't like it. (*Pause.*) But we'll be together. (*Pause.*) I'm tired, Dad. (*Pause.*) I'm so tired.

A long pause.

HENRY (*whispers*). Sylvia. (*He speaks, dully.*) Sylvia.

Sounds of the restaurant. PLACKETT *and* MICHAEL *are pulling on coats and setting off towards the door.*

PLACKETT. Forgot to ask, Michael: how did it go this afternoon?

MICHAEL. Oh fine, fine. No probs. I'd give the female with the implanted ganglion about twenty-four hours before she starts developing tumours in the gut.

PLACKETT. Excellent. Excellent. You know I can't begin to say how glad I am about Sylvia. There's such a bright future for her. She's made me so happy.

MICHAEL. And me.

PLACKETT. And somehow she's made me feel almost as if I could cope with anything. The thought of her's given me such strength.

MICHAEL. I know the feeling.

PLACKETT. D'you know, Michael, I was almost getting to the point of being depressed, till today. You know: a lot of damn fool philosophising and pseudo-spiritual speculation, wondering why it was all happening to us, and so on. Judgement, visitation sent by God. My oh my, what nonsense one can think. And I'll tell you, Michael, it's not healthy. Sort of stuff never did anyone any good. Just get on with it, that's what I say.

MICHAEL. Precisely.

PLACKETT. Ah well. The world's a fine old place really. Pop home for a drink? Lab can wait tonight.

MICHAEL. Wouldn't say no.

They start to go.

PLACKETT. Jolly good. Mary'll be glad to see you. Come along then.

They leave the restaurant.

And d'you know, Michael, what I've always thought is that . . .

But what PLACKETT *always thought is lost with their receding footsteps in the general fade. The last we hear is* PLACKETT's *cheerful laugh floating back to us as* MICHAEL *has said something which amuses him. Music fades up: 'Who is Silvia':.*

Then to Silvia let us sing,
That Silvia is excelling;
She excels each mortal thing
Upon the dull earth dwelling;
To her let us garlands bring.

TRANSFIGURED NIGHT

by Robert Ferguson

To Gertrude Margaret Ferguson

Robert Ferguson grew up near Blackpool in Lancashire and left school in 1968. He worked until 1976 and then began studying at UCL for a degree in Scandinavian Studies, specialising in Norwegian. He graduated in 1980. In 1983 he went to Norway on a scholarship from the Norwegian government and has been there since. He is writing a biography of Knut Hamsun.

Transfigured Night was first broadcast on BBC Radio 3 on 28 October 1984. The cast was as follows:

NARRATOR/X	Clive Francis
GIRL/BOY	Moir Leslie
POLICEMAN/COMPERE	Mark Rolston
NATHAN LEE	Anthony Hall

Director: John Tydeman

Running time, as broadcast: 44 minutes.

NARRATOR. I dismounted, leaning my bicycle against a tree, and stood watching her. She was looking away, in the opposite direction. A mountain rose tall and dark beyond us, and I seem to see her in my mind's eye turning, wandering slowly up its twisting pathway whilst I, casting about for some appropriate response, finally set my teeth to the bark of the slender birch beside me, biting at it with the abstracted ferocity of . . . (*Pause.*) With all the tenderness of . . . (*Pause.*) It was in the days when I was an actor. I worked for a company that spared no expense. Where the script spoke of real trees, real mountains, nothing would do for it but that we use real trees, real mountains. Even at rehearsal. And when we spoke of the river of grey water that came flooding down from the mountain, we did not content ourselves with a roll of oatmeal wallpaper strewn across the stage. Shame on the company that would perpetrate such shoddy illusions, that would make of disbelief a thing so slight that a mere trick might suspend it. The water was real, though for all the watchers could see our glasses might as well have been empty, for all the difference it would have made to them. For it was important that not merely the audience but we actors ourselves contrive for that brief hour or so to suspend our disbelief. (*Pause.*) There was a mountain. (*Pause.*) I imagine it had some kind of symbolic significance. It's only a guess, but I imagine its significance was symbolic, as was the river of grey water flowing from its heights. (*Pause.*) At this point, so close to the end, the script called upon us to improvise – a commonplace now, perhaps, but something of a novelty, in those pioneering days. I bit deep into the flesh of the silver birch, ghost among trees, and stood observing with theatrical intensity the blood, and the marks of the teeth etched in the green whiteness of the wood. The sun set. Earth's long shadow stretched out into space, and back she came, running back down the mountain track, and bowed low to the faces scattered pale across the darkness before us.

In the background the sound of applause from a large theatre with a full audience.

I made a quiet entrance. Leant my bike against a tree and stood watching as she waited, herself watching after someone making his exit on the far side of the stage. 'Sergei' she called, 'Sergei'. Then she turned and saw me. She stepped towards me. Took both my hands in hers.

GIRL (*in the theatre*). You came. Oh I'm so glad you could come. Thank you for coming.

NARRATOR. We spared no expense, in those days. Where the script called for a tree or a mountain to be real, then that's what we used, real trees, real mountains. Real water, where water was called for. Blood where blood, bread where bread. (*Pause.*) I tried to indicate in some way my awareness of the mountain there beside us, and this I did by standing quite still in its shadow, as though waiting for the right moment. For the sun to go down. For earth to cast her long cone of shadow. To throw up that black window and stand watching the stars scattered pale across the darkness before us. (*Pause.*) It was not a question of boots. We had boots adequate to the climb. Nor was it the height of the mountain, for as high as it was, it was not overhigh. (*Pause.*) And at the end of the show we parted, of course. We went our separate ways, as show-people do. A drink together, and then, 'Well, nice to be working with you again, old girl. Hope to work with you again soon. Old girl', and then off into the night, separate ways, the mountains and trees, the grey and tumbling waters of the river all but forgotten.

GIRL (*in the theatre*). You came. Oh I'm so glad you could come. Thank you for coming.

NARRATOR. We had the stage to ourselves. The sun lingering as though caught in the trees.

The sound of crows.

The lark spiralling above us. Just ourselves, and the bread, and the trees, and the mountain. There we sat by the grey river, safe in the shadow of the mountain, and there we broke bread, and laughing and mindless scooped the waters of the river to our mouths, lifting the waters of the river to our mouths, and for just a moment the water seemed clear and bright, sparkling as it flashed from the shadow into the light, sparkling like . . . (*Pause.*) like . . .

The theatre.

GIRL (*brightly*). I know – let's climb that mountain!

X (*patiently*). But dearest, we have not boots for such a climb.

There are titters from the audience.

GIRL (*astonished*). I beg your pardon?

NARRATOR. How I dreaded the need to improvise! And yet from somewhere I had found a response. My feeling was that the scene had worked well. I made a mental note to confer with her afterwards, to find out if she also felt that it had 'taken off'. But as things turned out, I did not. Show-people lead such strange lives – a smile, a kiss, a blow to the side of the head, whatever the script calls for – and then a quick drink round the corner. 'Nice to work with you again, old girl. Hope to work with you again some time. Old girl', and off into the night, separate ways. (*Pause.*) I carried a loaf of bread under my arm. My own idea, there was no mention of bread in the script. But since we were called upon to improvise – a commonplace now, perhaps, but in those far-off days a technique of considerable daring – it occurred to me that, should we run out of things to say, I might refer to the bread.

The theatre.

X. It's a lovely day, isn't it.

GIRL. Mm, yes. It is.

X (*pause*). Would you care for a slice of bread?

The audience titters.

GIRL. I beg your pardon?

NARRATOR. The loaf might serve as a prop, giving the easy verisimilitude of everyday life to what passed between us. As we talked on subjects quite remote from bread, my bicycle, perhaps, or the balloon stuck in the tree above us, or the inadvisability of the mountain venture, I might cut and butter a slice, and hand it to her in a casual, natural way, so that the scene would not seem at all grotesque – a policeman, a gypsy girl, flirting by a river, in the shadow of a mountain. (*Pause.*) It isn't easy to explain, the way in which an actor can become involved in a part to such an extent that presently a confusion arises between . . . (*Pause.*) To the point where it becomes difficult to . . . (*Pause.*) But it only takes the end for all to become clear, for all doubts to vanish as one's fellow performers run smiling forward, hands outstretched towards each other, to stand at the edge of the stage bowing to the darkness, to the faces scattered pale as stars across the darkness.

The audience applaud. As it dies down, there is the sound of crows.

A lark was singing. Oh there was music in the air all right. But at my age I felt it unwise to climb that mountain which, once climbed, at my age, could never be unclimbed. (*Pause.*) And yet at twenty, shod in brown brogues and devil-may care, I would have climbed the thing without a second thought. Given the proposal my whole-hearted assent in the loud, clear voice of youth.

The theatre.

GIRL. I know, let's climb that mountain!

X. Of course! Anything you say, old girl!

NARRATOR. Someone – perhaps it was that joker Don Sergei – developed a habit of switching the lights on and off during rehearsals, so that it was impossible for me to go on with my speeches. I give the name not from malice, not from any sense of bitterness, but because he was the only other character besides Maritana and myself, and because I knew that his involvement in the play ended with my entry. And while most actors in such a position would be glad of the chance of an early bath and a night home by the fireside, Don Sergei, known for his jokes, may well have taken it into his head to make life difficult for me. And what more natural, given the extent to which an actor can become involved in his part, what more natural – and why should she upon my entry be staring away after him? – what more natural than that – and why calling his name like that? – what more natural – if the man were no more than a name in her mind? – what more natural than that he should – if it were simply a name fed to her by the director? – what more natural than that an ex-lover – and if not, why was she staring away like that when I entered? – what more natural than that an ex-lover who makes his exit carrying with him still the memory unrequited, the unrequited memory, the unassuaged memory, the unassuaged memory, the unrequited, inassuagable memory of inexpressible things unlikely if not now than not ever to find expression, the inextinguishable memory of things left unsaid, and all that which must remain unsaid, words, words on words, mouldering, crumbling to the ground, subjected there to unspeakably, inexpressively massive geopsychological pressures over aeons of time until gradually an image crystallises, a mountain, perhaps, something having a purely symbolic existence, of the failures, perhaps, the disappointments, the sorrows, all the intolerable that cries out for the hiding shadow of symbol to fall upon it, subjected thus to the agony of leaving the stage with things unsaid, and the knowledge of memories in the making, and in his confusion, and because it's not always easy to describe but an actor may reach a point at which confusion blurs the distinction between, and in this confusion carrying his pain from the stage with him, what more natural than that an ex-lover should pursue a vendetta against me, not merely an image, in my policemanness, of high certainty of word, deed, and purpose, but his presumed successor in love, turning down the lights, as I struggled with my speeches? (*Pause.*) Whatever the truth of the matter, the result of the campaign against me was that I was never completely familiar with the part –

The sound of crows.

and in spite of my nerves was finally happiest at those points where the script indicated that the actors involved were to make up their own speeches.

The theatre.

X. It's a lovely day, isn't it?

GIRL. Mm, yes. It is.

X (*pause*). Would you care for a slice of bread?

The audience titters.

GIRL. I beg your pardon?

NARRATOR. Unforgettable scene. The bright sun. The grey water. The white bread. (*Pause.*) The pale face, the grey water, the bright white sun, the flash of, the flash of the pale bread flashing in sunlight before her grey face, grey against the grey of the water.

He tries again. The sound of crows.

The brilliant, the flashing brilliance of the sun on her pale face, the water trickling in veils from her fingers as she carried it in her hands from river to mouth. The scatter of her laughter as I sliced the bread. The two of us. The sun and the bread and the mountain and the water and the . . .

The crows stop.

There was talk in rehearsal that I might be too old for the part. My lapses into silence were seen as proof of a failing memory. There were references to bald patches visible beneath the spotlights. I could have defended myself. Told them about Don Sergei and his little tricks. But it seemed ungracious somehow, hitting a man when he's down, and I suggested instead that my silences had a very singular cause, namely, the peculiarly debilitating effects of happiness on me. (*Pause.*) And there was indeed an element of truth in this, for it sometimes happened that in the middle of my speeches a strange and irrational joy would take possession of me, and I would be struck dumb in celebration of its inner, causeless self. Or was it perhaps her nearness? Or no more than the sight of faces scattered pale over the darkness before us? (*Pause.*) I spoke persuasively, driven by fear of a return to the old parts. But my tale was derided as banal, and I won the day only by threatening to throw myself into the river were the part to be taken from me. (*Pause.*) For I had no wish to go back to the old parts, though an actor is glad, always glad of the work. Save in plays where, with an increasing frequency these days, he is called upon to improvise. And yet it seemed not to have occurred to her that the mountain might have a purely symbolic existence. Here, I felt, were grounds for a misunderstanding of the most basic sort. Of one's disappointments, for example. Or it might be one's failures. (*Pause.*) I suggested that certain parts be given the cello, as though the singer were too broken to continue. I could have started coughing, I suppose, but God knows, one cannot cough for ever. I added pointedly that I was a non-swimmer, for I had no wish to go back to the old roles, the old roles that filled the ache between halcyon days and Indian summer, when so often I played foil to those heroes I once played myself, in the clear, firm voice of youth.

The theatre.

GIRL. I know, let's climb that mountain!

X. Of course! Anything you say, old girl!

NARRATOR. Painful memories. Among many I recall one in which I was required to stride on stage in a ridiculous ill-fitting black uniform, properly the uniform of an inspector of buses, on this occasion passing as that of a park-keeper, and so in flagrant breach of our commitment to an authenticity complete almost to the point of redundancy. The part called for me forcibly to restrain a small boy, attempting by means of a pin stuck into the end of a stick, to burst a balloon caught fast in the branches of a tree. Quite a struggle the little rascal gave me. My cap fell off, and as I stooped to pick it up I received a sharp prick from the pin in the full of my bottom.

The theatre.

X. Ouch.

The audience titters.

Why, you little bleeder. Come 'ere.

He breaks the stick.

You come along with me you 'orrible vandalous little boy you.

BOY. Ouch. Yaroo. Leggo me ear mister!

NARRATOR. Turning on him with rapier swiftness I wrenched the implement from his hand, broke it in two across my knee and dragged him from the stage by his ear. A strange part, and a small one, and as any actor will tell you, the smaller the part, the less intrinsic interest one has in the meaning of the piece, or in its outcome, or in any damn part of it. Just deliver the line and then off, early bath, night by the fire. Soul-destroying. One such role after another led me in time to an indifference towards my art, and at length I decided to take matters into my own hands. It was during the performance of a play in which, simply to give a degree of verisimilitude to the proceedings, I was to sit on a park bench feeding bread to a pigeon while a nanny sat reading beside me. Presently I was to open a packet of cigarettes, put one in my mouth, feel about in my pockets for a light and, failing to find one, ask her. She was to say no. I was then to make my exit, leaving her to await the arrival of her lover. I should add that for the part I was dressed in the rather caddish fashion of the proprietor of a London sex-shop, leather coat, fur collar, astrakhan hat, this kind of thing, and the cigarette I was to thrust under her nose was black. (*Pause.*) I kept to the script throughout rehearsals. I gave no hint of my plans. Opening night, there I sat, the bread in my lap, rolling it into little balls between my fingers and tossing it to the pigeon, the nanny beside me engrossed in her book, now and then reaching out to rock the handle of the pram. With the scene then firmly established in our audience's mind I laid the bread aside and produced the black cigarette from my pocket.

The theatre.

X. Excuse me miss, do you have a light?

GIRL. No, I'm afraid I don't.

X. Oh. Oh.

NARRATOR. She waited for me to leave. The script did not call upon us to improvise at this point.

The theatre.

X. Would you care for a slice of bread?

GIRL. Er, no I wouldn't. Thank you.

X. Oh. (*Pause.*) See our little feathered-friend here, how he puts his claw up into his mouth whenever he's eaten? That's him scraping bread off his palate. It's because they refine all the roughage out of it, at the bakery. They make it into a kind of pulp. It's a disgrace. Don't you agree, miss?

GIRL. I beg your pardon?

X. I see you're reading a book there. What is it? Anything good?

NARRATOR. She turned the book the right way up and read the title to me, a look of outraged uncertainty on her face. Improvising is hell.

GIRL. Why yes, it's (*Pause.*) *The Death of Anton Webern: a drama in documents.*

X. Oh. (*Pause.*) Who's the author?

GIRL. Hans Molden-hauer.

X. Is it interesting?

GIRL. Fascinating.

NARRATOR. By this time she was directing frantic looks into the wings, hoping I don't know what, that perhaps someone would come and drag me off. But there was no stopping me. I had an almost mystical feeling that our scene was 'taking-off' in thrilling fashion.

X. Isn't it wonderful to see the signs of spring all about us! I saw a hen out walking this morning. Are you a nature lover, miss?

GIRL. No.

X. Ah, believe me, you don't know what you're missing. Just yesterday I saw a crow. Or was it the day before yesterday? No, no, as you were, it was yesterday. Are you fond of birds yourself?

GIRL. No.

X. Fascinating creatures. It's my hobby you know. I'm very interested in it. Talking of birds, do you remember when we did *The Wild Duck* by Ibsen?

NARRATOR. And so completely did I become immersed in the part that I forgot all about the audience in front of us, and began reminiscing at length about our performance of the play. Few will need reminding of the strain it puts upon our powers to suspend disbelief, and yet it takes but a small effort, and a little goodwill, to imagine a menagerie up there, in the Ekdal's loft . . . with chickens. And pigeons. And rabbits. And a duck. All up there, in the loft. And that on bad days old Ekdal goes up there with his gun and shoots himself a rabbit, to remind him of the good days, when he was young, when rabbits were bears, when . . .

X. . . . but don't you think it was a mistake to use real animals? Remember the noise? Like a farmyard. Clucking and cooing, rabbits thumping on the ceiling, bloody duck quack-quacking away. They were laughing, d'you remember? The audience were laughing. Ignoramuses. It seemed never to occur to them that the duck might have a purely symbolic existence.

The following dialogue continues through the narration.

POLICEMAN. Is this gentleman annoying you, miss?

GIRL. He most certainly is.

POLICEMAN. Come on then, let's be 'avin you.

X. But officer, I assure you, I was only trying to . . . ouch.

NARRATOR. My fun came to an end soon enough. Her lover, having with commendable initiative donned a policeman's uniform, entered, and displaying to the full his considerable talent for improvising, escorted me from the stage with my arm twisted behind my back. I had just time to grab what was left of the bread and stuff it into my pocket for later use. Perhaps as the focus for a little stage business. Eating it, for example, or talking about it. (*Pause.*) Simply for making something of the part like this I was threatened with dismissal. I argued that had I not built it up in this small way it might have seemed that I was indeed accosting the lady, foisting my attentions on her in hopes of the gratification of at least one of my sexual appetites. These improvisations of mine – casual, socially aware, and at the same time bracingly normal – went, in my opinion, a long way towards discouraging the audience from such suspicions. However, only under the most solemn promise that there would be no repetition was I allowed to remain with the company. (*Pause.*) This was not the happiest period of my acting career. The accusations of amnesia, the frequent references to my baldness, banishment into the half-world of the character actor, these personal difficulties took their toll of me, coinciding as they did with a general depression in the entertainments business. Takings at the box-office slumped, and with increasing frequency we resorted to the staging of guaranteed crowd-pleasers, *Murder in The Cathedral, Waiting for Godot,* this kind of thing. I blush to recall what was required of me in those days. How once, grotesquely attired in sunglasses and stetson, bermuda shorts, sandals and a large cigar, I played an American tourist, member of a coach party being shown a mountain for which extravagant claims were being made by some local, our guide to judge by his uniform. Tiring of his enthusiasm, I was to strike a belligerent pose, right leg planted firmly forward, stomach thrust out, shoulders back, and taking the cigar from my mouth, give him a piece of my mind.

X (*W.C. Fields voice*). You call that a mountain, why sir, back home in Texas we got mountains so tall if you set that down beside 'em, folks'd think they was walkin through a valley, why let me tell you sir we got mountains so tall it takes a man and two boys all day to look to the top of them, one lookin until he gets tired, an the other taking over where he left off from.

NARRATOR. One lost the desire to improvise in the face of such parts. Perhaps that's why I had such trouble, when my time came, when my time came again, when out of the blue my time came, and again I stood once again as in the old days watching her, dazzled by the brilliance of her, stunned into joy at the sight of her there by the water the wind shifting in her hair sun lingering in its westward drift mountain rearing into the blue –

The sounds of crows.

lark ascending water cupped laughing and mindless to her lips dripping like jewels from her lips. (*Pause.*) And the bread, the white bread in the white light, the sun on the bread on her face on the water, black mountain rising above us, sending down the water, taking back the path. (*Pause.*) There was a red balloon caught in the branches of the tree above us. The sight of it stirred in her some desire to improvise –

The crows become more insistent.

and she jumped to her feet and began trying to knock it free. I watched smiling until I could bear it no longer and jumping up in wild play took hold of her and held her arms against her sides, pleading with her to, suggesting that,

The crows fade.

pointing out to her the clear spring river running like quicksilver beside us, the rainbow and the brown trout jumping from it as though they had not freedom enough within it, the beat of a horse's hooves breaking the evening silence as it pulled a wagon along the twisting lanes, the bright sun dancing on the black paint . . . (*Pause.*) We tried everything to bring the crowds back – pantomime, music hall, variety, even a sex show. That was a hard part, humping the diva in the shadow of a cardboard birch, pale backs going through the motions for the benefit of watchers scattered silent in the darkness before us, humping and pumping and puffing up balloons in the shadow of a paper mountain, going through the motions, as the man said when . . . (*Pause.*) But the way she sang that high C was one of the strangest and most beautiful things I ever heard in my life. The note left her throat, it left her body, it seemed to float out over the audience like a star, drifting on up into the infinite.

The GIRL *gives a hacking cough.*

Then a crumb stuck in her throat, and she began to cough, hacking away like an old crow. I must've warned her a hundred times about eating on the job. We had to leave off for a moment while I gave her back a thump. 'How's that, old girl? Any better, old girl?' (*Pause.*) And when it was over, when she was gone off up the mountain, I searched in my mind for some appropriate means of expressing myself. In the grip of powerful and wounded instincts, I turned and bit savagely at the bark of the birch, the bitter sting of tinfoil blazing in the nerves of my teeth.

The audience applaud.

COMPERE. Thank you, thank you, thank you. And now, ladies and gentlemen will you give a warm welcome please to our next artiste, the internationally renowned masked conjuror, all the way from . . . (*Aside.*) Where you from this week, love?

X (*stage whisper*). Spain!

COMPERE. All the way from Spain! Senor X! The masked conjuror!

Band music. Applause.

Well, you got to have a gimmick 'avent you? I mean . . .

X (*atrocious accent*). Sank you sank you sank you.

Good-humoured boos, derision.

And good eevening ladees and yentlemen. (*Pause.*) Oh, come on, give us a chance!

NARRATOR. It went well, to begin with. I opened with the old balloon-and-stick trick, always a favourite, for some reason. With a pin embedded in the end of my wand I jabbed and prodded and stabbed away at a balloon, I beat it and smacked it from one end of the stage to the other. And yet miraculously, miraculously, miraculously, the pin appeared not to penetrate that delicate red membrane, to expose the nothingness within, the nothingness that might have shocked, that might have disappointed, and yet without which there could have been no red balloon. Over and over I performed the trick. But God knows, one cannot perform the same trick forever, whatever the heart's desire. I moved on. Things began to go wrong. A dove I took from my sleeve and threw fluttering into the air fell back to the stage with a thud, dead of a heart attack. But I had another pigeon up my sleeve, or to be more precise, in my waistcoat, or to be more precise, another dove. But when I reached for it the bird refused to come out, and clung with wretched fury to the lining of my pocket. In consternation I called for the curtain to be lowered. A few deep breaths to calm the beating heart, and then up with the curtain, on with the show. For my next trick I called on a volunteer from the audience to join me, and from the darkness there emerged a stout, swarthy man in a red waistcoat.

X (*Bruce Forsyth voice*). Your name, sir?

LEE. Nathan Lee.

X. And what do you do for a living, Nathan? As if we needed to ask!

LEE. I'm a Traveller. A Gypsy.

X. Got the family with you here tonight, Nathan?

LEE. My daughter Maritana's here with me.

X. Maritana, that's a lovely name. Isn't that a lovely name? Are you there, Maritana? Put your hand up so we can all see you love. (*Pause.*) There she is. Come on up love. Don't be shy. Come and join your old man. (*Pause.*) That's it. Right. There we are. So you're Maritana?

GIRL. Yes.

X. You know, I *do* like your name. I think it's a lovely name. A super name. (*To the audience.*) Isn't that a lovely name? Maritana?

There are sporadic yesses, assenting noises from the audience. There is a ticking noise, which continues.

NARRATOR. He had a pocket watch on a gold chain across his waistcoat. Having ascertained that it had both sentimental and practical value I took it from him, placed it in the palm of my hand, and draped a large handkerchief over it.

X. You don't mind if I smash your gold watch to pieces with this hammer, do you, Nathan?

The audience laugh.

LEE (*laughing*). No, not really.

X. Don't laugh! What you laughing for? He thinks I'm joking! No! I'm serious, I've never done this trick before. (*Pause.*) Right then . . .

NARRATOR. I took the watch from him and placed it in the palm of my hand, having first ascertained that it was of both sentimental and practical value. I then covered it with a large silk handkerchief, and struck it what appeared to be a firm blow with the hammer.

The sound of ticking stops.

With beating heart, my pulse racing, the sweat beading on my forehead, I removed the handkerchief. Had I succeeded? Had the trick worked? Indeed it had – the watch was annihilated. Pulverised, atomised, destroyed. Smashed beyond all hope of repair. Lee refused to leave the stage. He appeared to think – extraordinary notion – that I had not intended the destruction of the watch! As for Maritana, she simply laughed, and wandered off back into the darkness. Captivating laughter. Impelled by I know not what instinct, I ran to the front of the stage and called after her, 'Nice to work with you, old girl. Hope to work with you again some time. Old girl.' (*Pause.*) For it only takes the end, for all to become clear. You stand lost in thought, wondering what to say, wondering what to do. And suddenly they're running towards you, bright smiles on their faces, your fellow-players, beckoning you to the curtain call. And as you bow to the darkness, to the faces scattered pale as stars across the darkness, it all makes sense to you, the doubts and confusions just fly away. In a matter of moments it's a case of 'Nice to be working with you again, old girl. Hope to work with you again soon. Old girl', and off you go, separate ways, the what had passed between you all but forgotten, all but forgotten. (*Long pause.*) I saw a hen out walking this morning. (*Pause.*) Are you a nature lover, miss? (*Pause.*) Her father threatened to throw me in the water.

X. You mustn't do that.

LEE. Mustn't do that? Why not?

X. Because I can't swim.

LEE. Can't swim? Suppose you got shipwrecked?

X. Can you fly?

LEE. No.

X. Suppose your plane crashed?

LEE. Listen, if God meant us to fly he'd've given us the tickets. I think it's pathetic, grown man, can't swim. Suppose you get shipwrecked?

X. If God meant us to swim he'd've given us the flippers. I'd drown.

LEE. If you could swim you could at least go through the motions.

X. As the woman said when her old chap fell down the manhole.

LEE. Never mind all that, what're you going to do about my watch?

X. I'll reimburse you.

LEE. Don't you threaten me, mate!

X. I'll pay you back.

LEE. What with?

X. Money.

LEE. You haven't got any.

X. I'll make some. Open a boutique for hunchbacks. Call it 'Quasi Modes'. What d'you reckon?

LEE. No chance, no chance.

X. I'll write a TV series about impotent secret agents. Call it 'Emission Impossible'.

LEE. No chance, no chance.

X. What's the matter with you today, miserable sod?

LEE. I've just heard the Irish knock-knock joke. Want to hear it?

X. Not much.

LEE. You say 'knock-knock' to me.

X. Knock-knock.

LEE. Who's there?

Pause. LEE *snorts. The audience titters, the laughter swells.*

NARRATOR. Double acts, magic, sex shows, pantomime – we tried them all. Still our audiences declined. One by one the leading players packed their bags and left the company. And then out of the blue I received a summons from our director, a Mr Hobson. Our troubles were over, he announced – he had written an opera, a piece in the style of the 1840's, which decade he was convinced was 'due for a revival'. This one will run and run, he said. This will bring them flocking back. It's about a girl called Maritana, and her father. Gypsies, travelling people. They're illegally parked in a field somewhere out in the country. Maritana has a lover, a handsome dissipated roisterer by the name of Don Sergei, a cavalier at once shabby and yet debonair. Imprisoned for duelling during Holy Week he escapes, and makes his way to her side. As the curtain rises he sings a romantic aria in which he tells her how happy he is to see her again, and swears that they shall never again he parted. You are to play the part of a policeman, stationed at a little village not far from the scene of their joyful reunion. In the middle of his song you appear in the background, riding your bicycle towards them, carrying in your breast pocket a summons which you are to serve on them in connection with the illegal encampment. You are quite unaware of the drama surrounding Don Sergei. As far as you're concerned, this is just routine business. Naturally, the lovers are unaware of this. And when Maritana spots your dark form cycling towards them along the country lanes she takes you for a pursuing force, and in an aria of almost unbearable pathos tells Don Sergei that he must go, that their love can never be, that the obstacles in their way are insurmountable. But though she will never see him again, she will love him forever. Certain parts I have given here to the cello, as though the singers were too broken to continue. Don Sergei pleads with her to come with him, but she refuses, her mind is made up, and with dragging steps he leaves the stage as you enter from the other side and lean your bicycle up against a tree. You know at once, with your policeman's instinct, that something's wrong. You see tears streaked on Maritana's face, you sense her despairing indifference to all that surrounds her. What do you do? Do you follow your nose and investigate? Or do you serve the summons and leave it at that? (*Pause.*) 'Well,' I said, 'which is it to be?' He gestured helplessly towards a pile of bills on the desk in front of him. 'You'll have to decide for yourself, I haven't had time to finish it. Damn paperwork. Debts, duns, company falling to pieces in my hands – you'll have to improvise, X. Veteran like yourself shouldn't have any trouble.' (*Pause.*)

The sound of water flowing. Birds singing. Summer country sounds.

And so it came about that, just when I had thought it was all over, my hour came again, and again I stood once again I stood as in the old days I stood once again watching her dazzled by the brilliance of her stunned into joy at the sight of her, by the stream, by the tree, the wind lifting and shifting and lifting in her hair, sun lingering in its westward drift as though caught in the treetops, mountain sheering into the blue beyond while

A lark, very distinct.

a lark circled high above us, binding the hour in his silver chain of sound, and the river ran quick and clear at our feet, the rainbow and the brown trout jumping from it as though they had not freedom enough within it.

A distant horse and wagon on the road.

And from across the fields, breaking the evening silence, came the hollow iron music of distant hooves, the jingle and flutter of harness bells, the faint clatter of cartwheels, the dancing flash of the bright sun on the blue and red back of the wagon . . . (*Pause.*) For it only takes the end, for all to become clear.

X. Excuse me, miss. Would you care for a slice of bread?

NARRATOR. She did not hear me, as she was never meant to hear me. She stood looking off in the opposite direction, and then wandered slowly away up the twisting mountain track whilst I searched for an appropriate response, and finally set my teeth to the bark of the slender birch, biting at it with the abstracted ferocity of . . . (*Pause.*) With all the tenderness of . . . (*Pause.*)

Silence.

Some joker turned down the lights and left me standing there, with no lines to say, no one to say them to, with no tree, no river, no mountain, no bird, only the pale faces of the watchers scattered dim across the darkness before me. And the bare boards. And the bare walls trailing bare wires. I stood wondering what to say, wondering what to do. And it came into my head to sing.

DAYBREAK

by Don Haworth

To Jonathan

Don Haworth was born at Bacup, Lancashire, served in the Royal Air Force and worked as a journalist. This is his third Giles Cooper award. The earlier ones were for *Episode on a Thursday Evening* in 1978 and *Talk of Love and War* in 1981. He produces films for BBC Television and won the British Academy Award for documentary in 1980.

Daybreak was first broadcast on BBC Radio 3 on 12 January 1984. The cast was as follow:

HAROLD	David Threlfall
FRED	Christian Rodska

Director: Kay Patrick

Running time, as broadcast: 52 minutes.

It is 1944. HAROLD *and* FRED, *both aircraftmen, are travelling at night in a slow train.* HAROLD *is a burly country youth of twenty.* FRED *is an artisan ten years older.*

FRED. Going back off leave?

HAROLD. Yes.

FRED. R.A.F. Swetenhall?

HAROLD. How did you know?

FRED. Seen you in the cookhouse. You're a cook.

HAROLD. Are you stationed there as well?

FRED. Motor transport section. I'm one of your customers.

HAROLD. I've seen you in the dining hall.

FRED. I usually sit at the table by the door.

HAROLD. I didn't recognise you in this light.

FRED. These bulbs are no good. Landscape outside is brighter with the moon at the back of the clouds.

HAROLD. I don't see well anyway.

FRED. Do your specs not rectify that?

HAROLD. Not in this gloom. I can't see at all in t' blackout.

FRED. Nobody can see in the blackout.

HAROLD. Th' aircrews – they're passed for night vision, aren't they?

FRED. They say they are. Wing Commander came out of the mess in the blackout and fell down the steps.

They laugh, then fall silent for a moment.

You know we change at Retford?

HAROLD. Cold spot that in t' middle o' t' night.

FRED. Then we don't go on to Lincoln. There's no early bus on Tuesdays. We get out at Skellingford and walk.

HAROLD. I know.

FRED. Bags of time though. We'll be laughing.

HAROLD. You might.

FRED. Your pass is till 0800 hours, isn't it?

HAROLD. Yes . . . But yesterday. (*He laughs trying to conceal some nervousness.*) I shouldn't be surprised if they didn't put me on a charge.

FRED. Twenty-four hours adrift, that's nothing.

HAROLD. You reckon I might get off wi' seven days confined to camp?

FRED. Might not get even that . . . Have you an excuse?

HAROLD. Yes, I've got an excuse.

FRED. Tell 'em the tale then.

HAROLD. I'm not really bothered about being confined to camp.

FRED. If you're spent up, what difference does it make?

HAROLD. But I've a good conduct stripe coming up. I might lose that.

FRED. Not just for overstaying your leave.

HAROLD. I've long looked forward to having a good conduct stripe on my sleeve.

FRED. You will have.

HAROLD. To impress my dad.

FRED. Sure.

HAROLD. To please him.

FRED. He'd be proud of you.

HAROLD. And to show him that I'm not entirely worthless. (*He gives a slight laugh.*)

FRED. Does he say that?

HAROLD. Not always.

FRED. Because your cooking is very good.

HAROLD *pleased, laughs.*

Par excellence. Renowned.

HAROLD (*pleased, laughs*). There's a lot of us in t' cookhouse. I'm only one of 'em.

FRED. Renowned throughout the R.A.F. Blokes try to get posted to Swetenhall just for the grub.

HAROLD (*pleased*). You're kidding.

FRED. There's nothing else to get posted there for. Dump in the wilds of Lincolnshire with a mad C.O. and a shower of officers half way round the twist.

HAROLD. Some of th' aircrews are decent.

FRED. But they don't last five minutes.

HAROLD. They come and go.

FRED. You wouldn't get me flying.

HAROLD. You're better on t' ground.

FRED. Certainly. You and me are better off creeping along in this train than them poor blokes up in the moonlight getting hammered with flak and fighters at 20,000 feet.

HAROLD. It must be cold at that height.

FRED. Thirty degrees below.

HAROLD. It's cold even at th' height of our fellside. You need a warm by t' fire on a cold day.

FRED. Some of 'em get a warm they weren't expecting, them that go up in flames.

HAROLD. I wouldn't like that.

FRED. You're better on the ground.

HAROLD. Yes.

FRED. I'm called Fred.

HAROLD. I'm called Harold.

FRED. Fair enough. I'm glad to make your acquaintance, Harold.

They ride on for a time in silence.

HAROLD. This good conduct stripe.

FRED. It's not in jeopardy.

HAROLD. My dad, he's out of t' reckoning now, but there's a lass I want to impress.

FRED. Oh yes.

HAROLD. I keep trying but there's nowt doing.

FRED. Have you renewed your assaults this leave?

HAROLD. 'What if something goes wrong?' she says. Fair enough, that was an argument, but there's room for her now at our house.

FRED. No obstacles.

HAROLD. But if th' mare won't stand to t' stallion there's no remedying that.

FRED. Do you come from a farm?

HAROLD. Can you smell me?

FRED. No. You mentioned the fellside, and your bucolic allusion just now.

HAROLD. To my good conduct stripe?

FRED. No, to horses.

HAROLD. We only have th' owd cart horse.

FRED. Cows.

HAROLD. No. Sheep and pigs mainly. And fowl. I'm taking a dozen duck eggs back for t' lads and t' girls.

FRED. That'll make you popular.

HAROLD. I'm quite popular in t' cookhouse. I don't shirk my share o' t' work.

FRED. I know. I've seen you humping the tins round.

HAROLD. I wasn't always popular at home, not wi' my dad. (*He laughs.*) He called me Big Head.

FRED. But affectionately meant like?

HAROLD. Sometimes, but usually nasty. (*He laughs.*) He said I looked like a football with specs on. I must admit that's a very apt description. Can you descry me in this light?

FRED. I can descry you. Cherubic is what I'd say.

HAROLD. It's not what he said. His cough made him short-tempered at times. He punched folk.

FRED. Bit of a bruiser?

HAROLD. Not big like me. Little chap, quick as a rat. He had a way of clenching his fist wi' his thumb bent in behind his fingers so their joints stuck out like a row of toffee hammers.

FRED. Body puncher?

HAROLD. Yes.

FRED. Rib bruiser.

HAROLD. He once punched old Mr Banbridge, draper and agricultural clothing specialist; he once punched him t' length of th' aisle in t' methodist chapel.

FRED. Long way to punch an old draper, even if it weren't a big chapel.

HAROLD. My dad was playing th' organ.

FRED. Presides at the keyboard, eh?

HAROLD. Only when their regular organist's adrift, Mrs Salter, and she couldn't, as you say, preside this particular Sunday because she'd been tossed on t' Thursday by t' bull.

FRED. Reasonable excuse.

HAROLD. And her son who pumped bellows he had to stay at home and look after her hens and pound up and down stairs wi' hot drinks for her, so down at chapel reserve team were out, my dad at th' keyboard and old Bainbridge pumping t' bellows.

FRED. It's harder than you think.

HAROLD. And there's a knack.

FRED. There's a knack.

HAROLD. It were all that were in his capacity, poor old man, but he were simply playing with th' handle. My dad were getting no wind.

FRED. That's no good.

HAROLD. I knew his temper'd snap. Half out of his seat he were, yanking at t' stops and weighing down on t' keys and bollocking old Mr Bainbridge so vehement that even deaf old ladies with their mouth full of humbugs could hear him.

FRED *laughs.*

(*Laughing.*) Organ didn't offer to play a tune, it were just like a warbling groan, then Mr Bainbridge made a desperate effort and there were an explosion like an enormous fart, nearly took t' roof off.

They both laugh.

It's funny now but it weren't then. Mr Bainbridge, being a draper, had a starched collar on and my dad got hold of him wi' two fingers down it, same as you might grab a dog's collar, but wi' fingers down at t' front of his neck, not t' back, and he pummelled him with his free fist length of t' chapel and out past war memorial, and I think he'd have been pummelling him still if congregation hadn't run out and overborne him.

They both laugh.

HAROLD. People didn't like him for it, not outsiders. Inside the home you get more used to a person's quirks.

FRED. Did he set about you then?

HAROLD. Until I outgrew him. My mother's come in for regular pummelling, which isn't right or kind.

FRED. No.

HAROLD. But at least we understood t' cause of his moods. His chest got him down. Out toiling about fellside on a bitter day, that's a terrible trial to a man with bronchitis. Half dead he were in t' winter months, sat by t' fire wheezing.

FRED. And what stung him to rise and pitch into you?

HAROLD. Feeling ill and useless, having no money. He blew up at nothing, sudden and violent, like a fight breaking out in a hen house. (*He laughs.*) Over went t' table with all t' crockery, and biff, bang, wallop into my mother and me when I were little, then out he'd go gasping for breath and sit wi' his pigs.

FRED. Funny carry on.

HAROLD. That's what folk thought that didn't make allowance for his bronchitis. (*He laughs.*) I don't suppose they'd prevail on Mr Bainbridge to hazard a bout at pumping th' organ again.

FRED. He'd be wary.

HAROLD. It were agony for him to draw breath for a fortnight. I do believe it's a reason, these ructions, why I made no headway with this young woman. That and t' whiff of pigs about me.

FRED. You don't whiff of pigs.

HAROLD. And you reckon I won't lose my good conduct stripe?

FRED. They won't even put you on a charge.

HAROLD. I know a bloke who came back late and were let off because of his specs.

FRED. His specs?

HAROLD. He said his specs had been smashed and he'd had to wait to have new lenses put in.

FRED. Did they accept that?

HAROLD. He were just – what is it? – bollocked.

FRED. Reprimanded.

HAROLD. Yes.

FRED. You could say that.

HAROLD. They asked him why he hadn't telephoned.

FRED. What did he say?

HAROLD. I don't know. But I could deal with that. I could answer truthfully. We were busy burying my father.

The train whistles and rumbles on.

It is still night. They are alone in the unheated waiting room of a station, waiting for their connection. They rouse from dozing.

FRED. Your head.

HAROLD. What?

FRED. I've been weighing up your head while you were dozing.

HAROLD. What time is it?

FRED. Half-past two. Your head's not abnormally large.

HAROLD. You think not.

FRED. When you joined up, when you were kitted out, did they wheel you off to have your head measured for a special cap?

HAROLD. No.

FRED. They just chucked one at you out of the shelves?

HAROLD. Yes.

FRED. Standard issue. Stock size.

HAROLD (*pause*). I never thought of that. It's a misfortune I didn't travel with you sooner. I'd have liked to have put that to him before he slipped away.

Silence.

FRED. Bet you didn't know you were letting yourself in for this when you joined up.

HAROLD. I didn't.

FRED. Shivering in Retford waiting room in the middle of the night.

HAROLD. I said it were a parky spot.

FRED. But, as we said, not as parky as it is for the aircrew at 20,000 feet with only the flak to warm 'em up.

HAROLD. I wouldn't like to go up. I'd like your job, mechanicking.

FRED. Did you ask for it when you joined up?

HAROLD. Didn't know what there were going. I only joined on t' spur of the moment.

FRED (*laughs*). Moment of weakness.

HAROLD. I had to get another job any road. Once I were fully growed I were like out-eating my welcome at home.

FRED. Was that said?

HAROLD. No, he were very good, he never said that, but he thought it. He'd stare at this huge mound of potatoes and turnips and gravy my mother set before me, then he'd go wheezing out without a word and sit wi' his pigs.

FRED. You earned your grub.

HAROLD. Not on that scale. I would have done willingly had there been t' work to do, but our place were too small to keep us once I reached my full eating powers. Then t' war started and that put paid to any chance of renting any more fields because th' owners got more as subsidy for ploughing 'em up.

FRED. So you were like driven off the land?

HAROLD. I were better to go. On top of my eating we had my Uncle Leonard scrounging round – not scrounging really, he came to do th' electric as a favour.

FRED. The electric?

HAROLD. He's an electrician but he's all but give up to it. What wit' war, he couldn't get hold o' t' wire and things in sufficient quantity and then his arthritis in his knees got worse and he really weren't up to scrambling under floorboards, so he were like semi-retired, he had his pension, doing just like bits of jobs and when he come to do our electric it were lambing time and he helped with that and then he come up and did odd jobs most days and it were clear like somebody'd have to go.

FRED. And that were you?

HAROLD. I were eating t' most.

FRED. Were you not obliged to remain in agriculture?

HAROLD. No, I weren't obliged to remain in agriculture, because I weren't paid no regular wage and I didn't have no card wi' stamps on or nothing, so I weren't registered, which baffled 'em a bit at th' employment exchange, and it weren't entirely legal, but they had to let me go my own way.

FRED. And you were intent on the Air Force?

HAROLD (*laughs*). As you say, a moment of weakness. Thursdays I went wit' cart to hospitals and hotels and lunatic asylums and such picking up swill for t' pigs, kitchen waste. And one Thursday after my Uncle Leonard had took up his abode I happened to notice this R.A.F. poster outside th' employment exchange and I sailed in and after a certain amount of humming and hawing about whether I were a farm labourer within t' meaning of th' act they capitulated. There were two of 'em, one sent for his boss, they capitulated and I were signed on.

FRED. You out-argued 'em?

HAROLD (*laughs*). They hadn't much stomach for arguing. I were like well stuck up with kitchen waste and my boots were oozing on t' floor, and one of 'em were trying to tackle his tea and biscuits, so they were only too glad to bring proceedings to a conclusion and let th' Air Force have t' benefit of my company.

FRED. Per ardua ad astra.

HAROLD. Aye. He were retching, him wit' tea and biscuits.

FRED. And did they not offer you a trade?

HAROLD. They weren't disposed to prolong t' conversation and I didn't know owt about trades. It were passed over quickly.

Anything, I said, in th' open air and away from kitchen waste. So once I got in they made me a cook.

They both laugh.

I wouldn't change it now, mind. I'm good at it. I'm good at humping frozen carcases in t' back door and I'm good at delicate jobs like making trifles. I can do th' whole range.

FRED. Does the cooking smell not get you down?

HAROLD. If you came from where I come from no smell'd get you down.

They both laugh.

I know t' kitchen turns some folk up, but it's a clean smell. Catering officer comes round, M.O., orderly officer – do you get that amount of inspection?

FRED. No.

HAROLD. When we've scrubbed off and washed t' tiles down at night, king could live there if he were bombed out of his own premises. (*He laughs.*) And eat off th' floor.

FRED. It's a good kitchen.

HAROLD. And grand folk to work with. I'm quite popular with 'em.

FRED. You'd be popular anywhere, Harold.

HAROLD. I'm not quick on th' uptake but I'm thorough.

FRED. That's what counts.

HAROLD. You can take a pride. It's opened my eyes.

FRED. In terms of hygiene?

HAROLD. In terms of hygiene. (*He laughs.*) Never thought owt about it at home. Yard deep in dirt and droppings of every description and in through t' back door wi' your boots plastered. What can my mother do? It's tramped in with every comer and he could never like muster th' energy to shift midden perched at top side o' t' yard. In heavy rain it can actually ooze under th' house door.

FRED. Good God.

HAROLD. You won't have nothing like that to contend with where you come from?

FRED. No.

HAROLD. Then t' pigs –

FRED. I'd always heard pigs were clean animals.

HAROLD. Of themselves. But their feed isn't. Kitchen waste is nasty stuff to handle. It cakes to t' bins, it cakes to t' cart, it cakes everywhere. But things could be scrubbed and sluiced down like we do in t' cookhouse. Keeping pigs doesn't mean you've got to live like 'em.

FRED. You'll be able to change that.

HAROLD. I'd know how.

FRED. You'll get your ticket out of the Air Force now there's a farm with no proprietor.

HAROLD. I'd install taps, I'd shift t' midden, there's some walls that could do with knocking down and rebuilding. I might do away wi' pigs altogether, than if I fancied a woman I wouldn't have to restrict myself just to them capable of humping swill bins. I could range free.

FRED. You do it, mate.

HAROLD (*pause*). But I don't want to leave t' cookhouse, not just yet.

FRED. No.

HAROLD. My mother says she can manage along with my Uncle Leonard.

FRED. Fair enough then.

HAROLD. I'd like to stay for long enough to win my good conduct stripe.

FRED. Sure.

HAROLD. That is, if I haven't scuppered my chances.

FRED. Not for being 24 hours adrift.

HAROLD (*pause*). There are other things.

FRED. What other things?

HAROLD (*pause*). That might be took into account.

FRED (*waits*). I see.

They fall silent. A goods train passes through the station.

HAROLD. I hope I haven't painted a bad picture of my dad.

FRED. No.

HAROLD (*laughs*). In fact as we've only just become properly acquainted and you didn't know him it won't matter to you what picture I paint of him. You'll not be interested.

FRED. You talk, Harold. He's bound to be on your mind.

HAROLD. He is on my mind.

FRED. Bound to be. You've just come hot foot from interring him.

HAROLD. Haven't been to bed since.

FRED. No. And it's passing the night interestingly, anecdotes like punching the organ pumper.

HAROLD. That were an exception.

FRED. Of course.

HAROLD. Appearing in public. He stopped going anywhere, weren't fit for it. Choir, he used to sing once and brass band he played t' trumpet. Well, time came he hadn't wind for it.

FRED. Like the chapel organ.

HAROLD (*laughs*). Aye, they were both short of puff. And then he had this habit of black despair and coming over antagonistic, and folk didn't want owt to do wi' him and he didn't want owt to do wi' folk. So he became a recluse like, cleaving to his pigs.

FRED. Narrow kind of life for him.

HAROLD. It were . . . He were different when I was little. We had a big meadow then down by t' river. I think there were always something not quite right wi' his chest because he wore a scarf, a white silk scarf same as colliers do, and polished boots, and his face were a good colour, not white and drawn as it become.

FRED. I can picture him.

HAROLD. He taught me t' names of th' birds and t' fishes. I can remember seeing t' reflection of our faces in t' water, leaning over. Then he dropped a stone in and spread us out in ripples.

He laughs a little in fondness and FRED *laughs in sympathy.*

I didn't have my specs then. We had a young bitch, sheepdog, intelligent animal, that we trained in that field. First time he got her to lie down she lay in a puddle, cool her belly, and after that he'd a hard job to break her of th' trick of looking for a puddle every time he put her down.

They both laugh.

Everything seemed to go wrong at t' same time. I don't know which it were first, losing this meadow we rented or his chest, but I remember him laying into this little bitch wi' his stick, something she'd done wrong on t' fellside, and she yelped and howled and eventually he let go and stumbled over to t' wall fighting for his breath. He were mouthing at me to help him, but I didn't.

FRED. He'd brought it on himself.

HAROLD. Then t' young bitch came to him and licked his hand. I reckon she were a more Christian being than either him or me.

FRED. I like dogs. Not all, but some.

HAROLD. Same with pigs, I suppose. There's some likeable ones, I don't doubt, if you weren't biased. But I'm biased, I can't stand 'em. It all happened at once, my dad's health and t' meadow going and t' pigs coming to take up their abode. In fact it proceeded directly from losing t' let o' t' meadow. That left us with 25 acres of bottom land, which isn't enough for t' sheep when they're brought down off fellside, let alone keeping t' cows we had. You're scuppered for owt but pigs.

FRED. They just need their sty space, eh?

HAROLD. That's one way, but he threw everything into t' pig job. We put up a proper pig house that my Uncle Leonard wired for th' electric so it kept a good temperature and that way you don't lose litters in winter.

FRED. Does it pay for the outlay?

HAROLD. It's supposed to in t' long-run. In fact th' pigs were cosier in their stalls than we were in th' house. My dad used to go and sit with 'em – th' heat in there were better for his breathing – and me and my mother sat in th' house. We passed many a winter evening that way.

FRED. He must have been lonely.

HAROLD. He were very lonely. 'My best friends are in them stalls,' he used to say. But how can you expect to keep friends among humans if you're forever punching 'em?

FRED. Did he punch many?

HAROLD. Not outside th' house, no he didn't, that's misleading. But like his domestic punching were public knowledge long before he thumped Mr Bainbridge down the chapel. Years ago my Uncle Leonard told him he'd have to drop th' practice of going for my mother. Minister spoke to him and t' policeman, and me myself, once I'd joined up and seen things in a fresh light, I warned him every time I went on leave, I doubly warned him, he'd have to look out for himself if I caught him at it.

FRED. Did she nag him?

HAROLD. No . . . well, only about things that had to be decided about like overdue bills. And often enough he'd no power of decision because he'd no money to pay 'em.

FRED (*sympathetically*). So what could he do?

HAROLD. Nowt, could he? But even if it weren't money, if it were only like shifting t' midden, he were too sick and weary to contemplate it and t' mere mention were enough to make him ratty.

FRED. I can understand that.

HAROLD. Can you?

FRED. You've only to have a bad cold and it's hard to abide folk. We had a bloke poured a tin of oil over a Waaf fitter.

HAROLD. He never wasted no oil – that's one thing you couldn't hold against him. Sometimes it were like spontaneous combustion. He'd fly at my mother for nowt, and once when I'd grew too big to tackle he deliberately broke my specs, the frame, and till th' Air Force issued me this pair I went about wi' 'em held together wi' Elastoplast.

FRED. Did it throw you out of focus?

HAROLD (*laughs*). I was threw out of focus without that. He treated me as a blockhead and everybody else followed suit except my mother and my Uncle Leonard. Th' school tret me as a blockhead, t' bandmaster tret me as a blockhead when I wanted to learn t' trombone. (*He laughs.*) It was only when I come into th' Air Force, where they treat everybody as blockheads, that I felt normal.

FRED. It's them that's blockheads, not us. You'd travel a long way to find two bigger blockheads at one spot than the C.O. and the station warrant officer.

HAROLD. Lunatic asylum where we picked up t' swill had a good number of blockheads.

FRED. But some of 'em 'd be wise in their way, perhaps. Eccentric.

HAROLD. Yes.

FRED. Saintly, some of 'em, no doubt.

HAROLD. My mother's saintly. My Uncle Leonard said that. 'She's a saintly woman your mother.' And she is. She stood by my dad. And she stood by me and encouraged me wi' her words, quietly like when he were out of earshot so it didn't start no ructions.

FRED. Like walking a tightrope for her.

HAROLD. Sometimes, then other times when he were better side out he'd play th' old organ we have, play hymns and such, and he'd say, 'I don't know what I'd do without you both and I don't know why you put up wi' me.'

FRED. I'll bet you asked yourself that.

HAROLD. Well, he were my dad. But what he said were only t' truth. We did all his running for him. I were doing a man's work when I were a dozen. I sheared t' sheep from being ten because he couldn't stand th' heat and t' bending over. They all went shorn out of th' yard up t' fellside like a river flowing upwards, and he said, 'You're all right, Big Head. You'll finish up better than me.'

He breaks off, overcome, then masters himself and resumes.

He'd get peace sometimes from reading t' Bible.

FRED. That's what it's for, peace.

HAROLD. Once when he were playing th' organ he stood up and quoted t' scriptures at us. 'God so loved the world that he gave his only begotten Son that whosoever believeth in Him should not perish but have everlasting life.'

FRED (*pause*). That's what he's got now, Harold.

HAROLD. Yes.

FRED. That's what he was looking forward to, I suppose.

HAROLD. Yes.

FRED. Beyond pain and suffering, as you might say.

HAROLD. Yes . . . I have a vision of him in Paradise.

FRED. Paradise?

HAROLD. Aye. Not above t' clouds. I picture t' meadow we used to have by t' river and my dad in his white silk scarf teaching me t' names o' t' birds and t' fishes, and t' young bitch lying down in t' puddles to cool her belly. It was all right, was that.

Their train arrives at the platform. They climb into a compartment. The guard whistles, a couple of carriage doors bang to, and the train moves slowly off.

FRED. Harold . . . Harold. Are you all right.

HAROLD. Yes. Just thinking.

FRED. Sorry to interrupt.

HAROLD. This place where we get out.

FRED. Skellingford.

HAROLD. I'm not going to get out.

FRED. You'll be carried on to Lincoln.

HAROLD. I don't care where I'm carried on to. I can't face going back.

FRED. What's bothering you? They won't even put you on a charge in the circumstances.

HAROLD. But I'd have to explain t' circumstances. I'd have to watch my step. I'd have to watch what I were saying.

FRED. Tell the truth. You were burying your dad.

HAROLD. But what if they ask how it come to be necessary?

FRED (*puzzled*). You mean how he came to require interment?

HAROLD. There were nowt left of him.

FRED. You mean he'd wasted away?

HAROLD *does not reply.*

(FRED *waits for an explanation, then:*) Well, that's a private matter, Harold. It's nothing to do with the Air Force.

HAROLD. But they might ask. Flying Officer Tyson might ask.

FRED. Catering Officer?

HAROLD. Yes.

FRED. He seems a decent bloke.

HAROLD. He is. He wouldn't ask nasty, but he might ask sympathetic.

FRED. Well, tell him the truth.

HAROLD. But once you start telling t' truth you cannot say where it'll end.

FRED. You've nothing to hide.

HAROLD (*pause*). No . . . Except there were nowt left of him.

FRED. You mean reduced to skin and bone?

HAROLD. Reduced to nowt, just his boots on t' window sill and his belt buckle on t' floor.

FRED (*pause*). But you buried him.

HAROLD. Yes.

FRED. Committed him to the earth?

HAROLD. Yes.

FRED. You had a pukka funeral for him?

HAROLD. Except that it weren't him.

FRED (*puzzled*). Weren't him?

HAROLD. In the coffin.

FRED. Who was it then?

HAROLD. Nobody . . . It was a couple of sacks full of muck and bricks and some rotten cabbages wedged in to stop 'em rattling.

FRED. And the minister did his dust to dust performance over that consignment?

HAROLD. Yes. He didn't know.

FRED. Where's your dad then?

HAROLD. Eaten.

FRED. Who ate him?

HAROLD. The pigs.

FRED. You mean they literally snapped up the lot but for his boots and his belt buckle?

HAROLD. Th' owd sow mainly.

FRED. And the belt itself, they consumed that?

HAROLD. They like a bit of leather.

FRED. But not his boots?

HAROLD. No.

FRED. They ate him and his belt but spurned his footwear?

HAROLD. Yes.

FRED (*pause*). Funny do.

HAROLD. I knew you'd think it were a funny do. But Flying Officer Tyson, he might not leave it at that.

FRED (*pause*). Look, Harold, there's a death certificate, isn't there, that you have to produce to get the insurance?

HAROLD. He wasn't insured.

FRED. But whether he was insured or not, there's a death certificate. It says on it how he met his end.

HAROLD. Yes.

FRED. Well does it say 'Consumed by pigs'?

HAROLD. No.

FRED. What does it say?

HAROLD. Bronchitis.

FRED. Well then, tell 'em bronchitis if they want to go into it.

HAROLD. My Uncle Leonard told me just to say bronchitis.

FRED. That's all they'd ask.

HAROLD. Yes.

FRED. And that'd be a sufficient reason.

HAROLD. Yes.

FRED. Don't worry, Harold. You'll be laughing.

They ride on in silence.

Is it true then that pigs eat anything?

HAROLD. Yes.

FRED. As a matter of interest.

HAROLD. Reject nowt.

FRED. Bones and everything?

HAROLD. Bones and everything. They've jaws like dinosaurs.

FRED. Ugh! Just stick to bronchitis.

HAROLD. I will . . . If they offered me a gold clock there's nowt I'd want to add.

FRED. Add nowt.

HAROLD. I wasn't drunk but I'd had a few pints.

FRED. You mean when you found his boots and his belt buckle?

HAROLD. No, earlier, when I got back from t' pub. He were sat in t' corner wheezing and my mother were hunched in t' rocking chair, dead silent they were so I knew there'd been a hullaballoo. She got up to get my supper, rose from t' chair, but she collapsed and she grabbed t' table cloth and t' jam and bread and everything went on t' floor. I said. 'Has he been at you?' and she said, 'No', because I'd warned him, I'd doubly warned him, and I couldn't feel through her corsets whether there were bones broke so I got her upstairs and I shouted down to him to stay where he was till I'd time to attend to him. He didn't do that, though, he slipped out.

FRED. He might well.

HAROLD. Her ribs were bruised which she was used to but he'd punched her in t' kidneys.

FRED. That's rough.

HAROLD. And her back it were agony.

FRED. You think he threw himself to the pigs in contrition?

HAROLD. In what?

FRED. Contrition. He was sorry about carrying his domestic pugilism to them lengths.

HAROLD. He often said he were sorry afterwards.

FRED. That explains it then.

HAROLD. Does it?

FRED. Yes.

HAROLD. So I could put that, if matters were gone into, to Flying Officer Tyson?

FRED. You could, but there's no need to. If Tyson asks you cause of death say bronchitis.

HAROLD. And what if th' station warrant officer asks me?

FRED. Just say a cough.

They are silent for a moment.

If you don't mind me asking.

HAROLD. No. You've helped me, Fred. You've cleared my head.

FRED. Good . . . But, if only to make sure you don't slip up on it, Harold, how did you get bronchitis on the death certificate when he'd actually been despatched as spoken?

HAROLD. My Uncle Leonard did it. He's well informed, he knows th' ins and outs, and he got a death certificate for bronchitis signed by my dad's regular medical attendant – that's what's required – Dr Farlane.

FRED. No inquest?

HAROLD. No, because he'd seen him t' previous week. He's friendly disposed and usually drunk, and my Uncle Leonard also collected a second autograph from another doctor from Braithfell who goes round on a horse. That was Friday night and we had t' funeral yesterday afternoon.

FRED. That's going some.

HAROLD. Th' only fly in th' ointment was th' undertaker.

FRED. Awkward blokes, some of 'em.

HAROLD. They are, some of 'em. Some of 'em come to look like corpses same as old women come to look like their cats. But Mr Barnes isn't one of that type. Big red-faced chap, voice you can hear at t' other side o' t' fell. He weren't disposed to let us just have a coffin without his other services.

FRED. Had he anything to fit?

HAROLD. One he'd just finished. 'We'll have it,' my Uncle Leonard said. 'How much?' Course that's not their style, flogging you a coffin to take home under your arm. 'You will not have it', he said. 'The late Mr Metcalf deceased is expecting to go in there.'

FRED (*laughs*). Ridiculous. How can a late Mr Anybody deceased expect anything?

HAROLD. Except, as my Uncle Leonard said, a harp.

FRED *laughs*.

It were a good crack like but it were impolitic. It put Mr Barnes's back right up and he sailed into us wi' some very awkward questions – what were our game, what were we hiding, why couldn't we call him up to th' house and have it done in t' normal manner, you know in a loud booming voice you could hear t' other end o' t' village.

FRED. Tricky.

HAROLD. It were tricky. If th' policeman hadn't had t' wireless on he might have heard and come and handcuffed us on t' spot.

FRED. And you just had to ride the storm?

HAROLD. Aye, let it blow out. And then my Uncle Leonard buttered him up a bit, put his specs on to admire his handywork. 'You make a good coffin, Mr Barnes,' he said, 'It's a shame they're destined for t' clay.'

FRED. It is when you come to think about it.

HAROLD. Any road that turned him on to t' rules of his craft. A coffin ought to be bespoke.

FRED. Bespoke?

HAROLD. Made to measure. 'Otherwise', he said, 'you'll either have to cram t'client in wit' sole of your boot or you'll be shoving in packing pieces to stop him rattling about.'

They both laugh.

It weren't funny at time. Late at night, ghoulish wi' his dog padding round and getting up on its hind legs to have a sniff to see who he'd got in t' boxes. Then he found a new line, he started on about *habeas corpus.*

FRED. That's got to do with the law, hasn't it?

HAROLD. It means let's see the body.

FRED. Let the dog see the rabbit.

HAROLD. Yes, and even my Uncle Leonard was out of his depth wi' that one.

FRED. So how did he cope?

HAROLD. He said: 'Give us t' box at t' usual price and I'll come and rewire your lighting free.'

FRED. He wouldn't be expecting that.

HAROLD. It needed doing. He had bulbs hanging everywhere on frayed old bits of wire. So like it were a bargain to him and it put paid to *habeas corpus.* He said, 'Install me a plug socket as well and you're on.' So that were it. We made off with t' coffin at dead of night and th' other irregularity apart, everything were done, as you might say, according to standing orders.

FRED. Reverent and proper.

HAROLD. Aye. And my Uncle Leonard's going to slaughter that old sow today what downed my dad.

FRED. Quite right. That'll put the final stamp on the whole business.

HAROLD. I've a 48-hour pass due in three weeks. It'll be fat bacon by then. It'll be hung from a hook in t' ceiling.

FRED. Fair enough. It asked for it, Harold.

They have left the train and are now walking from the wayside station along a country road towards the airfield three miles away. The wind whistles through the trees.

FRED. Keep at this side of the road, Harold. It's drier.

HAROLD. I'll be all right when we get past t' trees and back into t' moonlight. I'll see better then.

FRED. It'll be daybreak shortly.

They walk for a time in silence.

HAROLD. I'm glad you told me what to say.

FRED. You'll be all right.

HAROLD. It spoiled t' funeral tea worrying what to say.

FRED. The bare facts.

HAROLD. And bronchitis, if asked.

FRED. If asked.

HAROLD. Then it won't jeopardise my good conduct stripe.

FRED. It won't jeopardise your good conduct stripe in any case, it's irrelevant. But it's best to keep it simple.

HAROLD. I know I blurt things out.

FRED. You're honest, Harold. You're straightforward.

HAROLD. But I shalln't have to blurt things out when I get back.

FRED. The less said the better.

HAROLD. That's it.

A heavy bomber which has been approaching now passes low overhead. Their conversation resumes as the engine noise tails away.

FRED. So that one got back, landing lights on.

HAROLD. Yes.

FRED. It's a mug's game. Even when they get back half of 'em on board can be dead.

The bomber is heard going in to land.

HAROLD. These duck eggs I've brought with me.

FRED. Yes.

HAROLD. There's a new lass come to t' cookhouse.

FRED. Oh yes.

HAROLD. It has passed through my mind she might be a better bet than this lass at home.

FRED. You've been hammering away there long enough with nothing to show for it.

HAROLD. And her in t' cookhouse, Mavis.

FRED. Nice name.

HAROLD. Aye. She comes to me if she wants a big pile of tins humping.

FRED. You reckon she fancies you?

HAROLD. She passes other blokes that could lift for her. She always comes to me.

FRED. It's your good nature, Harold.

HAROLD. Well, I was thinking, these duck eggs, instead of distributing 'em round, I could give her t' lot, th' whole dozen.

FRED. Concentrated attack?

HAROLD (*laughs*). Aye.

FRED. Saturation bombing.

HAROLD (*laughs*). Aye.

FRED. You've nothing to lose.

HAROLD. She couldn't hump swill bins but she wouldn't need to. I shall do away wit' pigs.

FRED. Could you make a living without 'em?

HAROLD. I'd get that meadow back by t' river. I'd take her down there. I'd show her t' fishes. I'd tell her t' names of t' birds.

FRED. She'd like that. You could lay her down in the buttercups.

HAROLD. It'd be an ideal spot.

Another heavy bomber passes overhead, interrupting their conversation.

My dad.

FRED. Yes.

HAROLD. I wouldn't like to leave a bad impression of him.

FRED. You haven't. You've given a very balanced picture.

HAROLD. He once stumped t' squire out. That were his big triumph, stumping t' squire.

FRED. At cricket?

HAROLD. He couldn't play in th' outfield because he hadn't breath to run so they made him t' wicketkeeper. Squire were a redoubtable batsman, he'd played for t' county, and he'd keep 'em sweating in t' field all afternoon while he knocked up numerous centuries. But not this Saturday. First ball, he went halfway down t' wicket to a short 'un, missed it completely and my dad had his bails off quick as a rat.

They both laugh.

There were repercussions. Squire hurled his bat into t' pavilion and everybody's rent went up. But he'd done right, me dad.

FRED. He had done right.

HAROLD. To whip his bails off, dismiss him for a duck. It were his only triumph but it was a big 'un. He stood on t' fellside, top side of t' farm, and he said, 'This is a view you couldn't buy for a million pounds, Big Head.'

FRED. Content.

HAROLD. Content . . . Well this lass, Mavis, I could show her that view.

Coming from t' town she won't be used to views. I could bull t' place up. I could install hot water. There's nowt now to hold me back.

FRED. You apply for your ticket out of the Air Force.

HAROLD. But I'll wait to get my good conduct stripe.

FRED. It might take you that long to win her heart.

HAROLD. It might well. I'll try t' duck eggs for a start.

A heavy bomber passes over. They walk in silence as the engine noise recedes.

FRED. The Air Force knows all about this business, you know.

HAROLD. What business, Fred?

FRED. Blokes, nothing left of them. When they come back from operations, there's often blokes in the gunners' turrets with so little left of 'em they get 'em out with a vacuum cleaner.

HAROLD. That's rough.

FRED. And sometimes if they've had two or three cannon shells through 'em there's nothing, just nothing. So that side of the story's not new in these parts. And as for packing coffins, that Lancaster that crashed on take-off last month –

HAROLD. It shook the saucepans.

FRED. And it shook the poor sods inside, seven of 'em. I believe the bits they found wouldn't have filled one coffin, never mind seven.

HAROLD. So they'd be in t' same quandary as me and my Uncle Leonard.

FRED. That's what I'm saying. You're not breaking fresh ground.

HAROLD. No.

FRED. I want you to know that, Harold, so it doesn't bother you.

HAROLD. I'll tell my Uncle Leonard.

FRED. Nothing out of the ordinary. Routine.

HAROLD. Fair enough.

FRED. Don't feel you need say anything about it. They don't.

HAROLD. No . . . So even if it were to leak out they're not in a position to moralise?

FRED. Exactly. But don't let it leak out, Harold. Keep it simple.

HAROLD. Yes.

The wind whistles across the dark fields as they walk on.

FRED. Thing just come to my mind, if you don't mind me asking.

HAROLD. No.

FRED. There's always a bit of something left. You said his belt buckle.

HAROLD. It were shining in t' muck o' t' stall with th' owd sow grinning above it.

FRED. And his boots.

HAROLD. And his boots.

FRED. In the pig house.

HAROLD. Yes.

FRED. But on the window sill.

HAROLD (*pause*). Yes.

FRED. What's bothering me, Harold –

HAROLD. I know what's bothering you, Fred . . . My Uncle Leonard told me what to say.

FRED. What you've told me?

HAROLD. But it's come unstuck, hasn't it, wit' boots?

FRED. It didn't occur to me when you first mentioned it but it does raise the question.

HAROLD. Yes.

FRED. Did he remove his boots, place them on the window ledge then take a header into the pigs?

HAROLD. Doesn't sound likely, does it?

FRED. No, it doesn't.

HAROLD (*pause*). I shall have to stop. I shall have to sit down on t' wall.

FRED. Stop here. The camp gate's round the next corner . . . I've got some fags if you'd like one.

HAROLD. No. No thanks . . . He'd took 'em off.

FRED. Yes.

HAROLD. Unlaced 'em anyway. Always did. Ease his feet.

FRED. Yes.

HAROLD. It must have been me popped 'em on t' window ledge.

FRED. After he'd been consumed?

HAROLD (*long pause*). No . . . I've missed a bit out, Fred. My Uncle Leonard told me to miss that bit out. I haven't been direct with you.

FRED. You don't have to say anything you don't want, Harold.

HAROLD (*pause*). I'd better tell you. I'd better get it off my chest. Because if I harbour it, I might blurt it out at t' wrong time.

FRED. I shalln't pass anything on, Harold.

HAROLD. I know you won't, Fred. What I've told you is true except I omitted events between putting my mother to bed and finding his boots and his belt buckle in t' morning.

FRED. You said he nipped out while you were up with your mother.

HAROLD. Yes. Well, I forgot about him. I sat with her till she went to sleep and then I went down and read t' paper and had a bit of a doze in t' chair, like sleeping off th' beer I'd had earlier. When I came to it were past midnight and I went out locking up and there he were sat in his pig house resting his feet on a bale of straw, wi' his boots unlaced. I wasn't, as you might say, a hundred per cent sober, but I wasn't drunk and I wasn't mad, I don't think. He got up and said, 'It weren't me, Harold. Don't blame me.'

FRED. Pathetic.

HAROLD. It were pathetic. But it were Harold, calling me Harold, that did it. Not Big Head, Harold. And I can't remember except that I felled him and I knew he weren't going to get up, and I heaved him over to his pigs. I can't remember t' boots at all, but that's what I must have done, put 'em on t' window ledge.

He stops for a moment, then blurts out:

I'm not going round that corner, Fred. I'm not going back to camp.

The trees rustle in the wind.

FRED. Harold . . . Lift your head up, Harold . . . It's coming daylight.

HAROLD. I'm in bad bother.

FRED. No.

HAROLD. I could be hanged.

FRED. No. I've told you what to say.

HAROLD. My Uncle Leonard told me and look where it's landed me.

FRED. It was too elaborate. There were too many ins and outs.

HAROLD. I'm not going to report. I can't face it.

FRED (*pause*). You want to stay in the cookhouse, don't you?

HAROLD (*depressed*). For t' time being.

FRED. You want to win your good conduct stripe?

HAROLD. Yes.

FRED. You want to tempt this lass with your duck eggs?

HAROLD. Yes.

FRED. Bull your farm up. Install taps?

HAROLD. Yes.

FRED. You've ranging ambitions.

HAROLD. I had.

FRED. Don't bugger 'em up by running away now. Just stick to what we said.

HAROLD. It'd certainly jeopardise my good conduct stripe if they knew I'd threw my dad to t' pigs.

FRED. Which is why there must be no talk of pigs.

HAROLD. No.

FRED. Nobody's going to mention pigs unless you do.

HAROLD. No.

FRED. And you're not going to. You're going to abstain totally from the mention of pigs.

HAROLD. Yes.

FRED. You're clear about that aren't you, Harold, what I'm saying?

HAROLD. Yes.

FRED. He's dragged you down for long enough. Don't let him wreck your prospects now he's gone.

HAROLD (*long pause*). I won't. (*With determination*). I won't.

FRED. That's the spirit . . . So when they ask you why are you 24 hours adrift, what do you say?

HAROLD. We were burying my dad who –

FRED. That's enough. And why didn't you telephone?

HAROLD. Didn't think.

FRED. And what finished him?

HAROLD. Bronchitis finished him and we have a certificate to prove it.

FRED. That's it. But just end it at bronchitis.

HAROLD (*pause, then with determination*). I will. I can manage that.

FRED. You can if you try.

HAROLD. I can and I will.

FRED. One – burying him.

HAROLD. Yes.

FRED. Two – didn't think to go to the blower.

HAROLD. Yes.

FRED. Three – bronchitis.

HAROLD. Yes.

FRED. Now sit quiet and recite that in your head.

There is a moment of silence between them.

HAROLD. I've got it. Everything depends on that, doesn't it?

FRED. Yes.

HAROLD. I've got it clear.

FRED. I believe you have, Harold.

HAROLD. I'm clear, Fred. You've made me clear.

FRED. Good. Now there'll be no complications if you stick to that.

HAROLD. No.

FRED. But if any should arise about any matter whatever, I'm at the M.T. section or come to the counter when I'm in for my dinner.

HAROLD. I shalln't need, Fred. I'm clear.

FRED. Right. Give me half a minute to get in ahead of you, then you'll have a clear run to check in at the guardroom.

HAROLD. I'll know what to say.

FRED. You'll be OK, mate.

A dawn chorus of birds is heard.

The birds are waking. It's dawn, Harold, daybreak.

HAROLD (*laughs a little, reassured*). I don't panic t' same when I can see.

FRED. Going to be a nice day.

HAROLD. Yes.

FRED. That lass's eyes'll light up at the sight of your duck eggs.

HAROLD *laughs, at ease, with pleasure.*

FRED. So long, Harold.

HAROLD. So long, Fred.

FRED *moves away.*

(*Calls.*) Fred.

FRED. Yes.

HAROLD. You're a good pal, Fred. You've got me through this night.

FRED. Fine.

HAROLD. I'll bring you some duck eggs back when I get my 48-hour pass.

FRED. Thanks, Harold.

HAROLD (*calls*). And a nice piece of fat bacon, Fred, to help 'em down.

A heavy bomber passes over and goes in to land.

THE WASTED YEARS

by Caryl Phillips

Caryl Phillips was born on St Kitts, West Indies, in 1958. He came to England in July of the same year, settling first in Leeds, then Birmingham. Educated at Queen's College, Oxford, he graduated in 1979 with an honours degree in English Language and Literature. Since then he has written drama for both the theatre and television. Faber recently published his first novel, *The Final Passage*. *The Wasted Years* is his first play for radio.

The Wasted Years was first broadcast on BBC Radio 4 on 12 March 1984. The cast was as follows:

SOLLY DANIELS	Tony Armatrading
CYNTHIA DANIELS	Carmen Munroe
ROY DANIELS	Rudolph Walker
MR TEALE/VOX POP	Graham Padden
CHRIS DANIELS	Adrian Harvey
TAGGER	Mark Audley
TRACEY	Tracey Ann Bell
JENNY	Amanda Dainty
HEADMASTER/INTERVIEWER	Roger Hume
GYM TEACHER/VOX POP	Peter Brookes
BATES	David Hannah
JOHNSON	Dale Bayford
STATION ANNOUNCER/VOX POP	Shirley Stelfox
VOX POP	Tony McPherson
VOX POP	Cornel John
CHILDREN	Members of the Birmingham Youth Theatre

Director: Vanessa Whitburn

Running time, as broadcast: 87 minutes 50 seconds.

Noise coming from a classroom as the bell has just gone for the end of the day.

TEALE. I said quietly, 5C. This isn't Saturday afternoon down at the match, it's a school, and Deakin put that chair back where it belongs.

Sound of the kids jeering.

Shut up, all of you. I said put it back Deakin and put it back now.

SOLLY. He don't have to do it, for it's the end of school.

TAGGER. Well I wouldn't do it, I can tell you that much.

TEALE. What was that, Daniels?

SOLLY. Nothing.

TEALE. Don't 'nothing' me, lad, I'm a bit longer in the tooth than you.

TAGGER (*giggles and whispers*). A bit what?

TEALE. Tagley, shut your stupid mouth, boy.

TAGGER. Sir.

TEALE. Daniels, I'm still waiting.

SOLLY. I said he don't have to move it if he don't want to for it's the end of school now.

TEALE. I see. You're not by any chance trying to tell me my job are you, lad?

Sound of some of the kids starting to giggle.

The rest of you move, and move quickly and quietly or I'll have you all back here in detention tomorrow night. (*Groans.*) Go on. Daniels, you wait here.

We hear them disperse until only TEALE *and* SOLLY *are left.*

I think we better have a talk, don't you?

SOLLY. I don't see what for.

TEALE. I don't see what for, Mr Teale.

SOLLY. Mr Teale.

TEALE. Look Daniels, haven't you got rid of that chip on your shoulder yet? It'll not do you any good once you get out there.

SOLLY. I haven't got a chip on my shoulder.

TEALE. Hasn't it ever occurred to you, Daniels, that people notice when you misbehave. When Tagley and the other lads do it they . . . well they see them all as one, find it more difficult to single them out, but with you, it's as if you're a natural target and you will insist on placing yourself in the firing line won't you?

SOLLY. I'm no worse than anyone else.

TEALE. Well I'm not sure if I'd go that far but what I will say is if you're going to leave school at the end of the week and go out into society with a kind of 'come and get me' attitude, then they'll come and get you; and they'll swallow you whole.

SOLLY. Who will?

TEALE (*laughs*). Who will? Daniels, there isn't a lad in the country of your age who's not going to have to run the gauntlet of interviews, careers people, dole people, social security, police; it's not like it was when I first started teaching anymore: and don't look at me like that – it was only 9 or 10 years ago. These days we don't send you out to your apprenticeships and your office-boy jobs now. Everybody's head is on the block and I can promise you there are people out there happily doing the chopping. (*Pause.*) You've never liked school have you?

SOLLY. I did to start with but people started to get at me.

TEALE. And so you began to throw away all your talent and energy into causing trouble: don't you see that's playing the wrong game, Daniels, and if you try and play that out there you'll be eaten alive. Doesn't your mother want you to get on?

SOLLY. Course she does and I don't cause trouble, it's you lot. You pick on me.

TEALE. Why not try for her? Or for yourself even.

SOLLY (*gets upset*). I have been but there doesn't seem to be any point, does there? If Tagger or any of the others do something then you let them off. If it's me I get sent to the head or put in detention. If there's a load of us running down a corridor then I'm the one who'll get stopped and given lines. Always me like it's a big joke to you, then you always have a talk to try and made me feel bad, like I'm a crook or something.

TEALE. Nobody thinks you're a crook.

SOLLY. Well I'm not! (*He gets up and runs out obviously upset.*)

TEALE. Daniels, wait. Daniels . . .

Newsreel: voice over of West Indians arriving off the boats in the fifties and 'BBC' INTERVIEWER *talking.*

INTERVIEWER. . . . these dashing chaps in their colourful hats and big smiles all seem to be finding the cold a bit much as they file gingerly down the gang plank. Let's go and talk to one or two of them. How are you finding it here?

ANSWER. Well it's cold but I think I'm going to like it.

INTERVIEWER. And how long are you planning to stay with us?

ANSWER. A few years, three or four.

INTERVIEWER. I see, then back to the sunny Caribbean, eh?

ANSWER. I hope so.

INTERVIEWER. And your wife here, is it?

ANSWER. I think we'll both like it here. Everyone seems so friendly already.

INTERVIEWER. Ah good. And you, sir. First impressions favourable?

ANSWER. Well it's the motherland isn't it, and I'm just pleased to be here.

INTERVIEWER. Quite. You look well-prepared, sir.

ANSWER. Well I was over here in the war, RAF pilot, and I'm used to it.

INTERVIEWER. And how long are you planning on staying with us this time?

ANSWER. About five years should be sufficient, but who knows. I might stay longer.

INTERVIEWER. And I think I speak for the British public when I say as long as there is work to be done we'll always be pleased to have you here.

ANSWER. Thank you very much.

SOLLY *is running across a wide playground.*

SOLLY. Tagger! Tagger!

He nears TAGGER *and slows down out of breath.*

TAGGER. I thought you weren't coming.

SOLLY. I had to listen to Teale first.

TAGGER. What's he say?

SOLLY. Nothing much.

TAGGER. Oh come on, what's he say? He must have said something.

SOLLY. Normal stuff. Going on like he might expel me.

TAGGER. How come? We've only got three more days in this dump.

SOLLY. I dunno. Always bleeding picking on me. You wanna go behind the bogs for a quick fag?

TAGGER. What for? It's after school and we can have one in the street or on the bus if we want.

SOLLY. I know but if my brother sees me he might tell my mum and she'll kill me.

TAGGER. Then you'll kill him, won't you?

SOLLY. Well someone else might see us and tell her. A friend of hers or something.

TAGGER. All right then, but Batesy and Johnson are behind there. (*Pause.*) Well, still coming?

SOLLY. I don't know. Forget it then.

TAGGER. It's up to you.

They walk on a little and we hear the noise of traffic as they leave the school playground.

You coming down the club tonight, Solly?

SOLLY. Suppose so. Don't care really.

TAGGER. What's the matter with you? You've gone all funny.

SOLLY. How?

TAGGER. Sort of quiet.

SOLLY. It's just the club, it gets on my nerves sometimes.

TAGGER. I reckon that's coz you haven't got a bird. Still, you could get one if you wanted one though.

SOLLY. Yeah, I know I could but I don't want one.

TAGGER. Well there ain't much else to do down there except hope someone'll buy us a drink.

SOLLY. Haven't you got any money either?

TAGGER. Course not but someone might have.

SOLLY. I don't know if I want to go now.

TAGGER. Look, have a fag and shut up. It's getting dark and nobody will see us. Well they won't see you at least.

SOLLY. That ain't funny.

TAGGER. Just a joke that's all, just a joke. (*Pause.*) I forgot to ask you. Will you do that maths quiz for us? I'll give you another fag if you do.

SOLLY. Yeah, course I will.

TAGGER. Great. It's even worse than homework and its supposed to be a game. Hang on a minute. (*Lighting a fag.*)

SOLLY. Look, you coming or not?

TAGGER. Funny that; that's what my bird always asks me.

SOLLY. Very funny. Come on, will you?

TAGGER. No need to bite my head off you know.

SOLLY. I ain't feeling too bright.

TAGGER. You ain't the only one. My old man says if I don't have a job in 6 weeks he's kicking me out. I told him that if all dads acted like him then the streets would be teeming with millions of homeless teenagers. So he clouted me for cheek. (*Laughs.*) I know what I was going to ask you. What did your dad used to do, I mean for a job like?

SOLLY. I don't know.

TAGGER. Well he might have been a millionaire, or a footballer or something. You can never tell. Ain't you interested?

SOLLY. No. What you don't know you don't miss. There's loads of people like me, you know. It's nothing special.

TAGGER. Yeah I know, I never said there was anything special.

SOLLY. Well why do you keep going on about it?

TAGGER. I don't. I just mentioned it, that's all. There's nothing wrong with that is there?

SOLLY. Suppose not. (*Pause.*) Look come on let's run, no point in hanging around here.

TAGGER. All right then. (*He begins to run.*) Last one into Fairfax Road is a wanker.

SOLLY. Hang on a minute.

The front door slams and CYNTHIA *shouts through from the kitchen where she is listening to the radio news.*

CYNTHIA. Christopher? Solomon?

CHRIS (*shouting back*). It's me, Chris.

CYNTHIA. And where's your brother?

CHRIS. I don't know. I haven't seem him.

He moves to go upstairs.

CYNTHIA. Where are you going, Christopher?

CHRIS. Homework.

CYNTHIA. You mean you can't come through and kiss me or say hello or something like that. Is it a house of ghosts I'm living in now or what?

CHRIS (*beginning to run up the stairs*). I'm in a rush, Mum.

CYNTHIA (*tired*). Everybody's in a rush, everybody's busy, nobody's got time. I don't know what kind of a world you all think you're living in. Jet age this, and space age that, and all I'm beginning to feel is my old age. Jesus, if only I'd have realised what I was taking on.

On a train.

ROY. You still cold, darling?

CYNTHIA. I thought England in July would be warmer than this, Roy.

ROY. Well it's a different world over here, me dear.

CYNTHIA. Seems like it.

Pause.

ROY. Look at the cows over there in the field. Jesus Christ, most of them look better fed than the people back home.

CYNTHIA. That's not fair. We have ample food back there.

ROY. So why the people them look like stick insects?

CYNTHIA. Here it's a land of plenty, it's exciting, like your first day at school. A brave new world is what they call it on the radio.

ROY. In a way it is. You don't think so?

CYNTHIA. I'll wait and see but I'm glad we've come this far, we can't turn back now.

ROY. Turn back? We soon going reach London then pow! Things really start to take shape.

CYNTHIA. I hope so. I really hope so for I can see that unless you come Prime Minister by next year all you going do is moan.

Pause.

ROY. You feeling all right, Cynthia?

CYNTHIA. I guess I'm just a little frightened, Roy.

ROY. Well you don't think I'm frightened too?

CYNTHIA. Are you?

ROY. Course but . . . but there's hope here, space to grow and develop, and England is not a normal island, it's special.

CYNTHIA. I suppose it is.

ROY. And the way I see it we must work and save up some money, and put down a deposit on our own property. Then, when the time is ready and we are settled and secure – then, and only then, we can start to bring children into the world so they can take over where we started.

CYNTHIA. I want two children, Roy. To keep each other company. Solomon and Samantha.

ROY. And I want the boy to be a doctor and the girl to be a nurse.

CYNTHIA. I thought you wanted the boy to be a lawyer.

ROY. Or a lawyer. It's a fine profession for a young man, especially if what I hear of England is correct. For you can't go wrong if you have an education, and that he must have, they must both have it, and no matter what happens we must try and give them that at least. If nothing else some learning for a future.

CYNTHIA. In that case we make the right decision in coming here.

ROY. Of course we did. All they really going to learn back home was how to starve and suffer and live without a job.

CYNTHIA. The train's slowing down, Roy. This must be London.

ROY. Look! Look! A red double-decker bus. Well, Lord I never thought I'd live to see a red double-decker bus – and a policeman. A bobby with a helmet. And look, my arse, a bowler hat! (*Pause.*) Cynthia, I want one of them.

CYNTHIA. If you do, well, I don't see why not.

Announcement: voice over – This is London Waterloo! London Waterloo!

ROY. Well we've arrived and the second part of our life is just beginning.

CYNTHIA. But I'm still frightened, Roy. I don't know what's going to happen, you know.

ROY. But that's all part of the excitement, girl; that's what's meant by being on the move.

CYNTHIA. Lord, I can feel my blood pumping like its ready to just burst out of my body.

CYNTHIA *is in the kitchen sitting alone in the dark. It is so quiet that perhaps one can hear a clock ticking away on the wall.*

CYNTHIA (*in a very hushed whisper*). Well Roy, I'm still trying, you know, I really am, and the blood still pumping. (*Pause.*) They've become a bit like what you were, Roy. Headstrong boys. They always played rough, even as babies. Always covered in bruises but never crying. Neither of them. Well Solomon did to start with: You remember that, but he soon learned to hush up when his brother came along. Yes, a brother: I know we wanted a girl but I'm happy with Chris; he's a good boy. I'm more than happy with him. (*Pause.*) And I can't be too hard on them. I just can't, not after what happened.

CHRIS. Mum?

CYNTHIA. Who is it?

CHRIS. It's me, Chris. Why is the light off?

CYNTHIA. Christopher? Where are you? (*Light goes on.*) Oh good, I can see you now.

CHRIS. Who were you talking to, Mum?

CYNTHIA. Nobody. Just myself. I must have fallen asleep. (*Standing up to fill the kettle.*) Even a simple little secretary job seems to be starting to tell on me. At my age. (*She laughs.*)

CHRIS. Are you all right, Mum?

CYNTHIA. Yes, dear. Just tired. You go on and finish your homework and I'll bring you up a cup of tea.

CHRIS. I've finished.

CYNTHIA. Oh, I see. Well you can talk to me then.

She goes to put on the kettle.

CHRIS. What about?

CYNTHIA. Nothing. Just anything. Talk. Or maybe we have to draw up an agenda before you can talk with your mother.

CHRIS. But I can't think of anything to say.

CYNTHIA. Don't worry. I'm sure we'll manage to find something to say, something to talk about. (*Pause.*) Well, sit down then.

CHRIS. Why don't you give up work, Mum?

CYNTHIA. And then what will you eat, you tell me that?

CHRIS. Don't you get a pension?

CYNTHIA. I hope that's a joke.

CHRIS. Well some people get them before they're sixty.

CYNTHIA. Well not me.

CHRIS. Solly might get a job.

CYNTHIA. And I'll win the pools, eh?

CHRIS. I'm only trying to help.

CYNTHIA. I know you are. (*She kisses him.*) Tea or coffee?

CHRIS. Tea.

CYNTHIA. Tea what?

CHRIS. Please. (*Pause.*) Mum, what's a period?

CYNTHIA. Nothing that you'll have to worry about. Why?

CHRIS. It's just that I heard some girls talking about it and I thought it meant how long a lesson takes but they laughed at me.

CYNTHIA. What were they saying?

CHRIS. Just stuff about being late which is why I thought they were talking about lessons.

CYNTHIA. I see. And what do you think they were really talking about.

CHRIS. I'm not sure.

Pause.

CYNTHIA. Samantha. If we had a girl we were going to call her Samantha.

CHRIS. That's awful, sounds like a princess.

CYNTHIA (*laughs*). She would have been a princess and she'd have been able to tell you all about periods.

CHRIS. You tell me then.

CYNTHIA. I've got two princes instead and I'll tell you both when I'm ready and not before. Now take this and go to bed, you look tired.

CHRIS. But football's on tonight.

CYNTHIA. I said you look tired so you're going to bed.

CHRIS. No point cos Solly always wakes me up when he comes in.

CYNTHIA. Well you should tell him to come in more quietly.

CHRIS. I do but he never listens anymore. He just shouts. And at school he just ignores me. I think he's trying to pretend I'm not his brother.

CYNTHIA. All boys are like that but I'll talk to him if you like.

CHRIS. Do you think he'll listen.

CYNTHIA. Of course he'll listen, I'm his mother, aren't I?

CHRIS. Teachers keep saying things to me about him.

CYNTHIA. Like what?

CHRIS. Like why can't he be like me and stuff like that.

Pause.

CYNTHIA. Is it upsetting you, Christopher?

CHRIS. It gets to me a bit. Annoys me. It's like they think he's a freak or something, Mum. They talk about him like he's not real.

CYNTHIA. And what else do they say to you?

CHRIS. Nothing.

CYNTHIA. Are you sure?

CHRIS. Yes.

Pause.

CYNTHIA. Go to bed, son. I'll speak to your brother when he comes in.

CHRIS. All right, goodnight.

CYNTHIA. Goodnight, son.

We are at a discotheque where the music is loud and punkish. They are not really playing any black music.

SOLLY. But it's no good coming somewhere if you haven't got any money.

TAGGER. Well we've only just got here, Solly. What's the matter with you?

SOLLY. And what about the school disco on Friday night. I haven't got any money for that either.

TAGGER. Well nick some from your mum's handbag. That's where my dad gets his.

SOLLY. I ain't nicking it from home.

TAGGER. Well that's up to you, ain't it?

SOLLY. Yeah, and I ain't nicking none.

TAGGER. Well we can't have a drink till my bird gets here. But she might have a quid or something.

SOLLY. Tracey?

TAGGER. I've only got one bird, you know.

SOLLY. Yeah I know.

TAGGER. You should get one. At least you'd have someone to buy you a drink then. (*Laughs.*) What about Jenny Bates. You ain't trying to tell me you don't fancy her cos I know you do.

SOLLY. Who says?

TAGGER. I say. You never shut up about her but it'll only come to nothing cos you're too chicken to say anything in case she tells you to get lost.

SOLLY. I'm not scared.

TAGGER. I didn't even have to ask Tracey. Her mate Sandra or whatever her name is, she told me. And what's the first thing Tracey starts talking to me about when I took her out: kids and getting married. I said yeah I want all that Trace but there's a few more years to wait as yet. I'm only 16 for God's sake.

SOLLY. I know what you mean.

TAGGER. Do you, hell. If I didn't know you better I'd think you were . . .

SOLLY. Who me?

TAGGER. It's like you're scared of them. Is it cos you're coloured, you think they might tell you to get lost?

SOLLY. You don't know what you're on about. You sound pissed already.

TAGGER. Oh yeah? And what would you know about it.

SOLLY. As much as you.

TAGGER. Sure you do. Anyway shut up, here comes Tracey.

SOLLY. I'm off to the bog. I'll see you later.

TAGGER. Why, are you thinking of moving in there or something?

SOLLY. Get stuffed, Tagger.

We mix back to the discotheque later where the music is still playing and the scene seems to be in full swing. SOLLY *is standing on his own and* TAGGER *comes across with* TRACEY.

TRACEY. Hello Solly. Where have you been?

TAGGER (*a bit pissed*). Watcher Sol, me old mate. What you doing over here all by your tod then?

SOLLY. Same as usual. I couldn't find you. And how come you've been drinking?

TRACEY. Yeah that's what I want to know. Me dad got laid off this morning and he gave me and me mum a fiver each to go and commiserate for him as he was going out with his mates. I've got about forty pence left cos he's gone and drunk it all in record time.

SOLLY. I might have guessed.

TAGGER. Not all of it. She had an orange juice. (*He laughs to himself.*)

TRACEY. How come you ain't dancing, Solly?

TAGGER. Cos it ain't 'roots, man', not vital music, that's right ain't it, Sol?

TRACEY. Shut up will you, Tagger.

SOLLY. I just don't feel like dancing. I'm going now anyway.

TAGGER. Well you're going to have to run quickly if you wanna catch her up for she left ten minutes ago.

TRACEY. Catch who up?

TAGGER. Jenny Bates of course. You mean you don't know about Solly fancing her?

SOLLY. On your bike will you Tagger. I'm off.

TAGGER. If you wanna go out with her ask her.

SOLLY. It ain't none of your business if I do.

TAGGER. You ain't ever had a bird have you?

TRACEY. Oh shut up Tagger.

TAGGER. You shut up! You're scared of asking her, aren't you?

SOLLY. Shut your face or I'll fill it for you.

TAGGER. Yeah, you and whose army? You think I'm scared of you just cos you're black.

TRACEY. Tagger! Shut up! He's just drunk, Solly. He don't even know what he's saying.

SOLLY. He better not say anymore or I'll hit him, mate or no mate.

TRACEY. Tagger, shut up. I'm going for my coat then we're off. See you later, Solly.

TAGGER. I wonder what it's like never to have been able to pull a bird.

TRACEY. Shut up Tagger! See you, Solly. You better go now.

SOLLY. Yeah see you, Tracey.

He goes.

TRACEY (*in a lower voice*). You behaved like a pig.

TAGGER. It's him and all his pretending about not wanting a bird. Makes me sick.

TRACEY (*in a lower voice*). He don't really fancy her, does he?

TAGGER. Course he does but he never says nothing about it. You can see in the way he just looks at her.

TRACEY. Oh God, speaking of Jenny Bates here comes her brother with that stupid git, Johnson.

TAGGER. They better not try anything cos I've got my flick-knife with me.

TRACEY. Don't be stupid. Put that away, Tagger.

TAGGER. I can handle myself.

TRACEY. And so can they but nobody has done anything so don't start any trouble, eh?

TAGGER. I don't want to start any trouble. Have we got enough money for another drink?

TRACEY. I suppose so if you have half.

TAGGER (*glumly*). All right then.

TRACEY. I'll get it. Wait here, and for God's sake behave.

CYNTHIA'*s bedroom. She is lying awake and we hear the bedroom clock ticking. We hear the sound of* SOLLY *creeping up the stairs but the steps are creaking despite his attempts to keep it quiet.*

CYNTHIA (*shouting through*). Solomon is that you trying to creep up the stairs without me hearing you?

SOLLY. I was just trying to keep quiet so I wouldn't wake you up.

CYNTHIA. Yes I'll bet you were. You'll have to grow wings, boy, before you can get past me like that. Come, I want to talk with you.

SOLLY (*he has come into the bedroom now*). What about?

CYNTHIA. What about? Haven't you got any manners?

SOLLY. I just asked you what you wanted to talk to me about.

CYNTHIA. I know what you asked me, Solomon.

SOLLY. Well what's the matter?

CYNTHIA. You, you're what's the matter.

SOLLY. I haven't done anything so I don't see why you're getting at me.

CYNTHIA. Who'se getting at you?

SOLLY. You, you are. Always bickering and telling me what's wrong with me, telling me what to believe and how to dress, and what to wear, and what to say, and none of it makes any sense does it?

CYNTHIA. You mean nothing I say makes any sense to you?

SOLLY. No, none of it. It's all just words, words, words, and it don't add up to anything real. Like when you keep saying don't I feel I owe you something.

CYNTHIA. Well don't you?

SOLLY. Like what?

CYNTHIA. Like the fact that you've got clothes on your back for instance.

SOLLY. And I'm supposed to feel grateful for that? I thought that's what you were supposed to do anyhow if you had kids.

CYNTHIA. Well open your eyes, Solomon. Some parents don't.

SOLLY. Well they're stupid then, aren't they?

CYNTHIA. And do you think I'm stupid? Well? Do you think there's something the matter with me?

SOLLY. No! I told you it's them. Not you.

CYNTHIA. You should feel proud, Solomon, you should hold your head up high and realise you're just as good as the other boys, you're just as English as them.

SOLLY. That's it! That's just it! You don't know what you're talking about, do you? I'm not just as English as they are and I don't know why you keep going on about it.

CYNTHIA. What do you mean you're not just as English as they are? Of course you are.

SOLLY. Well you go tell them that and see what they say to you.

CYNTHIA. 'Us', 'them', 'we', 'they': what's got into you, Solly? Why all the dividing all of a sudden? It's not the way I brought you up.

SOLLY. I know, Mum. But it's different from just straightening your tie, and grinning nicely! I am different! They can see that.

CYNTHIA. Don't shout or you'll wake up your brother.

SOLLY. I might as well wake him up cos he's gonna have to hear this sooner or later anyhow.

CYNTHIA. Hear what?

SOLLY. Hear that it's not the truth what you say.

CYNTHIA. Then what is the truth, Solly? What is it that I'm either too stupid or too ignorant to know?

SOLLY. I don't mean it like that.

CYNTHIA. Like what?

SOLLY. Like to tell you that you're stupid or anything.

CYNTHIA. Well don't stop now, you might as well go on. And what is it that you say your brother will have to learn?

SOLLY. He'll have to learn that they don't like him even if he does come top of the class every time. It don't make any difference in their eyes.

CYNTHIA. I see and you think it's all about wanting to be liked.

SOLLY. I never said that, what I meant was that it'll change for him too.

CYNTHIA. What'll change?

SOLLY. I don't know, Mum. (*Pause; he is getting upset.*) Why don't you ever explain things to us?

CYNTHIA. What do you want to know?

SOLLY. About you and Dad, for instance.

CYNTHIA. I don't see what that's got to do with your lack of interest in your schoolwork, do you?

SOLLY. No, but it's real talk isn't it? Isn't it?

CYNTHIA. Don't shout at me, Solomon. Just remember who you are and where you are.

SOLLY. I know that.

CYNTHIA. Well if you don't like it you're perfectly free to go, understand? I won't have you here any longer unless you have some respect, understand?

SOLLY. Why can't I ask questions?

CYNTHIA. Go to bed Solomon, it's late.

SOLLY. I said, why can't I ask questions?

CYNTHIA. You can but when I say bed I mean bed so please, go. And I expect an apology from you.

SOLLY. What for?

CYNTHIA. You'd better think about that yourself. Well? (*Pause.*) Well?

SOLLY. I'm sorry.

CYNTHIA. Go to bed, Solomon. I sometimes wonder just who it is you really think you are.

In the brothers' bedroom.

CHRIS. Is that you, Solly?

SOLLY. No it's the Ghost of Christmas Past.

CHRIS. What time is it?

SOLLY. I don't know, do I? I'm turning the light on.

CHRIS. What for?

SOLLY. So I can see, dummy. (*He turns it on.*)

CHRIS. God it's bright, Solly.

SOLLY. Light bulbs usually are.

CHRIS. Aren't you coming to bed?

SOLLY. No I've got to write a letter first.

CHRIS. Who to?

SOLLY. Prime Minister. Asking her for a job in parliament.

CHRIS. Doing what?

SOLLY. Oh shut up will you.

Pause.

CHRIS. You been arguing with her again?

SOLLY. Brilliant, so you've got two ears.

CHRIS. What about?

SOLLY. About why you're such a dick.

CHRIS. No, really.

SOLLY. About how she keeps on about how the sun shines out of Britain's backside.

CHRIS. No she don't.

SOLLY. Just listen and you'll hear her. She's got her job with Dr Chandra but she must leave his place and travel in a sealed capsule to get to work and back home. She never sees or feels anything.

CHRIS. Yes she does.

SOLLY. Like what, creep? Like the number of gold stars in your report book?

CHRIS. No, I don't know. (*Pause.*) Will you be long?

SOLLY. Why?

CHRIS. Cos I can't sleep with the light on.

SOLLY. Well put your head under the blankets.

CHRIS. Then I can't sleep cos I'll suffocate.

SOLLY. Well you'll have to suffocate then.

CHRIS. Is it a love letter?

SOLLY. Shut your face, is it hell.

CHRIS. We get our exam results tomorrow.

SOLLY. I said shut your face I'm writing.

CHRIS (*whispers*). You shut yours.

SOLLY. You what?

CHRIS. Nothing. I had a talk with Mum today.

SOLLY. So, you're not the first and you won't be the last.

CHRIS. Did she tell you about it?

SOLLY. About what?

CHRIS. The talk.

SOLLY. No, why should she?

CHRIS. No reason.

SOLLY. Well shut up then.

Pause.

CHRIS. Solly?

SOLLY. For God's sake.

CHRIS. What's a period?

SOLLY. A what?

CHRIS. A period. I heard some girls talking about it today.

SOLLY. It's what they get when they're not going to have a kid.

CHRIS. Is that all?

SOLLY. Well what did you think it was?

CHRIS. I didn't know.

SOLLY. Just shut up now, will you? I want to finish this.

CHRIS. Then will you turn the light out?

SOLLY. No I'm going to sit here all night until the bulb blows up, goodnight.

CHRIS. I'm not thick you know, Solly. You don't have to talk to me like that.

SOLLY. Who told you that or did you learn it in general studies?

CHRIS. That's not funny.

SOLLY. And neither are you so shut up or go back to sleep.

Pause.

CHRIS. You always wake me up.

SOLLY. Well if you don't shut up I'll put you to sleep for good, right?

Newsreel type interview: in the street.

INTERVIEWER. And sir, can I ask you what you think of our coloured brethren?

ANSWER. I think there's far too many coloureds over here and they ought to be sent back to the jungle or wherever it is they come from.

INTERVIEWER. The West Indies.

ANSWER. I don't give a damn where it is. All I know is I didn't fight a war for this country just to see the likes of your sort handing over our spoils to niggers and watching them take our women from us.

INTERVIEWER. Thank you, sir. And you madam, what do you think?

ANSWER. Well they're dirty for a start off. Never see any washing on the lines outside of their houses. And they let their children run around with hardly any clothes on.

INTERVIEWER. And you, sir. Do you think there's a colour bar problem?

ANSWER. Don't know do I?

INTERVIEWER. Well then do you work or socialise with any coloureds?

ANSWER. A few and they're all right. Keep themselves to themselves.

INTERVIEWER. So you don't have any complaints against them?

ANSWER. A spade's a spade. A white man's a white man, that's all there is to it.

INTERVIEWER. Thank you, sir. Madam. Can I ask you about the coloured folk over here. Do you have any contact with them at all?

ANSWER. What?

INTERVIEWER. I mean at work, or in the local pub.

ANSWER. I don't mix with darkies. I was against letting 'em in and I still am.

1966: ROY *and* CYNTHIA *are lying in bed.*

CYNTHIA. Roy? (*Pause.*) Are you awake?

ROY. I can't sleep, Cynthia.

CYNTHIA. What's worrying you?

ROY. I don't know. Seven years in this country and we still don't get no place as yet. I guess that could be worrying me.

CYNTHIA. But at least you're working. We have a nice bedsit and soon we can maybe put down a deposit on a house.

ROY (*laughs*). When? I could have built a house by now with my own two hands.

CYNTHIA. When things pick up a bit.

ROY. I sometimes wonder if things ever going to pick up, you know, England just win the world cup, hippies in the street, everything peace and love, and we still ain't going no place. How come everybody else is happy and we still in the shit?

CYNTHIA. We have to give it time, Roy. I think we maybe expected too much too soon from England. Maybe we place too much burden upon her.

ROY. Well if that's the case she's certainly getting her own back now. Today, at work, the foreman asked me if I fancy doing some overtime but not to tell any of the others. When I ask him why he just wink at me and say that it's a secret between the two of us for they don't like spades. Well I let that one slip by, but when he bowl me the one about he's only paying me half rate for the overtime for is he doing me a favour, I have to drive the ball back down the wicket and into his damn mouth because he must think I'm a fool or something.

CYNTHIA. Why didn't you tell me this before, Roy?

ROY. Why? (*He laughs.*) Do you tell me every time someone push you in the back, or drop your change on the counter, or call you nigger, or push you off the bus, do you tell me every time? No you don't and you know why not? It's because if you did we'd be talking all day and we'd never get any peace of any kind in the evening. There would be too much misery between us.

CYNTHIA. So nobody talks to you at work?

ROY. Yes man, people say things like 'Bring the hammer, Roy', and 'Take the hammer, Roy', and 'Bring the spanner, Roy', and 'Take the spanner, Roy', they talk to me all right.

CYNTHIA. Well, you can always change the job, can't you?

ROY. And do what? We have enough problems saving up as it is at the moment and I can't risk a less secure post than this otherwise we never going be able to afford to have some children and bring them up nice and properly. All I've got to look forward to at the moment is more, 'Bring the godamn hammer, Roy', 'Take the godamn hammer, Roy'.

CYNTHIA. I could go out to work, Roy.

ROY. How many times I must tell you that I prefer it if you stay at home for the man should support the woman like back home.

CYNTHIA. But we can save faster if I work too, don't you see that?

ROY. Yes I see it but I don't know if it's right, you know. I just can't tell, Cynthia.

Classroom just before the start of the day and all the commotion of the kids arriving.

TAGGER. Give it us here. I'll do it.

Voices of the classroom: No, let Steve . . . It's only a knife . . . etc.

Only the 'Y' to do now. Anyone coming?

VOICE. Not yet, Tagger. He's bound to notice when he opens his desk.

TAGGER. Well that's the whole idea isn't it, birdbrain?

VOICE. Hang on a minute, here he comes.

We hear the sound of a terrible commotion and chairs scraping etc. as they try to get into place.

TAGGER. All right, Solly.

SOLLY. Yeah. Why, what's up?

We hear the sound of sniggering.

TAGGER. Nothing. What makes you think there is?

SOLLY. Because I know you and I can tell when something's up.

VOICE. There's nothing up, Sol. It's just Tagger still smashed from last night.

SOLLY. Yeah, noticed you didn't come across and offer me a drink.

TAGGER. I told you it wasn't my money that I was spending otherwise I'd have been the first across. You know me.

SOLLY. Yeah I know, Tagger. Better than you think.

VOICE. Hold up a minute, Teale's coming.

Sound of TEALE *coming in and closing the door.*

TEALE. Morning. (*Murmured reply, hardly audible.*) It's happened at last. You've all lost your tongues. Well? I said 'morning'.

CLASS. 'Morning.' (*In various shades of protest.*)

TEALE. 'Morning Mr. Teale, or 'Morning Sir' would have been better but I suppose I'll have to be thankful for what little I get from you lot.

VOICE. Don't be like that, sir.

TEALE (*mimics*). Don't be like that, sir. There's no spark in you lot is there? No spirit? A wasted generation.

VOICE. We're not wasted, sir.

TEALE. Well prove it then, behave, work, dress smartly, take some pride in yourselves and all the rest.

VOICE. You sound like the man from the Army Recruiting Office, sir.

TEALE. Well that's not exactly what I had in mind, thank you very much. Right. Register. Andrews . . .

VOICE. Sir.

TEALE. Askew . . .

VOICE. Sir.

TEALE. Bates . . . Where's Bates, anybody?

VOICE. Late, sir. I saw him coming to school but . . .

TEALE. I know. I know. Had to stop for a quick fag.

They all laugh.

Collins . . . Daniels . . . Deakin . . . Evans . . . Fairbairn . . . Francis . . . Grahams . . . Harris . . . Hawley . . .

The register fades, then we go back to the classroom where TEALE *is still taking the register.*

TEALE. Tagley . . .

TAGGER. Sir.

TEALE. Tattersall . . .

VOICE. Sir.

TEALE. Thompson . . .

VOICE. Sir.

TEALE. Watson . . .

VOICE. Sir.

TEALE. And last and by all means least, (*The class laughs.*) Williams.

VOICE. Sir?

The class laughs even more.

TEALE. Quiet, quieten down now. The joke's over with. (*They shut up.*) Now then, as you may or may not be aware there is a school disco on Friday night to celebrate the releasing of your horrible selves onto the unsuspecting world out there. (*A cheer.*) I don't know what you're all so happy about. I'll give it a week and you'll all be begging at the school gates to be let back in.

VOICES. 'No chance, sir' – 'You've got to be kidding' – 'What, into this dump?' etc.

VOICE (*in a quiet voice*). Here, Tagger, look.

TAGGER. Oh God, he's opening it. (*Suppressed laughter.*)

TEALE. Well anyway, when you have a discotheque you need people to do exciting things like serve soft drinks, serve food, prepare the school hall, hang up decorations, do some disc-jockeying, and lots of other thrilling things, and seeing as it's for your benefit we, the staff that is, don't see why we should have to be bothered with such details. I'm sure you all agree. (*Boos.*) So we need some volunteers. (*Silence.*) Well come on then. Don't crush me to death in the rush. Solomon Daniels, how about you?

SOLLY. Eh?

TEALE. Eh? What kind of an answer is that? And what are you doing lad?

The class bursts out laughing.

SOLLY. Nothing.

TEALE. It doesn't look like nothing to me. (*Moves toward him.*)

SOLLY. I'm not doing anything.

TEALE. Well I'd like to see what's in your desk too. (*He lifts up the desk lid.*) I see. You do know how to write with a pen and a piece of paper don't you, Daniels?

SOLLY. Course I do.

TEALE. Course you do. Why, then, carve 'Jenny' into your desk lid like some imbecillic, love-sick ten year old?

SOLLY. I didn't carve it into my desk.

TEALE. Well somebody did and it's you who was poring over it when I was asking for volunteers?

SOLLY. I wasn't poring over it.

The school bell goes.

TEALE. All right, you lot hoppit to your lesson. Daniels you stay here. I'd like a word with you yet again.

TAGGER. See you later, Solly.

TEALE. I said hoppit and that means all of you. And fast.

They all leave and then it goes quiet and we are left with the sound of the two of them alone in the room.

TEALE. So, you didn't carve the name into your desk then?

SOLLY. No, I just said I didn't.

TEALE. Then who did?

SOLLY. I don't know.

TEALE. Let's try it from another angle then. How long has it been there?

SOLLY. I've never seen it before.

TEALE. So it must have been done either last night or this morning, right?

SOLLY. I suppose so.

TEALE. And who is this Jenny girl anyway? Your girlfriend I presume.

SOLLY. I don't know.

TEALE. You mean you don't know who the 'Jenny' might be referring to?

SOLLY. I said I didn't do it, all right, so I didn't do it.

TEALE. And I'm saying that somebody did it and it's wilful damage to school property and whether you like it or not, or whether I like it or not, it's part of my job to find out who it was.

SOLLY. Well I don't know what you're asking me for cos I didn't bleeding do it.

TEALE. I don't think there's any reason to adopt that tone of voice.

SOLLY. What tone of voice?

TEALE. You know what I'm referring to.

SOLLY. No I don't. All I know is that you're calling me a liar and if you call me a liar I'm gonna tell you to piss off, cos I'm not a liar.

TEALE. I'm sorry, Daniels, but your behaviour's becoming a bit too arrogant even for me. I'll meet you outside the head's study in five minutes. If you can't or won't talk to me then you'll have to talk to him otherwise you'll be in very serious trouble, understand? Understand?

SOLLY. No, I don't understand.

TEALE. Well to be quite frank with you I'm a little baffled myself, Daniels. Tell me, is it that you don't trust me, you think I can't relate to whatever it is that's getting to you?

SOLLY. Nothing's getting to me.

TEALE. Oh come on, I was your age once myself. Girls, getting a job, convincing your parents of the most basic and obvious things, younger brothers and sisters, it's all common, but it seems to have hit you harder than most, doesn't it?

SOLLY. I don't think so.

TEALE. Look, I'll be frank with you. I know I'm not coloured but I think I do understand some of what you're talking about.

SOLLY. Like what?

TEALE. Like, well, like . . . Well you're not really talking, are you?

SOLLY. No.

TEALE. Just plain insolence and stubborness.

SOLLY. I don't want to talk to you, don't you understand?

TEALE. I think I'm beginning to. Outside the headmaster's study in five minutes.

Inside the HEADMASTER*'s study.*

HEAD. But you actually have no proof that the boy did it.

TEALE. It's not so much the desk itself that worries me, Headmaster, it's his attitude in general.

HEAD. Well from what I've been hearing you're not the only one worried by the boy's behaviour.

TEALE. Fair enough but I think it would be good for him if you tried to talk with him, not so much as a judicial figure of authority, but more as a friend, a counsellor. He's standing outside waiting.

HEAD (*laughs slightly*). Mr Teale, I appreciate your concern for the boy's welfare. Indeed I think it's admirable, but if I were to waste my time as counsellor to all the boys, and indeed some of the staff too, then I'd have no time left to run the school. I think it's perhaps time you took the bull by the horns and dealt with an issue yourself, Mr Teale, instead of delegating like some Lily-livored community worker.

TEALE. Instead of what?

HEAD. Instead of delegating, Mr Teale. Instead of passing the buck.

TEALE. But there comes a time, Headmaster, when a boy needs to be pushed slightly more rigorously, especially when things are going wrong for him.

HEAD. And you have my full permission to do so, and to discipline the boy as you see fit.

TEALE. But I'm not asking for your permission to punish, I'm asking for your co-operation in guiding the boy as safely as possible out of this school and into the world out there. I'm asking you to back me up.

HEAD. To do your job for you?

TEALE. No, dammit, to help me do my job!

HEAD. I think you had better calm down Mr Teale, or else resume your duties – that is, after all what the Local Authority pay you to do.

TEALE. I see.

HEAD. And when they promote you through the various scales, head of department, then deputy head, then finally, possibly, to headmaster, then I think you'll begin to understand what it is that I am talking about.

TEALE. Maybe.

HEAD. Yes indeed, maybe, but one can but hope. Good morning, Mr Teale.

TEALE. I haven't finished yet.

HEAD. Well I have. Good morning, Mr Teale (*Pause.*) Oh and you can send the boy on his way. There seems little point in his propping up the wall outside all day, wouldn't you say.

TEALE. Yes, Headmaster.

Girls' toilet.

TRACEY. Here, Jenny, I've been looking everywhere for you. (*Pause.*) What you doing in the bogs?

JENNY. Nothing.

TRACEY. Yes you are. What are you doing?

JENNY. I'm just reading, Tracey. Just leave us alone.

TRACEY. Let's see.

JENNY. No, leave off.

TRACEY. Let's see. (*She snatches.*) Oh God, it's not a letter from Solly Daniels, is it? I don't believe it.

JENNY. Give us it back. It might be.

TRACEY. You don't like him, do you?

JENNY. I don't know him.

TRACEY. But you don't fancy him?

JENNY. He's all right.

TRACEY. But what'll your mum and dad say?

JENNY. I haven't done anything yet.

TRACEY. I know but what would they say? And what about your brother?

JENNY. I said I haven't done anything yet.

TRACEY. I know, but I was just wondering, that's all.

JENNY. I heard you and I don't want to hear anymore.

TRACEY. Well it's up to you.

Pause.

JENNY. Give us it back, Tracey.

TRACEY. 'Dear Jenny, I know that I don't know you very well so please forgive me for just writing to you like this.' Where did he learn to write like that?

JENNY. I don't know, do I?

TRACEY. 'You see, I'm a bit shy of saying anything right out to you in case you tell me to get lost or something. I suppose I'm being a bit cowardly about it, aren't I?' Too right he is.

JENNY. Give us it back, Tracey.

TRACEY. 'But I'd really like to go out with you after school tonight, to the pictures, or just a walk if you like. Please let me know what you think and I'm sorry for not just asking you straight out. Yours sincerely, Solomon Daniels.' Solomon Daniels!

JENNY. Well that's his name, isn't it?

TRACEY. No it's not, his name is Solly.

JENNY. Which is short for Solomon, stupid. You know like Tagger's last name is Tagley but everyone calls him Tagger.

TRACEY. All right I know, I know. You don't have to go on.

JENNY. Well if you know how come you're pretending you don't. And anyhow it's up to me, isn't it, if I want to see him or not?

TRACEY. Course it is, but I've already said I think you're mad. Here, you can have your letter but for God's sake hurry up or we're gonna be late for the next lesson.

JENNY. All right I'm coming, don't bite my head off.

TRACEY. You're day-dreaming like you're in love already.

JENNY. Oh shut up, Tracey. You must have an electric mouth the amount you talk.

Behind the toilets in the playground.

TAGGER. Hi, Sol, all right?

SOLLY. No, I'm not.

TAGGER. Do you want a fag?

SOLLY. No, I wanna know why you got me into all that with Teale and don't say it wasn't you cos I know you.

TAGGER. It was only a joke, Solly.

SOLLY. I might have known.

TAGGER. No need to be like that, how was I supposed to know that Teale would come and have a look.

SOLLY. That ain't the point, is it?

TAGGER. Yeah, I know, but anyhow what happened?

SOLLY. Give us a fag and I'll tell you.

TAGGER. Here, have one.

SOLLY. Cheers.

TAGGER. Well what happened then?

SOLLY. Hang on a minute. Let me get it lit will you.

TAGGER. Okay. (*He lights the cigarette.*)

SOLLY. Well he just kept asking me who done it and I just kept telling him to mind his own business cos it wasn't me. Eventually I must have told him to piss off once too many times cos he sent me to see the Head. I stood outside while he went in then he just came out and told me to get lost.

TAGGER. What, you reckon the Head must have told him to get lost?

SOLLY. I don't know what happened but that's the end of that as far as I'm concerned.

TAGGER. You didn't split on me then?

SOLLY. Course I didn't split. I'm no grass, you should know that by now.

TAGGER. I knew you wouldn't split. Not you. Come on I'm off to the shop. Coming?

SOLLY. Yeah, I want some chewing gum.

TAGGER. Chewing gum? What do you want that for?

SOLLY. It's games this afternoon. Helps you concentrate when you're playing.

TAGGER. You've been watching too much *Match of the Day* mate. You'll be wanting vaseline to rub on your legs next.

SOLLY. At least I can kick a ball which is more than you can do, you slob.

TAGGER. You must think you're Luther Blissett.

SOLLY. Who says?

TAGGER. I says.

SOLLY. On your bike, Tagger. Let's go.

TAGGER. Hey, Solly?

SOLLY. What?

TAGGER. I was a bit pissed last night. Tracey says I should say sorry.

SOLLY. Don't worry about it, it's okay.

TAGGER. And will you still do that maths quiz for me?

SOLLY. Yeah, don't worry, loads of time.

TAGGER. Great. I haven't got a clue.

SOLLY. Okay.

TAGGER. You don't mind do you?

SOLLY. I wouldn't be doing it if I minded, would I?

TAGGER. No, suppose not.

SOLLY. Well there you are then. Come on, man. Let's go.

1969: We are in a room somewhere. We can hear noise from another room. A bedsitter of some sort. The noise is a football match with a radio commentary. Then a baby starts to cry in the room.

ROY. But I can't take this place anymore, it's killing me, it's driving me mad. After 10 years I'm about to become a madman in England. They can put a man on the moon but I'm still living in a bedsitter with a wife and child.

CYNTHIA (*comforting the crying baby – about 18 months old.*) Quiet, Solomon, your father's tired too.

ROY. Still trapped in the same damn stupid nothing dead-end job and every place you turn these damn evil people calling you name this and name that. And you can't go out and find a next job to double the money because of that child, and we can't find the money to put down a deposit on our own property – you know I don't know what the hell we still doing here, you know I just can't figure it out.

CYNTHIA. Roy, you're just tired.

ROY. Course I'm just tired, woman, but you have to ask yourself what it is I'm tired of. I'm not a young man any more, you know, I can feel the years slipping away from me, the best years of my life going down the drain and passing out of sight: in this place: in England!

CYNTHIA. But we can't go back home. What about Solomon, he has to have his education here. There's nothing back there for him, we both know that, Roy, that's why we're here in the first place.

ROY. But we're not going anywhere in this country, we're going backwards.

CYNTHIA. But we've got to keep trying. We've got to make sure that we don't fail, for our sakes, but more so for Solomon; we owe him success of some kind.

ROY. And we owe ourselves something too. Sanity in England. Solomon shouldn't have been born so soon then we could just dig up and try a next place for work, a next city, or America even.

CYNTHIA. Solomon is the best accident that ever happened to me. I don't regret anything so please don't talk that way about our child.

ROY. Don't 'Please' me any more, woman, I've had it. I turn up early for work I have the union on my back. I turn up late I have the boss on my back. My child is ill so I stay at home and I have everybody on my back, and this country don't have as many spare jobs as they like to make out so I can't just tell them to go to hell or otherwise what we going to eat? (*Pause.*) I can't take my child in the park for the loose dogs come and chase us and one of us end up stepping in filth, and if we go out together is only a matter of time before somebody shouting at us 'Nigger go home' or 'Jungle Jim do us a dance', and the Beatles's singing 'Get Back' and people singing it to us, and you want us to stay here? We can't even go out together cos nobody will babysit for us so I mean what the hell am I supposed to do, eh? I mean you want to go mad in England? You want our child to go mad here, to get used to being called 'nigger' in England? Eh? Eh?

CYNTHIA. Roy, I'm having another baby.

ROY. You doing what?

CYNTHIA. I'm pregnant.

ROY. Why?

CYNTHIA. What you mean why?

ROY. When you find this out?

CYNTHIA. This morning.

ROY. Well that's it, then you must get rid of it.

CYNTHIA. I can't kill it, Roy.

ROY. You must get rid of it! We can't afford to feed a next mouth and I don't want another child in this country. One going be enough of a problem as it is.

CYNTHIA. Roy I can't just get rid of it: It belongs to us, for better or for worse; it's our baby.

ROY. You crazy or what? I kill you before I see you bring a next child into this world.

CYNTHIA. Roy I want to have the child.

ROY. And how you going feed it? It's only one pair of hands I have.

CYNTHIA. We'll find a way.

ROY. What you mean 'we': you didn't hear what I say? I gone now for sure woman. I'm going home if you have a next child.

CYNTHIA. But you talk to me as if it had nothing to do with you.

ROY. And I could say the same about you and your decision to have the thing.

CYNTHIA. But it's wrong to . . .

ROY. And it's just as wrong to bring a coloured child into this damn world as it is at the moment. You don't see that? Well?

CYNTHIA. But I've waited ten years for our two children. Roy, I'm getting too old to wait for a next chance.

ROY. Well it's you who must make your decision. I've said what I've got to say, understand? Well?

CYNTHIA. Roy, please . . . (*The door slams.*) Roy . . .

The baby starts to cry.

We are in a noisy school changing-room and the kids are getting changed for an afternoon game of soccer.

SOLLY. Whose side are you on, Tag?

TAGGER. I don't care. I don't feel like playing anyway.

SOLLY. That's cos you can't.

TAGGER. Here we go again.

SOLLY. Boring you am I?

TAGGER. Yeah, but I nearly forgot. I've got something for you.

SOLLY. What?

TAGGER. You'll have to cross my palm with silver first.

SOLLY. Sod off. What is it?

TAGGER. A letter from Tracey.

SOLLY. Tracey?

TAGGER. Given to her by none other than, Miss Jenny Bates. As opposed to Master Bates.

SOLLY. Give us it here.

TAGGER. Well aren't you going to open it up then?

SOLLY. Yeah, when you've gone.

TEACHER. Right you lot. Out there now! And that means now.

TAGGER. See you in a minute then, Solly, and try and control yourself as you read it.

We hear them all trooping off out leaving SOLLY *alone.*

JENNY (*voice over, reading the letter*). Dear Solly, thank you for your letter. I would like to go to the pictures with you tonight and I'll be at the Odeon at seven if you still want to go. Maybe it's best not to tell anybody at the moment cos my dad's a bit funny about me going out with boys. Sorry it's so short but I've got to rush. Yours sincerely, Jennifer Bates.

TEACHER. Well, Daniels? Waiting for Christmas are we? Get out, lad! Get out there, show us some of that old black magic.

On the football pitch. We hear the whistle, shouting, etc. The sound of the ball being kicked.

VOICE. Here! Pass it over here!

VOICE. Through ball! Through ball!

SOLLY. Here! Here!

VOICE. Solly!

SOLLY. Aghh!

VOICE. That's a foul, sir. Penalty!

The whistle goes and voices are raised in anger.

TEACHER. What kind of a tackle was that, Bates?

BATES. It was an accident, sir.

TAGGER. Send him off, sir. That was disgusting.

BATES. Shut your gob, Tagger.

TEACHER. Bates! If I hear anymore from you, or see another tackle like that, you'll be off, okay?

BATES. It was a professional foul, sir.

TEACHER. There was nothing professional about thuggery even before the Jimmy Hills of this world gave it a nice label, understand?

BATES. Sir.

TEACHER. Are you all right, Daniels?

SOLLY. I think I might have twisted my ankle.

TEACHER. It's just a bit bruised but you better go off. Can you walk?

SOLLY. I think so.

TEACHER. Give him a hand, Tagger.

SOLLY. No, I'll manage, honest.

TEACHER. Okay. (*He blows the whistle.*) Penalty.

There is argument.

SOLLY *goes into the house and slams the door.*

CHRIS. You limping, Solly?

SOLLY. No, I fell in a puddle and one of my legs shrunk.

CHRIS (*hushing him up*). Quiet Solly, Mum's ill.

SOLLY. What do you mean ill?

CHRIS. She's in bed not feeling too good. I had to ring up Dr Chandra and he came round and said we had to stay with her.

SOLLY. What's up with her?

CHRIS. Nothing serious, just exhaustion, he said, and worry.

SOLLY. Exhaustion? She works for him doesn't she. Trying to work her to death is he?

CHRIS. He said it was worry really. She's got too much on her mind.

SOLLY. So where is she now?

CHRIS. Upstairs asleep. He gave her some sleeping pills and said we had to check on her from time to time.

SOLLY. What, all night?

CHRIS. Yeah, why, were you off out?

SOLLY. Pictures.

CHRIS. Where you get the money from?

SOLLY. None of your business.

CHRIS. I bet some bird's paying for you.

SOLLY. Well that's how much you know.

CHRIS. Well you're not still gonna go are you, Sol?

SOLLY. Why not? You're here to look after her.

CHRIS. It ain't fair, Solly. She's your mum too. (*Pause.*) Don't go Sol. Phone up whoever it is and say you can't.

SOLLY. Don't tell me what to do.

CHRIS. I'm not.

Pause.

SOLLY. Is there anything to eat?

CHRIS. Beans on toast. You're not going then?

SOLLY. Let's have some of that. I'll go and sit with her first.

CHRIS. Okay.

SOLLY. Hey.

CHRIS. What?

SOLLY. Did he say there was anything else the matter with her?

CHRIS. No, he said she'd be all right as long as she got some rest, that's all. Just some rest.

SOLLY. What you looking at me like that for then?

CHRIS. Like what?

SOLLY. Like it was my fault she's ill.

CHRIS. I'm not.

SOLLY. Yes you are.

CHRIS. You keep shouting at her. (*Pause.*) I heard you last night.

SOLLY. I wasn't shouting, it was her.

CHRIS. I only heard you.

SOLLY. So you think it's my fault.

CHRIS. I didn't say that.

SOLLY. You think I've made her ill just cos I ain't a creep.

CHRIS. It's more you than me.

Pause.

SOLLY. You say that again and I'm gonna kick your head in.

CHRIS. So what?

SOLLY. You know what. And your beginning to get on my tits as well so shut it.

CHRIS. I won't.

SOLLY. I said shut up!

We hear CHRIS *coming downstairs and into the kitchen.*

CHRIS. I said it's your turn to go and sit with her now, Solly. Were you asleep?

SOLLY. Let me finish my cup of coffee first. It's like being on guard duty outside Buckingham Palace. What time is it?

CHRIS. Nearly eleven. You could take your coffee with you if you wanted.

SOLLY. I wanna drink it here.

CHRIS. I don't reckon she should go to work tomorrow.

SOLLY. It's up to her.

CHRIS. Don't you care?

SOLLY. Course I care or how come I'm here.

Pause.

CHRIS. Was it that Jenny bird that you were supposed to be going out with.

SOLLY. Why?

CHRIS. Someone told me you fancied her.

SOLLY. Who?

CHRIS. I can't remember. (*Pause.*) She's okay though, isn't she?

SOLLY. Suppose so.

Pause.

CHRIS. Are you glad to be leaving school?

SOLLY. Can't wait. Hate the bloody place.

CHRIS. But you didn't always used to though, did you?

SOLLY. So what? They treat you like you're a kid.

CHRIS. Not all of them though. Tealy's okay, isn't he?

SOLLY. Used to be but he's getting just like the rest of them. Even asked me about Mum and how things were at home.

CHRIS. What did you say?

SOLLY. Nothing. None of his business, is it?

CHRIS. No. Suppose not. (*Pause.*) I came top of our class in the exams.

SOLLY. I could have been top of our class if I'd have wanted.

CHRIS. Yeah, I know.

CYNTHIA (*voice very faint from upstairs*). Chris? Christopher?

SOLLY. She's woken up. I'll go.

CHRIS. Tell me when it's my turn.

SOLLY. I will, don't worry.

CHRIS. No need to be like that is there? It's not my fault you couldn't go out.

SOLLY. It don't matter. She's more important than any bird, isn't she?

CHRIS. Yeah I know she is. You don't have to tell me.

SOLLY. And what do you mean by that?

CHRIS. I don't mean anything, why?

SOLLY. Well you better not.

CHRIS. I don't.

In CYNTHIA'*s bedroom.*

SOLLY. Mum?

CYNTHIA. Solomon. Pass me some water from over the side there. (*He does so.*) Thank you.

SOLLY. You want anything else?

CYNTHIA. No. I just wanted to make sure you were all right.

SOLLY. We're fine.

CYNTHIA. You had something to eat?

SOLLY. Yeah.

CYNTHIA. Good. You can go back downstairs now if you want.

SOLLY. No, it's all right I'll wait here. You go back to sleep.

CYNTHIA. You can be a good boy. Both of you can be. (*Pause.*) It's late so don't stay up too late, and make sure Christopher goes to bed before you.

SOLLY. I will. Go to sleep now.

CYNTHIA. I'm just tired that's all, Solomon. Nothing to worry about. Nothing at all.

SOLLY (*concerned*). You'll be all right, won't you?

CYNTHIA (*laughs painfully*). I've done all right so far. I think.

In the bedsitter.

ROY. I don't care what you say woman, I'm going.

CYNTHIA. But you can't leave me and Solomon and a next child on its way, Roy. How the hell we going to eat? How are we going to live with no money coming into the home?

ROY. Well you'll just have to start working. This damn country just about grind me down to nothing and unless I'm leaving now there don't going be nothing left of me to grind down any further. I've already told the man at work that Friday is my last day.

CYNTHIA. How you going explain to our family back home, Roy? How you going tell them that you just walk out on me like that, you just leave me?

ROY. You think I'm afraid of what people think? You think you can blackmail me into staying here with you? You must be crazy . . .

CYNTHIA. Well maybe I am crazy, but I can't just rip a child out of me body and throw it in the trashcan just because you say to me that I must do so for you don't like England. All I'm interested in Roy is the education of my children. I never stood a chance and neither did you on an island where your opportunities stopped when you were 15 or 16, unless you had money or you could win one of the big scholarships, and although we both had brains in our heads just look at the jobs that we end up doing, well? And in England why is it that we can't find the money after over ten years of struggle, we can't even find the money to own even the smallest of houses, we can't go out and enjoy ourselves, we can't do anything, Roy, except shout and curse each other, and lately I notice that we don't even do that because you too drunk by the time you come back in from the pub. All you care about is yourself and how things are bad for you. What you're forgetting is Solomon and the next child, Samantha, maybe. You forgetting what will happen to them. At least here they have a chance to get some qualifications, even if it means we must send them to school out of this one room, at least here they have a chance to be somebody, to be something and they don't have to go through all the pain and the humiliation of having to leave the island and their family to do so. You, Roy, you just trying to force me to kill so you can stay but you can go now, I don't care, you can go but I can't take them back to that.

ROY. And you know why? It's because deep down you're just ashamed of what you are, that's all. You're ashamed of the people you came from, the place you came from, you're ashamed of real life, aren't you?

CYNTHIA. No Roy, I'm ashamed of you. You've tried but only for yourself. It's not good enough for me and my children.

ROY. Well in that case I gone then! I can't stay here with you for you'll only be happy on the day when you wake up in the morning and look in the mirror and find you've turned white. Until that day comes you always going be unhappy, aren't you, always thinking you're something you aren't. You can keep the children for I going reclaim the sunshine and a real life.

SOLLY *is in the kitchen pouring out his cornflakes into a bowl. It is morning.*

SOLLY (*shouting*). Chris, hurry up will you? It's half past eight. Chris!

CHRIS *comes in.*

CHRIS. What?

SOLLY. How come you aren't dressed then?

CHRIS. Cos I ain't going to school today.

SOLLY. How come?

CHRIS. I'm staying at home with Mum.

SOLLY. Does she want you to?

CHRIS. No, I want to. Just in case she faints again.

SOLLY. Do you want me to ring Chandra and tell him she ain't coming in.

CHRIS. No, I'll do it when she wakes up.

SOLLY. Okay.

CHRIS. Have you got any money I can lend, Sol?

SOLLY. What for?

CHRIS. Milk and stuff like that. I don't want to wake Mum up.

SOLLY. I've got a quid. Here.

CHRIS. Who give you it?

SOLLY. Do you want it or not?

CHRIS. Thanks. (*Pause.*) I'll see you tonight then.

SOLLY. I'll be back to take over. Make sure you look after her properly.

CHRIS. Course I will! What do you think I'm gonna do to her?

SOLLY. I don't know do I?

Pause.

CHRIS. Solly?

SOLLY. What do you want now?

CHRIS. Remember when she told us that we weren't called Daniels any more.

SOLLY. Yeah, so what?

CHRIS. Why did she change her mind back again?

SOLLY. I don't know. (*Pause.*) I think it was cos of Dad. Why, are you thinking of changing it?

CHRIS. Well it's silly to have his name isn't it: if he's dead we might as well be called after Mum.

SOLLY. You don't half talk some rubbish, you know. Her name is Mrs Daniels cos she's called after him: We're Daniels cos she is, all right?

CHRIS. I just wondered that's all.

SOLLY. Well you can keep wondering because that's all there is to it. Keep an eye on her and I'll see you later, okay.

CHRIS. Okay.

In the classroom.

TEALE. Now 5C I've called you all back here after assembly for I've got a very serious and sad announcement to make.

VOICE. Is Thatcher dead, sir?

They all laugh.

TEALE. Quiet! When I say serious I mean serious. Yesterday afternoon, during the games period, two boys in this room, I won't say who they are for it's not important, what is important is that these two boys had money taken from their pockets by somebody, or some people in this room.

A murmur goes around the boys.

Now, unless any of you are unaware, this is known as stealing and I don't care much for thieves so will the culprits, or culprit, please make themselves known. (*Long pause.*) All right, seeing as nobody has the courage to speak out I'll be having the whole lot of you back here tonight until somebody does own up, is that understood?

TAGGER. Oh God.

SOLLY. I ain't staying back.

TEALE. Did you say something, Daniels?

SOLLY. I said I can't stay back tonight cos me Mum's ill.

TEALE. I see. Well I'm sorry to hear that but when I say the whole class I mean the whole class, and that includes you. Now all of you get to your lesson quickly and quietly.

They all begin to move off noisily.

I said quietly.

The playground behind the toilets.

JENNY. Did you go to the bingo with your mum last night, Tracey?

TRACEY. Yeah, but it was dead boring seeing as you decided that you didn't want to go.

JENNY. I never said I was going in the first place.

TRACEY. But you never said you wasn't going either so I thought you were, didn't I?

JENNY. Well you thought wrong.

TRACEY. And I suppose you went out with Solomon Romeo Daniels instead.

JENNY. No, as a matter of fact I didn't.

TRACEY. What happened? Your Dad wouldn't let you out as usual?

JENNY. No. He didn't turn up.

TRACEY. He stood you up?

JENNY. He might not have been able to make it.

TRACEY. Well he could have phoned you.

JENNY. He didn't know the number.

TRACEY. It's in the phone book. He can read, can't he?

JENNY. Course. I don't care anyhow.

TRACEY. I'll bet you do, anyone would. I'd kill Tagger if he tried that on with me.

JENNY. I don't know why. He gets away with everything else he tries on.

TRACEY. Get lost. (*Pause.*) So what happens if he asks again?

JENNY. What do you mean what happens?

TRACEY. I mean are you gonna tell him to get lost or what, cos he can't just not turn up.

JENNY. I don't know what'll happen do I. It's not easy to tell.

TRACEY. Yeah, well I know what I'd do. Wasting a night like that.

JENNY. You can't just . . .

TRACEY. Hey, hang on a minute. I don't believe it. Look who's coming over. He's got some front, hasn't he?

JENNY. Don't be like that.

SOLLY. Hello, I've come to explain about last night.

TRACEY. Yeah, I should think so as well.

JENNY. Shut up Tracey, will you?

TRACEY. Well he can't go round doing that to people.

JENNY. Shut up will you.

SOLLY. You see . . .

JENNY. Hang on a minute. Why don't you leave us alone for a minute, Trace?

TRACEY. Oh hark at her lovebird.

JENNY. It's not that, it's . . .

TRACEY. Yeah, I know. I know when I'm not wanted.

She leaves.

JENNY. I'm sorry about that.

SOLLY. I'm sorry about last night. You see it's my Mum. When I got home she was collapsed and I had to stay with her.

JENNY. Oh God, is she all right now?

SOLLY. Yeah, well a bit weak but I reckon she'll be all right soon.

JENNY. I thought it must be something like that.

SOLLY. You see I haven't got a Dad.

JENNY. Why not?

SOLLY. I just haven't. He's dead. Chris and me have to look after her.

JENNY. I didn't know.

SOLLY. It's not your fault, I don't really talk about it much.

JENNY. I see. I'm sorry.

SOLLY. What for?

JENNY. That you haven't got a Dad.

Pause.

SOLLY. Did you wait for long?

JENNY. About an hour.

SOLLY. Oh God.

JENNY. But it wasn't that bad though. This old man gave me a paper to read. Really boring. (*She laughs.*)

SOLLY. Well how about tonight then?

JENNY. I can't. I've got netball practice.

SOLLY. Well, Friday then?

JENNY. That's the disco isn't it?

SOLLY. Yeah, how about meeting up at eight for the disco?

JENNY. Okay great.

Pause.

SOLLY. Do you still mind about everyone knowing?

JENNY. Not now. Should I?

SOLLY. No. (*Pause.*) Sure?

JENNY. Course I'm sure. I'd better go now otherwise I'm gonna be late.

SOLLY. What's your Mum and Dad do?

JENNY. That's a weird thing to ask, isn't it?

SOLLY. Is it?

JENNY. No one's ever asked me that before.

SOLLY. You been out with someone else?

JENNY. Well sort of, but not properly. I meant nobody, not even a girl has ever asked me that.

SOLLY. Sorry.

JENNY. I don't mind. My Mum's a housewife and my Dad's a carpenter. Boring isn't it?

SOLLY. Sounds all right to me. At least he's working.

JENNY. Just, or so he says. Have you thought about what you're going to do yet?

SOLLY. Thought about it but not really done too much about it, if you see what I mean. Not a lot I can do except hope and wait and all the rest of those things.

JENNY. Suppose not. (*Pause.*) I've really got to go now, Solly.

SOLLY. Okay then. See you tomorrow. About eight.

JENNY. Okay then, see you.

In the classroom.

VOICE. How long's this detention going on for, sir?

TEALE. Till I tell you it's over.

VOICE. And how come Daniels is allowed to get away with it?

VOICE. Yeah, we all know who was in the showers first.

TAGGER. Shut your face, Marsh, or I'll push it in for you.

VOICE. You and whose army, Tagger?

TEALE. Quiet! All of you. That's enough. You've been here nearly an hour now so you can go.

The noise of them all about to leave.

I said quiet – I'm going to have to think whether or not you lot deserve an end of term discotheque.

The noise of jeering.

And even if you do, I want you all on your best behaviour, otherwise it'll be one dance then hoppit for the lot of you.

The noise of them jeering etc.

Now go quietly.

In the front room.

TEALE. Seems like you've a very nice front room here, Daniels. I can see why you prefer coming here and putting up your feet rather than being in detention.

SOLLY. It's not my front room, it's me Mum's.

TEALE. Well then, how's your mother?

SOLLY. Better I suppose. She's gone off to work. Why, did you want to talk to her?

TEALE. No, No. It's you I came to talk with.

SOLLY. Well?

TEALE. Why did you take the money?

SOLLY. I didn't take it.

TEALE. Well who do you think did then?

SOLLY. I don't know.

TEALE. Well some people think it was you.

SOLLY. What people?

TEALE. It doesn't really matter what people, just some people. And I think it could have been you but I don't know why you would want to take money.

SOLLY. I didn't take any money.

TEALE. Look, Solly, when I was younger I used to take things too you know. Sweets from the corner shop and things like that. Why? Sometimes just because I wanted them, which is a stupid reason. Now you're not stupid like I was. You must have had a reason. And the rest of your behaviour of late, it's like you're angry but you don't know what you're angry about. Is it the prospect of leaving school?

SOLLY. No.

TEALE. Has something happened at home? With your mother?

SOLLY. I told you she's poorly.

TEALE. Is that what's been worrying you?

SOLLY. No.

TEALE. Has anybody said anything to you? Is somebody calling you names for instance?

SOLLY. No.

TEALE. Well, what about this girl, Jenny? Presumably the Jenny is Jenny Bates?

SOLLY. Might be.

TEALE. How long have you two been seeing each other?

SOLLY. We don't.

TEALE. But you'd like to.

SOLLY. I don't want to talk to you anymore.

TEALE. But you'd like to go out with this Jenny Bates, is that it?

SOLLY. I want you to go now. I don't want to talk with you.

TEALE. Did you take the money for her? So you could impress her perhaps.

SOLLY. I want you to go I said.

TEALE. I don't think there's any need to get quite so upset about it, Daniels.

SOLLY. I said I want you to go.

TEALE. I'll see you tomorrow then I expect.

SOLLY. You might.

TEALE. Oh come on, Daniels. Last day at school. You'll want to be there for that won't you.

SOLLY. I've told you I don't want to talk to you.

TEALE. There's no need to shout. I'm going. (*Pause.*) Maybe I ought to have a talk with your mother. What do you think?

SOLLY. You can't talk to her cos she's out and I don't want you to talk with her, all right.

TEALE. I'll see you tomorrow then.

SOLLY *slams the door behind him.*

SOLLY. Yeah, but that'll be the last time, then you can get stuffed.

In the boys' bedroom.

CHRIS. Can I have one of your blankets, I'm cold.

SOLLY. Yeah, take it.

CHRIS. Did you think Mum looked tired tonight when she came in?

SOLLY. Course. You would if you'd gone and fainted the day before and just spent all day at work.

CHRIS. What are you doing? I want to go to sleep now.

SOLLY. Well I'm not stopping you.

CHRIS. Are you writing poetry?

SOLLY. No I'm not and stop trying to look.

CHRIS. You are, aren't you? (*Pause.*) Why won't you tell me what Teale wanted to know?

SOLLY. Cos it's none of your business.

CHRIS. Are you in trouble with him or something?

SOLLY. Course not.

CHRIS. Well how come he comes to our house then?

SOLLY. None of your business.

CHRIS. Can you turn out the lights please, I want to go to sleep.

SOLLY. I'll be finished in a minute.

CHRIS. Good, I'm tired.

SOLLY. I said I'll be finished in a minute, didn't I?

CHRIS. Okay.

Pause.

SOLLY. You ask too many questions.

CHRIS. That's cos you don't give any answers.

SOLLY. You reckon?

CHRIS. Yeah. Finished?

SOLLY. No. Shut up.

CHRIS. I heard you crying, Solly. After Teale had gone.

SOLLY. Who me?

CHRIS. Yeah.

SOLLY. No you didn't.

CHRIS. I did.

SOLLY. You didn't, all right.

Pause.

CHRIS. What's up?

SOLLY. Nothing.

CHRIS. Why don't you talk to me anymore, Solly?

SOLLY. Cos I'm tired.

CHRIS. No, I mean all the time. Not just now. All the time, you never do, never. (*He begins to cry.*)

SOLLY. Whose crying now?

CHRIS. Stop getting at me.

SOLLY. I'm sorry, Chris.

CHRIS. No you're not.

SOLLY. I am. I didn't mean to make you cry.

CHRIS. You always do this to me, you're just not my friend anymore, are you?

SOLLY. Course I am. Chris?

CHRIS. I don't want to talk, I want to go to sleep now.

SOLLY. Chris?

CHRIS. I want to go to sleep, I'm tired now. Just let me go to sleep, Solly.

The HEADMASTER*'s office.*

HEAD. But are you saying the boy took the money, Mr Teale? Or are you saying something else? I have to be frank with you, it sounds like another of your 'scratching on the desk' games.

TEALE. I'm saying that I'm not sure if Daniels took the money but it's symptomatic of the hysteria his presence causes that almost all of his peer group seem to feel he did.

HEAD. And what do you propose to do about this?

TEALE. I was hoping that a stiff letter to his mother might help. I tried to talk with her when I visited the boy's home yesterday afternoon.

HEAD. And presumably she would not talk with you either.

TEALE. She was not in when I called round.

HEAD. Then write the letter, Mr Teale.

TEALE. I was hoping that you might write it, Headmaster.

HEAD (*sighs*). There seems little point, Mr Teale, I hardly know the boy and neither his mother nor the circumstances of his home life are even vaguely familiar to me.

TEALE. So you refuse?

HEAD. You come in here with some half-baked story about a shower-room theft and a boy who has been causing you and the rest of my school trouble and you seem either incapable or unwilling to put the two pieces together.

TEALE. So that's the end of that then, is it?

HEAD. Not quite Mr Teale. Take a seat again, please. I've been watching your own conduct over the last term with some interest and I'm not sure if you're the right sort of teacher for a school of this sort.

TEALE. What do you mean?

HEAD. I mean, Mr Teale, that this is a tough comprehensive school with, I have to admit it, a rather second-rate academic track record. It would seem to me that you'd be happier in a school with less demanding disciplinary problems where your liberal studies skills might flourish a little more easily. Have you thought about a transfer?

TEALE. Well, when you put it like that, no.

HEAD. Well might I suggest you do. It shouldn't be at all difficult to arrange, and there might even be a promotion involved if we were to choose the right school for you.

A train station.

ROY. You didn't have to come and see me off, you know.

CYNTHIA. I wanted to.

Train announcement.

ROY. I feel stupid, Cynthia.

CYNTHIA. If it's what you want then do it, just go.

ROY. It's not what I want.

CYNTHIA. Then why do it?

ROY. Ssh. Don't shout.

CYNTHIA. I'll shout if I want to.

Train announcement.

What am I supposed to tell the children?

ROY. Tell them their father was going mad in England and he left before he killed somebody.

CYNTHIA. And what kind of sense is that supposed to make to them, Roy? What kind of sense is it supposed to make to me?

ROY. I don't know.

CYNTHIA. Solomon, you understand your father?

ROY. Please . . .

CYNTHIA. Look good at him for it's the last time you'll ever see him.

ROY. Don't threaten me, woman.

CYNTHIA. I'll do what I like Roy, you've no right to tell me anything anymore. Never! Never!

Train announcement.

ROY. I've got to go now.

CYNTHIA. Then go. But look good at your child and remember. And the one in my belly that you can't see is the same one you said you never wanted to see, and I going to make sure the child never going see you so go! It's never going know nothing about you so just go – go!

In the kitchen – the clock – silence.

SOLLY. Who were you talking to Mum?

CYNTHIA. Solomon?

SOLLY. Who were you talking to, Mum?

CYNTHIA. Your father. I sometimes hear his voice and . . . and it comforts me.

SOLLY. But you were shouting.

CYNTHIA. Was I?

SOLLY. Why don't you ever take us to his grave, Mum?

CYNTHIA. Please, Solomon.

SOLLY. Why don't you ever talk about him, Mum?

CYNTHIA. I don't know, dear. Don't you have to be at school?

SOLLY. I leave school today, Mum, to start up on my own. I've finished with all that. I'm big now.

CYNTHIA. I suppose you are.

Pause.

SOLLY. Just tell me one thing about him.

CYNTHIA. What?

SOLLY. Just one thing. Anything.

CYNTHIA. Your father was going mad in England and he left before he killed somebody. (*She begins to cry.*)

SOLLY. I don't understand. Why are you crying, Mum?

CYNTHIA. He was going mad in this country, Solomon. Working himself stupid for nothing – but you two, both of you, you've got a real chance to make good here. Please, for my sake, make use of it.

SOLLY. What do you mean he was going mad?

CYNTHIA. I'll tell you Solomon, but not now. I'm too tired. Too tired to think anymore.

SOLLY. Do you want anything?

CYNTHIA. Come here and hold me, son. Just hold me.

SOLLY. All right, Mum. All right.

She continues to cry.

CYNTHIA. Solomon why do you shout at me, son?

SOLLY. I don't mean to, Mum, it just happens.

CYNTHIA. It's been happening for a while now, hasn't it?

SOLLY. I know, I'm sorry, Mum.

CYNTHIA. Sometimes what I think is best for you isn't always best.

SOLLY. What do you mean?

CYNTHIA (*laughs*). I don't know. (*Pause.*) Do you think I've brought you up badly, Solomon? Do you think I've neglected you?

SOLLY. No, who says you have?

CYNTHIA. Nobody, it's just that I sometimes wonder. I sometimes wonder if I've failed.

SOLLY. You haven't failed, Mum. Nobody could have done what you've done. I know that and so does Chris. It don't really matter if nobody else does, does it?

CYNTHIA. No I suppose not.

SOLLY. It doesn't. I don't care what they say.

CYNTHIA. I love you both. (*Pause.*) I'm very proud of you.

In the school playground.

TRACEY. What you reading, Jenny?

JENNY. Nothing.

TRACEY. Yeah you are, I can see you, can't I? I'm not blind. (*She snatches.*) Let's have a look.

JENNY. Give us it back.

TRACEY. Oh my God, I don't believe this. Poetry. Is it from him?

JENNY. Who else?

TRACEY. He's a nutter.

'My heart cries out for you,
And I feel blue,
But the sun in the sky,
And the warmth in your eye,
Turns the world a brighter hue.'

(*She laughs.*) What a load of crap. If Tagger wrote anything like that I'd tell him where to get off straight away.

JENNY. Give us it back.

TRACEY. I haven't upset you, have I?

JENNY. No you haven't.

TRACEY. I thought you were going out with him.

JENNY. No I'm not. I'm thinking of changing my mind.

TRACEY. Why? Just cos we've been taking the mickey a bit?

JENNY. Maybe.

TRACEY. Well I think you're better off without him. I keep telling you it will just cause trouble.

JENNY. Maybe . . . but . . .

TRACEY. But nothing. You'd get in a right mess. Come on, we're off to the shop. Coming?

JENNY. All right, I suppose so.

TRACEY. He must think he's a poet or something, sending you poetry. Off his rocker.

JENNY. He's not off his rocker.

TRACEY. Can I have the poem?

JENNY. What for?

TRACEY. To show Tagger.

JENNY. No, it's mine.

TRACEY. But I thought you said you might not go out with him no more or anything.

JENNY. I might not but it's mine, he gave it to me.

TRACEY. But I only want to show Tagger.

JENNY. I still like him. I don't want you making fun of him.

TRACEY. I'm not making fun.

JENNY. It's my Mum and Dad, Tracey. They'd kill me, they really would. It's pathetic but I suddenly realised that it's serious. It'll never work, will it?

TRACEY. You already know what I think.

JENNY. I suppose I'm just a coward. I feel terrible about it, Tracey. Honest. Really bad.

TRACEY. There's nothing to worry about. It didn't even start really did it?

JENNY. I suppose not . . . but . . .

TRACEY. But nothing, come on.

JENNY. I don't like giving up. I don't really want to.

TRACEY. You don't know what you want, do you?

JENNY. I don't know. Maybe I'll think about it a bit more.

TRACEY. Come on. I'm in a rush.

JENNY. I'll not come tonight, will you tell him?

TRACEY. Yeah.

JENNY. But I think I will keep going out with him. I've got to stand up to my parents some time, haven't I?

TRACEY. Well I'm glad I'm not you.

JENNY. I am or else I wouldn't have Solly.

TRACEY. Oh God. When are you gonna start the family?

At home in the Daniels' house.

CHRIS. Have you been at home all afternoon?

SOLLY. Yeah. Just reading and stuff.

CHRIS. Where's Mum?

SOLLY. Gone out to work.

CHRIS. She leave us anything to eat?

SOLLY. Normal.

CHRIS. I've got a letter for you.

SOLLY. Who's it from?

CHRIS. Mr Teale gave it to me.

SOLLY. Teale? (*He opens it.*)

CHRIS. What's it say?

SOLLY (*tearing it up*). Nothing.

CHRIS. It must say something.

SOLLY. Yeah, it says the school is full of rubbish which I know already.

CHRIS. Is that all?

SOLLY. Yeah. Make us some tea will you? I've got to go get ready.

CHRIS. You going to the disco tonight?

SOLLY. Yeah.

CHRIS. You're going with Jenny Bates, aren't you?

SOLLY. Might be.

CHRIS. She's all right, she is.

SOLLY. What do you know about it?

CHRIS. Same as you.

SOLLY. Oh yeah. Make the tea, shrimp. (*Pause.*) Chris?

CHRIS. What?

SOLLY. What's a period?

CHRIS. Get stuffed.

Pause.

SOLLY. Chris?

CHRIS. What?

SOLLY. Don't tell Mum.

CHRIS. Don't tell Mum what?

SOLLY. That I'm going out with her.

CHRIS. You mean you really are?

SOLLY. Don't sound so surprised.

CHRIS. That's great. I like her.

SOLLY. So what if you like her. And you don't even know her.

CHRIS. But it's good, though.

SOLLY. I suppose so. It's all right.

CHRIS. All right?

SOLLY. Don't shout. And don't tell Mum just yet.

CHRIS. Don't worry, I won't tell her. (*Pause.*) I won't split on you.

At the school disco. Music is playing loudly and it is in full swing.

TAGGER. All right, Sol?

SOLLY. All right, I suppose.

TAGGER. You don't sound it. (*Pause.*) I'm off to the bar. You want anything?

SOLLY. Yeah, coke please. You want the cash?

TAGGER. No, it's okay. If they sold pints here I might say 'yeah'.

SOLLY. I know you would.

TAGGER. Anyhow, I came into a bit of money, if you know what I mean?

SOLLY. I know what you mean. I thought it was you.

TAGGER *laughs. Then he goes off and leaves* SOLLY. *The music continues then* TEALE *comes across.*

TEALE. Didn't see you with the other helpers at six o'clock Daniels.

SOLLY. Don't remember ever saying I'd come.

TEALE. And I don't remember giving you permission to leave school early either. (*Pause.*) Well? Did your brother give you the letter?

SOLLY. Yeah.

TEALE. And I suppose you gave it to your mother.

SOLLY. I'll give it to her later.

TEALE. I bet. (*Pause.*) Well what's to become of you now? A first brush with the police? Or have you already had a brush with them?

SOLLY. I've never been in any sort of trouble.

TEALE. Well one way and another you've certainly been trying hard enough this term.

SOLLY. I haven't got anything to say to you.

TEALE. I did notice, but I could have helped you, you know. I can still help if you'll let me.

SOLLY. I don't need your help.

TEALE. Maybe not but if you ever do then take this card. It has got my home phone number on it. You see the headmaster is trying to get rid of me as well. Thinks I take too much interest in boys like you. And my wife, she thinks I'm a coward and I can't make up my mind whether you're coloured or black or West Indian *or* an ethnic minority *or* Black British, and she reckons that's where I go wrong, but I've always said to her that you're just a lad to me, Daniels, and maybe that's where I've been going wrong with you.

SOLLY. Maybe.

TEALE. But you see it's when I start to think of you as something different from just an ordinary lad that I'll pack it in. Does that make sense to you?

SOLLY. Maybe.

TEALE. Yeah, I know. My problem. (*Pause.*) Go on take it. Put it in your pocket before your mates come back.

SOLLY. Okay.

Pause.

TEALE. See you around then.

SOLLY. All right.

TEALE. Good, I hope so. And stay out of trouble.

TEALE *goes off and* TAGGER *comes back.*

TAGGER. Did he give you a going over?

SOLLY. Wanted to know where I was all day.

TAGGER. Don't matter now, does it, you've left.

SOLLY. That's what I told him.

TAGGER. Yeah, I'd have told him that too. (*Pause.*) Hang on, here's my bird.

TRACEY. All right, Solly.

SOLLY. Yeah, how you doing, Tracey?

TRACEY. Yeah, I'm all right but Jenny's not coming. She asked me to tell you.

SOLLY. What's the matter with her?

TRACEY. Parents. She'll ring you tomorrow. You're onto a winner there.

BATES. Nothing's the matter with her, Daniels but there will be if I catch her with you. I don't like coons round my sister, right?

TRACEY. Oh God. Push off, Bates.

BATES. Shut your face, slag.

SOLLY. You can't tell Jenny what to do.

BATES. I can tell who I like what to do, right, Daniels?

TAGGER. Leave it out, Batesy.

BATES. You shut your mouth, Tagger. It's nothing to do with you.

TRACEY. Yes it is, he's Solly's mate and my mate too.

BATES. I don't care if he's Solly's grandad. It's between Jungle Boy and me.

SOLLY. I've got nothing to say to you, it's between me and Jenny.

BATES. You what?

SOLLY. I said it's between me and her and you keep your nose out.

BATES. You're off your head, Daniels you wog.

He hits SOLLY *who immediately hits him back and there is a fracas.*

TAGGER. Leave off him, Batesy . . . Hit him Sol, hit him.

TRACEY. You bully, bully. Stop him, Tagger, stop him.

We hear a hell of a commotion but get the idea that SOLLY *is losing.* TEALE *comes tearing across.*

TEALE. Break it up right away. You want to try it on with me too do you, Bates?

BATES. No I don't, so get off me.

TEALE. You telling me what to do, Bates?

BATES. No.

TEALE. No what?

BATES. No, sir.

TEALE. Right, stand there. You all right Daniels?

SOLLY. Yes, sir.

TEALE. Now who started this?

TRACEY. It was Bates sir. He's just a bully. A big stupid bully.

TAGGER. Yeah it was. Solly didn't do nothing.

TEALE. I think you better leave Bates and I don't want to see your stupid face around here again, understand?

BATES. You won't have to cos I won't be round here again. Come on Johnson, let's go.

TRACEY. Bloody animals.

TEALE. Are you sure you're all right Daniels, that's a nasty bruise you've got there.

SOLLY. I'm all right.

TEALE. Maybe you should go home and get it dressed.

TAGGER. I'll go home with him, sir.

TRACEY. And me.

SOLLY. No, it's okay I'll go by myself.

TEALE. Are you sure?

SOLLY. I'll be okay.

TAGGER. I'll call by tomorrow see how you are, Sol.

SOLLY. Okay then.

TRACEY. See you, Sol.

SOLLY. Yeah, bye.

SOLLY *goes.*

TEALE. All right, let's get back to the disco.

TRACEY. I hate that Bates you know. I wish someone would kill him.

TAGGER. Yeah me too, but I don't know who. Clint Eastwood maybe.

In the kitchen.

CYNTHIA (*bathing his wound*). So which boy hit you in the face?

SOLLY. It doesn't matter, Mum. Its finished with.

CHRIS. I bet I know who it was.

CYNTHIA. Who?

CHRIS. I'm not sure.

SOLLY. Good.

CYNTHIA. There, does that hurt?

SOLLY. No.

CYNTHIA. Well sleep with your head the other way on the pillow tonight and you'll be fine.

CHRIS. Have you told him yet, Mum?

CYNTHIA. No.

SOLLY. Told me what?

CYNTHIA. We're going away together for a week as from tomorrow.

SOLLY. Going away? Where?

CYNTHIA. I don't know. The country, the seaside. Wherever you want to go.

CHRIS. Great, eh?

CYNTHIA. We all need a rest, and we need to talk, don't we Solomon?

SOLLY. Yeah, we need to talk.

CHRIS. About what?

SOLLY. About everything.

CYNTHIA. Everything, Chris. You're big lads now. You've grown up practically before I've had time to blink. We need to spend some time together.

CHRIS. Well what we gonna do? What we gonna talk about?

SOLLY. Dad.

CHRIS. Really? And what else?

SOLLY. There ain't anything else is there?

CHRIS. Yeah there is.

SOLLY. Like what?

CHRIS. I don't know, do I?

CYNTHIA. Right, that's enough of that. I think you ought to go to bed now.

CHRIS. But Mum . . .

CYNTHIA. No argument. We've got to be up early in the morning, all right?

CHRIS. All right.

CYNTHIA. I'll wake you both up.

SOLLY. Goodnight.

CYNTHIA. Goodnight. Both of you, sleep well.

In the boys' bedroom.

CHRIS. Are you still gonna go out with Jenny Bates now that you've left, Solly?

SOLLY. Yeah. Why?

CHRIS. I just wondered that's all. (*Pause.*) You're not saying much.

SOLLY. I'm tired.

Cut to CYNTHIA *sitting alone.*

CYNTHIA. You see, Roy, you were right. It's not for us. It was never for us. But that's what you never fought for. Nobody left for just themselves. Nobody stayed for just themselves. We came to fight for them.

In the boys' bedroom.

CHRIS. Do you wanna play soccer tomorrow?

SOLLY. I'll think about it. (*Pause.*) We can't.

CHRIS. Why not?

SOLLY. Because we're going away, aren't we?

CHRIS. We can play when we get there.

SOLLY. I suppose so. (*Pause.*) Yeah, I suppose we can.

In the kitchen.

CYNTHIA. And eventually the boys will find you in themselves, and in each other, and if they want to find you they can and I won't stop them, but I don't regret anything, Roy. I regret nothing. They'll never cut cane, or spend their lives herding scrawny goat, do you understand?

In the boys' bedroom.

SOLLY. I want to sleep.

CHRIS. Is your face still hurting?

SOLLY. No.

CHRIS. Good.

SOLLY. Yeah, I'll see you in the morning, Chris. In the morning, man.

He is falling asleep.

In the kitchen.

CYNTHIA. And as you always used to say, Roy, you get nothing for nothing. But when I look at our two boys, I know the price I paid was cheap. They've got a life now, Roy. We don't matter anymore. At least coming to England has given them a chance.

SWIMMER

by Christopher Russell

Christopher Russell was born in 1947 and grew up on the Isle of Wight. On leaving school he joined the civil service but left in 1973 to do shift work as a postman and write in his spare time. His first radio play, *Harvey's Festival*, was broadcast in 1975, and since becoming a full-time writer in 1980 he has written widely for both radio and television. He lives in South London with his wife and three young children.

Swimmer was first broadcast on BBC Radio 3 on 1 April 1984. The cast was as follows:

NEIL	Julian Firth
MICHELLE	Tillie Vosburgh
KEN	John Rowe
MOTHER	Jane Wenham
FATHER	James Bryce
JACKO	Alex Jennings
1ST BOY	Michael Jenner
2ND BOY	Ian Hoare
OFFICIAL	John Rowe

Director: Richard Wortley

Running time, as broadcast: 51 minutes 4 seconds.

A living-room. Air bubbles up through the water of a tropical fish tank.

NEIL (*very close, voice over, his face close to the tank*). Neon tetra . . . Barb . . . Dwarf Gourami . . . Cardinal . . . Moving so efficiently . . . Effortlessly . . . Gliding . . . Darting . . . Like flying only better. More graceful. The air's untidy, unpredictable. But underwater's not like that . . . they have complete control. Even gravity doesn't bother them . . .

A loud splash. We are in an echoing indoor swimming pool.

KEN (*walking briskly along edge of swimming pool, pushing one person after another into the water*). In . . . In . . . In . . . In . . . In . . .

There are five more splashes in quick succession as five more people hit the water. NEIL *is the last to go. We go with him. The water closes and boils over his head. He comes up, gasping for air.*

KEN (*a little away, standing at the poolside, authoritative*). Now, back to the rail. Come on, we don't want anyone drowning in their first lesson. You all right, Crosby?

NEIL (*in the water, gasps*). I think so . . . (*Very close.*) Cold . . . it feels cold. Not like the therapy pool used to be. . . .

KEN. Okay, we've proved the first law of learning to swim – you don't melt when you get wet. So we're not afraid anymore, are we?

The voice of MOTHER, FATHER *and* KEN *fade in and out over the swimming pool.*

KEN (*voice over*). Well, I think it sounds like a great idea, Mrs Crosby. It'll be good for the lad's confidence. Particularly as he's shown an interest –

MOTHER (*voice over*). Good for his confidence? When it means undressing in front of normal people?

KEN. Uh, normal people?

MOTHER. Normal people have two normal legs. . . .

NEIL (*very close*). Looking down through the water you'd hardly know anything was wrong. . . . the distortion's distorted. Funny how something as clean and clear as water can distort . . . change things. . . .

MOTHER. I've never tried to pretend Neil's not different and I don't intend to start now.

KEN. A disability's nothing to be ashamed of, Mrs Crosby. Not nowadays.

MOTHER. It's not something to flaunt either.

KEN. But you say he's sixteen. He's a young man. You can't shut him away for ever just because he was born with a damaged leg.

NEIL (*very close*). My right foot won't stay on the bottom. It just floats up . . . like a piece of cork. . . .

FATHER (*voice over*). We don't want to shut Neil away . . . We're not ashamed of him, we're proud. He's done well at his lessons, and he's got hobbies. . . .

KEN. Uh, yeh, tropical fish, you say?

FATHER. They've been a great success. Ever since he was ten. He watches them for hours.

KEN. But there's more to life than watching, Mr Crosby.

NEIL (*very close*). If I push my knee down with my hand, the foot goes down to the bottom again. But I can't really tell when it gets there. It has no feeling.

MOTHER. We are his parents. We do know his needs. And his limitations. . . .

FATHER. We care. We want what's best for Neil, that's all.

KEN *blows a short blast on a whistle at the swimming pool.*

KEN (*at the swimming pool*). Right, heads under the water, open your eyes, and look at your feet. . . . Eyes down!

NEIL *submerges. We go with him: The air pressure roars briefly in his ears. When* NEIL *speaks he does so with slight distortion and slight echo.*

NEIL (*very close, under the water*). Clean and clear . . . And down here, under the surface, everything outside your head so quiet . . .

Back in the swimming pool.

KEN (*at the swimming pool*). Okay, heads up . . .

FATHER. We used to take him to water therapy when he was little, of course. He used to like splashing about.

KEN (*voice over*). Why did you stop?

Pause.

MOTHER. It wasn't doing any good.

KEN (*at the swimming pool*). Crosby!

KEN (*voice over*). But surely if he enjoyed it . . .?

MOTHER. It was in everybody's interests to stop.

KEN (*at the swimming pool, alarmed*). Crosby!

He blows the whistle hard. NEIL *breaks the surface a little away and gasps.*

What the hell d'you think you're playing at, Crosby?

NEIL (*a little away, in the water*). Just getting used to the water.

KEN. You're not deep sea diving, laddie – five seconds is long enough . . .

NEIL. Yeh, sorry.

KEN (*voice over*). Look, why not bring him along and see how it works out, Mrs Crosby. I mean, think of the satisfaction you'll *all* feel if he actually learns to swim.

The living-room. We are close to the fish tank.

FATHER. So, uh, how did it go, Neil?

NEIL (*facing the tank, absorbed*). Uh?

FATHER. Your swimming lesson.

NEIL. I enjoyed it. I felt different in the water.

MOTHER (*a little away*). His hair's still wet. I told him when I collected him – if we can't trust him to dry his hair properly he won't go again.

FATHER. Your mother's right, Neil. Wet hair leads to pneumonia.

NEIL. Did you get more worms, Dad?

FATHER. Sorry?

NEIL. You were going to the aqua shop. These new Gouramis are feeding now. . . . (*Closer, quieter.*) See how they hang there, browsing. . . . just the merest fin movement keeping them in position . . . (*He laughs and turns to* FATHER *and* MOTHER.) D'you think I'll ever swim like that?

At the swimming pool. Loud splashes as people jump in.

KEN (*standing at the poolside, addressing the class*). It's quite easy for the human body to float. There's no mystery about it. It's all down to specific gravity, which, translated for the ignorant, means the density of an object compared with the density of water.

The living-room. The fish tank bubbles. KEN*'s voice fades in and out.*

FATHER. The instructor seems very competent. And the whole thing's well supervised. I'm sure if there was any . . . trouble, they'd, well, they'd be able to cope.

MOTHER (*sharply*). I don't want them to have to cope. That's our job, coping. It's nothing to do with anyone else.

KEN (*voice over*). Water has a specific gravity of 1. Objects with an S.G. of less than 1 will float. Those with an S.G. of more than 1 will sink.

FATHER. Well, we can't stop him now. It wouldn't be right. His mind's set on it.

MOTHER. Because of you and your wonderful aquarium!

FATHER. We don't know that. We don't know. . . .

KEN (*voice over*). By a stroke of good luck the average human body with an average amount of air inside it has a specific gravity of 0.98, which means it will float. Just . . .

FATHER. And anyway, if it's supervised and one of us is always there to meet him afterwards, what harm can it do?

At the swimming pool.

KEN (*a little way away, at the poolside*). Crosby?

NEIL (*in the water*). Yeh?

KEN. We're gonna try floating. You all right or d'you want me to come in and help?

NEIL. I'll manage. (*Very close.*) I'll manage.

KEN. Okay, let's all float then, shall we? First, relax. Hold your arms out in front of you, palms of hands downwards. Keep your legs straight. Now, lean forward, everybody . . . go on . . . forward until your face is in the water . . . Do it properly and you'll find you're leaning on the water, supported by the buoyancy. Good. . . . Right, heads up again. . . . Now, from this position we can also glide . . . Stand up straight and raise your hands above your head. Take a normal breath and hold it. Bend your knees until your head's under the water, then lean forward and push off with your feet against the bottom of the pool. Okay? Try it. Let's glide. . . .

NEIL (*very close, intense*). Yes. . . . (*He grunts as he plunges forward.*) Yes . . .!

The water closes and boils over his head. FATHER*'s voice fades in.*

FATHER. It's only therapy, that's all.

The swimming pool. The lesson is over. Only NEIL *and* KEN *remain near the pool.*

KEN (*a little away*). Crosby? (*He pauses then approaches.*) Oi, Crosby. Lesson's over, laddie. Crosby?

NEIL (*sitting at the poolside, roused from reverie*). What?

KEN. Lesson's over.

NEIL. Yeh, I know.

KEN. What you sitting there for then? Can't you get up?

NEIL. I was just looking at the water.

KEN. What's wrong with it?

NEIL. Nothing. (*He pauses.*) D'you know something? When we did that gliding just now, it was the first time in my life I'd ever moved, y'know from A to B, without being aware of this leg. . . .

KEN. Oh. (*He pauses.*) Well, that's good then.

NEIL (*laughs*). Good? Here on dry land it's like a lead weight – like a ball and chain. I have to drag it around with me everywhere. What's the point? In the water it seems to just . . . melt away – d'you see what I mean?

KEN. Yeh. A lot of disabled people find movement easier –

NEIL (*intense*). I don't mean that. I mean it melts away. It doesn't exist anymore. (*He pauses.*) How long before I can swim?

KEN. Not long. You're built for it from the waist up. Strong arms and shoulders –

NEIL. How long?

KEN. Four weeks.

NEIL. What if I had lessons every day?

KEN. Every day?

NEIL. Yes.

The living-room. The fish tank bubbles.

MOTHER (*a little away*). No.

NEIL (*very close. Voice over. His face close to the tank*). Some kinds of fish prefer to swim at a particular level. . . .

MOTHER. I said no.

NEIL. Upper water . . . mid water . . . lower water . . . Some, like the swordtail, go anywhere. . . .

MOTHER. D'you hear me, Neil?

NEIL (*to* MOTHER, *but facing tank*). They change the water regularly, Mum. It's a very healthy environment. . . .

MOTHER. One lesson a week is enough. More than enough.

FATHER. You mother's right, Neil. You don't want to tire yourself out.

NEIL. Swimming doesn't tire me.

FATHER. It wouldn't leave time for other things.

NEIL. What other things?

MOTHER (*firmly*). It's not convenient.

NEIL. Who for?

FATHER. We do have to come and collect you, Neil.

NEIL (*turns to face them*). Why?

Pause.

FATHER. To make sure you're all right. You're our responsiblity.

Pause.

NEIL (*facing the tank again*). One of the swordtails looks pregnant, Dad. Is the breeding tank ready?

The swimming pool. NEIL *is thrashing clumsily through the water, swimming front crawl. He gulps in air rhythmically every time his head breaks the surface.*

KEN (*a little away. Standing at the poolside shouting encouragement*). That's it, Neil, keep going. Keep going . . .!

NEIL (*very close. He speaks intensely, in between gulps of air*). In the crawl stroke . . . the legs act mainly . . . as stabilisers . . . and assist buoyancy . . . the main drive . . . comes from the arms . . . the arms . . . the arms . . . (*He gives a final grunt of exertion and grabs the rail at the edge of the pool, his swim completed. He breathes heavily.*) How did I do?

KEN. Congratulations. You just swam.

The living-room. The fish tank bubbles.

FATHER. That's great, Neil, really great. Isn't it, Jean? In less than a week, too.

MOTHER (*a little away*). Very single-minded.

NEIL. Ken says I'm a born swimmer.

FATHER. Ken?

NEIL. The instructor. Another few days and I'll be doing a length. I'll be safe in the water. (*He pauses.*) Unsupervised.

The swimming pool. Heavy splash as NEIL *jumps in and submerges. We go with him. The air pressure roars briefly in his ears. When* NEIL *speaks he does so with slight distortion and slight echo. There is no other sound except for occasional bubbles.* MOTHER *and* FATHER*'s voices fade in and out.*

NEIL (*very close*). Down, down, down. . . .

MOTHER. Well?

FATHER. It'll be all right.

MOTHER. Will it?

NEIL (*very close*). Upper water . . . mid water . . . lower water . . .

FATHER. They have people watching all the time. Not just during the lessons – all the time . . . he's got this far without any trouble, hasn't he? Besides, he's sixteen now.

MOTHER. Does that make it better?

NEIL (*very close*). There's a shaft of sunlight so thick you feel you could lean against it . . . it strikes down through the water and makes a golden square on the bottom of the pool. As I swim through it I feel the warmth of the sun passing along my body, strong and healing. . . . I feel I just want to stay here in this golden square, basking in the warm silence. . . .

Silence except for the few bubbles then NEIL *breaks the surface a little away.*

KEN (*at the poolside*). Christ, Neil, I wish you wouldn't do that.

NEIL (*hoisting himself out of the water*). What's the matter?

KEN. You were down there over a minute.

NEIL (*sitting at the poolside*). I like being down there. (*He takes a deep breath.*) It makes me feel good.

KEN. Well be a bit careful, that's all –

NEIL. When can I join the Sharks, Ken?

KEN (*surprised*). What?

NEIL. The Sharks. When can I join?

KEN. Who said anything about –

NEIL. I can swim five lengths now.

KEN. Yeh, you can swim five lengths –

NEIL. That's the minimum for joining, so when can I join?

KEN (*laughs*). Look, Neil. . . .

NEIL. What's the matter?

KEN. Nothing's the matter. It's just that the Sharks are a bit special, right?

NEIL. And I'm just a gimp.

Underwater acoustic. The voices of JACKO *and the other boys have slight distortion and slight echo. They seem to circle around. The voices of* KEN *and* NEIL *fade in and out.*

KEN. I never said that.

JACKO. Who . . .?

1ST BOY. Crosby . . .

NEIL. All right for special classes. Hidden away. . . .

JACKO. Neil Crosby?

KEN. It's not any old swimming club, Neil. It's not just for fun. It's serious stuff.

1ST BOY. Yeh, Neil Crosby.

KEN. It's training, it's competitions. . . .

JACKO. Leave it out. He's a gimp.

2ND BOY. He's a gimp.

KEN. You're still a novice. You couldn't cope . . .

JACKO. A bloody spastic.

NEIL. I could cope.

2ND BOY. An abortion.

KEN. Look, there are other clubs, Neil . . .

NEIL. I could cope!

JACKO. We don't want him.

KEN. The rest of the lads put a lot of time in. They've got a lot of pride. They're motivated to win. They're a crack team, Neil. They've won the regional gala for the last three years.

NEIL. And they don't like gimps. Wrong image.

JACKO. Who ever heard of a spastic shark?

JACKO *and the boys laugh. The laughter echoes in the underwater acoustic.*

KEN. They know they're the best, that's all.

NEIL. They're wrong! I'm the best!

A muffled explosion – NEIL *has plunged underwater. His voice is now distorted with slight echo.*

NEIL (*coming very close, intense*). I'm the best. . . .

The changing-room. Metal lockers, background chatter.

1ST BOY. Wear that thing in the water, do yuh?

NEIL (*seated*). What?

1ST BOY. The leg iron. D'you wear it in the water?

JACKO. Course he doesn't. Go rusty, wouldn't it?

The boys laugh.

JACKO. What's your best stroke?

2ND BOY. The front limp.

More laughter.

NEIL. I do front crawl.

1ST BOY. And that's only on dry land.

The boys laugh and go out barefoot. Short pause.

KEN. Welcome to the Sharks.

NEIL. I can cope.

NEIL *stands up, throws his leg iron into a locker and limps barefoot after the others, dragging his bad leg. Fade to the swimming pool acoustic. A sharp blast on the whistle.* NEIL *and* JACKO *plunge into the water and start to race. Jeers and shouts of encouragement from the other boys echo round the pool.* NEIL *ploughs through the water doing front crawl. He does not gulp any air.*

NEIL (*very close, swimming hard*). The arms work alternately. While one is under the water propelling you forward, the other is recovering out of the water. The hand enters the water ahead of and in line with the shoulder, fingers leading and wrist relaxed. The arm is slightly bent, with the elbow higher than the shoulder. You then force your hand forward and downward. As your hand gets a grip on the water, it starts to pull you forward. . . .

The jeering and cheering in the background becomes louder, more excited as the race reaches its climax.

(*Even more intense*). It pulls you forward. . . . The movement is continued in a backward direction and from a point below the shoulder the pull turns into a push. When the elbow breaks the surface at the end of the stroke, the hand must be carried forward out of the water on the recovery. The process is then repeated . . . repeated . . . repeated . . . repeated . . .!

As the jeering and cheering peaks, NEIL *explodes from the water, the race complete. He gulps in air for a second or two.*

1ST BOY (*a little away, at poolside. Laughs*). Nice one, Jacko. Beaten by a gimp.

The other boys laugh.

JACKO (*in the water, breathless*). What, one length? Don't call that a race, do yuh? Kiddies' stuff . . .

The boys jeer.

Anyway . . . (*He hauls himself out of the water.*) Supposed to be kind to cripples, ain't yuh?

Fade to the changing-room. Whistling, laughter, chatter. NEIL *approaches barefoot, dragging his bad leg. Background noise subsides.*

NEIL (*cool*). All right, where is it?

JACKO (*seated*). Do what?

NEIL. You know what I'm talking about.

JACKO (*laughs*). Yeh?

NEIL. Where's my leg iron?

JACKO. What? You haven't lost your leg iron, have you? Hear that, lads? Crosby's lost his leg iron.

The boys are full of mock concern.

NEIL. It was in my locker.

JACKO. Locked, was it? Your locker?

NEIL. No.

JACKO. Well, there you are then. Some thieving cripple's probably had it away. Still, you can always hop.

The boys are greatly amused.

NEIL (*shouting*). Where is it?

The laughter ceases.

JACKO (*stands up, then close*). Don't shout at me, Crosby. Don't ever shout at me . . . not unless you want the other leg smashed. Okay? (*He pauses.*) Oh, look. Well, I never – there's a leg iron on top of that cupboard over there.

The boys share JACKO*'s surprise.*

1ST BOY (*a little away*). I wonder if it's yours, Crosby. Hang on, let's see if it fits.

JACKO (*sharply*). No. (*quietly*). Let him get it. Handicapped people like to do things for themselves. Isn't that right, gimp? (*He laughs, then moving away.*) Come on . . .

BOYS (*following* JACKO *and singing*). Any old iron, any old iron, any, any, any old iron . . .

Their singing and laughter fade. We hear NEIL *crossing to the cupboard then grunting and banging against it, as he vainly attempts to jump and reach the leg iron.*

KEN (*a little away*). What the hell are you up to now, Neil?

NEIL. My leg iron's up there.

Short pause while KEN *approaches, reaches down the leg iron, and gives it to* NEIL.

KEN. Here.

NEIL. Thanks. (*He sits down heavily.*)

KEN. Jacko put it up there?

NEIL. How should I know? Maybe it just flew . . .

He starts replacing the leg iron.

KEN. I did try to warn you, Neil.

NEIL. Yeh.

A short pause.

KEN. D'you want a hand with that thing?

NEIL. I can manage, thanks.

KEN. Jacko's a toe-rag, but he's a good swimmer.

NEIL. I beat him.

KEN. I doubt you will next time. He doesn't like losing.

NEIL. Toe-rags never do.

KEN. Channelled aggression I think you call it. All right, they're a rough crowd, I know that, but I take the view they're better off in here thrashing up and down a swimming pool than out on the streets beating up coloureds.

NEIL. And gimps.

KEN. Don't go out of your way looking for trouble, mate, okay? Your life's difficult enough as it is.

NEIL. Difficult? (*He pauses.*) My life's only just beginning. (*He stands up.*) See you. (*He starts to limp away.*)

KEN. Neil.

NEIL (*stops a little away and turns*). Yeh?

KEN. You swam that length against Jacko without a breath. That's pretty unusual.

Short pause.

NEIL. Maybe I should've been born a fish, yeh?

A loud splash then underwater, as NEIL *plunges in and submerges.*

NEIL (*very close, with slight distortion and echo*). Down . . . down . . . down . . . clean . . . streamlined . . . free . . . This is my world now . . . Up above the Saturday crowd splash and wallow about, their legs and arms thrusting down towards me . . . weird . . . like disembodied limbs stuck through a ceiling . . . Occasionally a face . . . Jacko ploughs by on his thirty-third length. Implacable . . . his hands seem to grab and tear at the water on the forward stroke. He has no feel for water. It isn't his element. Just something else to be beaten . . . I twist and glide away towards the peace of the deep end . . . Here, in the six metres of the diving pit, sheltered from the sunlight, my world is opaque and cool . . . a world of shadows and possibilities. I rest like a pike, hove to in the dimness of the dense green weed at the bottom of the pond . . . waiting . . . If Jacko was a roach I could strike upwards and take him in one snap!

He bursts to the surface, colliding with JACKO *in the water. Back into the noisy swimming pool.*

JACKO (*yells in surprise, then struggling to right himself*). You bloody great berk!

NEIL (*in water, breathless*). Sorry, Jacko. Didn't see you.

JACKO. Do that again and I'll drown you – like you mother shoulda done. Go on, sod off down the shallow end with the other dimbos!

NEIL *submerges.*

NEIL (*very close, with slight distortion and echo*). The shallow end's not for me, Jacko. Only when there's no-one else there . . . when they've all gone home and the tide is out. then I'll come into the shallows, into the rock pools that catch the evening sun. Then I'll rest among the limpet-covered rocks, smelling the kelp, watching the sea anemones gently swaying, listening to the music of the sea . . . you'll never hear that, Jacko, because the water's not yours. You have no place here. The mermaids sing for me . . .!

Slowly fade up strange but gentle underwater music. It has about it something of the melancholy call of whales mingled with the beauty of a celestial choir. The music peaks as NEIL *bursts to the surface and into the noisy swimming pool. The underwater music instantly changes to loud pop music on a transistor a little away.*

MICHELLE (*seated at the poolside*). Here, watch who you're splashing! (*She pauses then laughs.*) What you staring at? (*Pause.*) What's up, d'you want me to throw you a fish or something? (*She laughs.*)

NEIL *submerges. As he does so the laughter echoes, becomes lighter and crossfades into the underwater music. It gradually fades out. In the empty changing-room.*

KEN (*a little away*). Still here then, Neil? (*He approaches.*) First in, last out, as usual.

NEIL (*seated, putting on shoes*). I suppose Dad's outside, fretting.

KEN. No, he's not. He's gone.

A short pause.

NEIL (*laughs*). He's what?

KEN. He's gone home. I told him I'd drop you off. It's on my way.

NEIL (*surprised*). Oh.

KEN. That's all right with you, is it?

NEIL. Yeh. Yeh, it's fine with me. I just –

KEN. I thought it might make you feel a bit easier about things – not having your mum and dad always hovering about waiting to take you home. It can't help.

NEIL. And he agreed?

KEN. Yeh, with a bit of persuasion.

The living-room. The fish tank bubbles a little away.

MOTHER. You're a fool!

FATHER. But look . . . we can trust Ken.

MOTHER. And Neil's out of our control that much longer –

FATHER. For God's sake, Jean . . .

MOTHER. He practically lives at that swimming pool as it is.

FATHER. A journey home, ten minutes in a car. Is that so dangerous?

In KEN*'s moving car.* KEN *is driving,* NEIL *is sitting next to him.*

KEN. I've chatted to your dad before. He seems a nice guy. Just a bit . . . over-protective.

NEIL. They don't like me out of their sight. They like to know what I'm doing.

KEN. Well, understandable, I suppose. Only child. And your leg –

NEIL. They'd like to know what I'm thinking.

The underwater music slowly fades up and continues to build under the ensuing:

NEIL. There was a girl . . . at the pool this evening . . .

KEN (*laughs*). Oh yeh? Interested in girls, are you? Do your mum and dad know?

NEIL (*absorbed*). She had a green swimsuit. She was sitting at the side of the pool . . . She had the most beautiful hair, like a mermaid . . .

KEN. Yeh, just like a mermaid – she spends half her life combing it. Her name's Michelle.

The music fades quickly.

NEIL (*surprised*). Do you know her?

KEN. Ought to. (*He laughs.*) She's my daughter.

The car slows down.

Fourth house on the left your dad said . . .

The car stops. The handbrake is applied.

KEN. Neil?

NEIL (*startled*). Uh?

KEN. This it?

NEIL. Oh, yeh.

KEN. Shall I help you out?

NEIL. I can manage, thanks.

The car door opens.

KEN. Right. See you tomorrow, I suppose?

NEIL. Yeh. (*He starts to clamber out of the car.*)

KEN. Oh, and Neil.

NEIL. Yeh?

KEN. If you fancy Michelle, watch out for the competition.

Slowly fade up the underwater music. Then it fades to become the background to NEIL *reading. Towards the end of the speech the music crossfades to the living room with the fish tank bubbling.*

NEIL (*voice over. Close. Quiet. Almost reverent*). Her hair was as a wet fleece of gold, and each separate hair as a thread of fine gold in a cup of glass. Her body was as white ivory, and her tail was of silver and pearl. Silver and pearl was her tail, and the green weeds of the sea coiled round it; and like sea-shells were her ears, and her lips like sea-coral. The cold waves dashed over her cold breasts, and the salt glistened upon her eyelids. . . .

MOTHER (*a little away*). What are you reading, Neil?

NEIL (*seated*). A book.

MOTHER (*restrained*). What book?

NEIL. It's a story by Oscar Wilde. About a mermaid . . . (*Half aloud, half to himself.*) The cold waves dashed over her cold breasts, and the salt glistened upon her eyelids . . .

MICHELLE (*voice over with slight distortion and echo*). Here, watch who you're splashing. . . .

MICHELLE *laughs. The laughter echoes, becomes lighter and crossfades into the underwater music. Fade up the music. It peaks as* NEIL *bursts to the surface. There is pop music on a transistor.*

NEIL (*a little away*). Hello.

MICHELLE (*seated at the poolside*). Oh, you can speak then.

NEIL. Your name Michelle?

MICHELLE. Yeh, why?

NEIL. Can you swim?

1ST BOY (*a little away, in the water*). She can swim better than you can walk, gimp.

The other boys laugh a little away in water.

MICHELLE. What's so funny?

1ST BOY. Haven't you seen his leg?

2ND BOY. It's enough to make you throw up.

NEIL *submerges. We go with him. The water closes and boils over his head. Underwater music fades up.*

1ST BOY (*voice over*). He's a spastic, love.

MICHELLE (*voice over*). Oh. (*She pauses.*) He's got nice shoulders. . . .

In the empty changing room. NEIL *approaches with shoes on. He stops abruptly as* JACKO *steps out in front of him.*

JACKO. Hello gimp. I've been waiting for you.

NEIL. Oh yeh?

JACKO. I hear you've been bothering people.

NEIL. Eh?

JACKO. Deaf as well as crippled, are you? I said you've been bothering people.

NEIL. What people?

JACKO. Michelle Prescott.

NEIL. I haven't been bothering her –

JACKO. You calling me a liar? (*He pauses.*) Just keep away. All right? Caliper brains. (*He laughs.*)

NEIL *limps away. His footsteps echo.*

NEIL (*very close, as he walks*). The red-tailed black shark isn't a true shark at all. . . . Though boisterous in defence of its territory, it likes plenty of rockwork and roots among which to hide. . . . (*He giggles.*)

The giggle echoes and crossfades to underwater with underwater music. NEIL *bursts to the surface into the swimming pool.*

NEIL. Hello, Michelle.

MICHELLE (*a little away, at the poolside*). Oh, hello.

NEIL. No radio today?

MICHELLE. Ruined it, haven't you? Got it wet.

NEIL. Sorry. Fancy a swim then?

MICHELLE. No thanks, I've already been in.

NEIL. You're allowed in twice. (*Pause.*) What's the matter – scared of Jacko?

There is a short pause then a loud splash as MICHELLE *jumps in.*

MICHELLE (*in the water, shudders*). It's cold.

NEIL. No it's not. Not to you . . . (*Very close, voice over.*) Her eyes are a deep mauve colour. I knew they would be. All mermaids have mauve eyes. . . . (*Aloud.*) Mermaids don't feel the cold.

MICHELLE (*laughs*). Mermaids?

NEIL. Have a race?

MICHELLE. If you like, but I'm not very good. I can only swim a couple of lengths.

NEIL (*very close, voice over*). Below the waves you could swim all day . . . Faster than the tunny, further than the salmon, then rest and sing upon the surf . . . (*Aloud.*) Come on then, I'll give you a five second start. Ready?

MICHELLE (*laughs*). Hang about.

NEIL. Go!

MICHELLE *plunges off and starts swimming.*

NEIL (*very close, voice over*). She moves so beautifully . . . her white limbs caress the water and it in turn caresses her . . . the golden hair is dark now, streaming behind her in the foam. If only I could touch that hair, curl it around my fingers. . . .

MICHELLE (*a little away*). Are you swimming or not?

NEIL (*aloud*). Yes. I'm swimming.

He submerges.

(*Very close, with slight distortion and echo.*) I'm swimming for ever . . . in the land of mermaids. . . .

The voices of KEN *and* MICHELLE *fade in and out as the underwater music begins and slowly builds in the background.*

KEN (*voice over*). Neil Crosby reckons you're a mermaid.

MICHELLE (*voice over, laughs*). Yeh, he told me. I've been called worse.

KEN. He meant it as a compliment.

MICHELLE. I know. (*Pauses.*) I know. He's quite nice really. . . .

NEIL. Swimming down deep where everything is possible because nobody can touch you or hear you or see you. . . .

KEN. I don't mind you being friendly with him. With parents like his he needs friends. Just don't get over-sentimental, okay? He doesn't want pity.

NEIL. At 700 metres the sunlight no longer penetrates and nor do the eyes of the world . . .

The underwater music grows louder, gradually becoming distorted and nightmarish.

NEIL. Down . . . down . . . down . . . Deeper than the mackerel and the whiting . . . deeper than the clown fish and twinspot wrasse . . . deeper than the giant blue whale and the ghost-like manta ray . . .

MOTHER *and* FATHER*'s voices fade in and out.*

FATHER (*voice over*). But it's perfectly natural that he should take an interest.

MOTHER (*voice over*). Is it?

FATHER. Of course. He's a different person now. We should stop worrying once and for all. About everything. . . .

NEIL (*becoming intense*). Down . . . down . . . into the darkness where the viper fish and the great swallowers live undisturbed . . . where the gulpers and bristle-mouths and rat tails will brush against us and call us friend. . . .

The music fades up loud then we fade into the living-room. The fish tank bubbles.

MOTHER (*a little away*). About this girl, Neil.

NEIL (*facing the fish tank*). What girl?

MOTHER. The girl at the swimming pool.

FATHER (*a little away*). Michelle, Neil.

NEIL (*still facing the fish tank*). What about her?

FATHER (*approaching, tentative*). We were wondering why you hadn't mentioned her, that's all. (*He laughs.*) I felt a bit of a fool when Ken told me.

MOTHER. You mustn't be afraid to tell us things, Neil.

FATHER. No, because we're pleased.

NEIL (*very close, voice over*). The fire-mouth cichlids hatch their eggs in their mouths to protect them from predators. . . .

FATHER. Very pleased. It's time you had some friends of your own age.

NEIL (*very close, voice over*). For a while afterwards the young will return to the adult's mouth when danger threatens. . . .

FATHER. You must invite her home for tea.

NEIL (*turns*). What for?

FATHER. Well, we'd like to meet her. And I'm sure she'd be interested in the aquarium. . . .

Crossfade underwater. The underwater music is just audible in the background. The boys' voices have slight echo and distortion. They seem to approach close and veer away like fish.

1ST BOY. She fancies him, Jacko.

2ND BOY. She's going home to meet Mum and Dad, Jacko.

1ST BOY. Gonna have a look at his aquarium.

They both laugh.

2ND BOY. Second best to a gimp, Jacko.

1ST BOY. What you gonna do . . .?

2ND BOY. He can't be dead from the waist down, Jacko . . .

1ST BOY (*very close*). She's a mermaid. . . . But that's no problem . . .

2ND BOY. That's no problem. . . .

They both laugh and the laughter echoes. Then into the living-room. with the fish tank.

KEN (*close, facing tank*). Isn't it a bit cruel?

FATHER (*laughs*). Cruel, why?

KEN. Well, keeping all these fish in a glass tank. Bit like a cage really, isn't it? Doesn't seem much of a life.

NEIL (*sharply*). How would you know?

MOTHER (*a little away*). Neil.

KEN. It's all right Mrs Crosby. (*He laughs.*) Neil's the expert.

NEIL. Fish only move far enough to get what they need to survive. . . .

KEN. Oh well, that's –

NEIL (*coming close, facing the tank, his voice becomes flatter, quieter*). In a well-balanced aquarium they have light and shade, cover and open water, food at the right intervals. And the opportunity to reproduce. . . .

KEN (*laughs*). Sounds all right. When do I join?

NEIL (*very close, quiet*). And they're safe from predators. . . .

1ST BOY. }
2ND BOY. } (*voice over, with slight distortion and echo*). What you gonna do, Jacko. . .?

MICHELLE (*close, facing the tank*). Well, I think they're all beautiful. . . .

FATHER (*approaching*). Yes, I thought you'd like them, Michelle. These in here are swordtails – they're about to give birth as a matter of fact. Could be anything from seventy-five to a hundred live young.

MICHELLE (*laughs*). Good job they don't need nappies. (*Turning away*.) What's in that tank over there?

FATHER (*moving a little away*). Ah, that's an interesting one. It's called an archer fish. In the wild it obtains its food by squirting a jet of water at insects on overhanging plants, you see. . . .

NEIL (*very close, voice over*). If only you could see, Michelle. . . .

FATHER. The insects fall into the water and the archer fish gobbles them up. That's why you have to have these plants growing above the surface of the tank. . . .

NEIL (*very close, voice over, longing*). If only you could look up from my world into this. Look up from below the mirror horizon of water and see everything above it fringed with all the colours of the spectrum . . . everything shines, Michelle . . . everything shines seven times over . . . red, orange, yellow, green, blue, indigo, and violet. The colours glow and run into one another like a glorious melting rainbow . . . the archer fish sees all that . . . it stares up with what you think are vacant eyes, but it sees all that . . . when will you see it too . . .?

There is a loud splash as NEIL *dives into the swimming-pool and submerges.*

NEIL (*very close with slight distortion and echo, intense*). When? (*Further away and plaintive*.) When . . .?

The underwater music becomes audible in the background, the voices of KEN *and* MICHELLE *fade in and out.*

MICHELLE (*voice over, awed*). He stays under so long. . . . Don't you think he's fantastic . . .?

KEN (*voice over*). Yeh, quite a swimmer. But he gives me the creeps.

MICHELLE. Why? Because of his leg?

KEN. No, not just because of his leg . . . oh, it's not his fault, I know. . . .

MICHELLE. I don't think he's creepy. His mum is though. She was watching me like a hawk.

KEN. Over-protective, that's all. Probably doesn't trust mermaids.

MICHELLE. Not like Neil . . . (*The words echo*.)

NEIL (*as if answering*). Michelle. . . . Michelle. . . .

The swimming pool.

KEN (*sighs*). You're a funny kid, you are – you could have your pick. But first you take up with a head case like Jacko and now it's a cripple with water on the brain.

MICHELLE. Maybe I just like being a mermaid.

KEN. Yeh, all right –

MICHELLE. You said he didn't want pity.

KEN. He doesn't want leading on either, the poor sod.

MICHELLE. How do you know what he wants?

NEIL (*a little away in the water*). Michelle? (*Pause*.) You coming in?

A short pause.

MICHELLE. I'll see you later, Dad.

A short pause then a loud splash as MICHELLE *plunges into the water. We go with her. She and* NEIL *laugh and splutter as they splash about.*

NEIL (*very close, voice over*). She smiles at me and takes my hand . . . we gambol like the sea children who play amid the surf, rolling and laughing, she clinging to my back as if I were a playful dolphin . . . her skin is wet and cold but her breath on my neck is warm . . . so warm . . . oh, Michelle . . . Michelle . . . it won't be long now, I promise you. . . .

MICHELLE *squeals with laughter as* NEIL *submerges. The water closes and boils above his head. The laughter echoes as we fade underwater then it crossfades into the underwater music. The music fades up loud. Then in the quiet changing room. The boys are gathered in a close expectant crowd.*

JACKO (*approaching*). You didn't listen to me, gimp.

NEIL (*seated*). Hello, Jacko. When are we going to have another race?

The boys titter.

JACKO. I told you to keep away from Michelle Prescott. (*Coming close.*) She's clean . . . she doesn't want anything to do with an abortion like you.

NEIL. You're never in the water when I am now, Jacko. What's up, got a verruca?

JACKO *grabs* NEIL *and bangs his head against a locker.*

1ST BOY (*alarmed*). Not here, Jacko, for Christ's sake!

JACKO (*kicking* NEIL). It's gotta be here . . . the bastard's never anywhere else without a bloody armed guard!

2ND BOY (*a little away*). Look out!

The fight stops. There is some quick uneasy shuffling of feet. KEN's *footsteps approach.*

KEN. Well . . . When two or more sharks are gathered together it's usually a sign of blood. . . . Everything all right?

A murmur of confirmation.

Where's Neil?

A short pause. The boys move aside.

KEN. Jesus, what happened to you?

NEIL. The floor's wet. I slipped over. (*Pause.*) I slipped.

KEN. Oh. Well, I hope you're okay for Saturday. You're in the team for the gala. In the freestyle. With Jacko. That should give you both something to chat about. All right?

KEN *slowly walks off. There is a short pause.*

NEIL (*stands up, close*). Think you can beat me in the water, Jacko? Eh? If you can, she's yours.

JACKO (*laughs*). What?

NEIL. She's yours. If she wants you.

JACKO. Sod off.

NEIL. Winner takes all. Come on, Jacko. . . . I say I'm the best. If not, then I'll sod off. But you've got to prove it . . . in the water. She likes me, Jacko. She doesn't mind the leg. It doesn't interfere with anything.

JACKO *grabs* NEIL *again. The other boys pull him off.*

2ND BOY. Leave it, Jacko! Leave it!

1ST BOY. You can take him over two lengths.

NEIL (*breathing hard*). Can you, Jacko? Can you take the gimp over two lengths? What if you can't? If I'm an abortion, what does that make you?

JACKO. I'll take you. . . .

NEIL *laughs.*

(*Shouting.*) I'll take you!

In the living-room. The fish tank bubbles.

FATHER. So you're in the regional gala, Neil.

NEIL. Yeh, the 100 metres freestyle.

FATHER. Ken says you're in the team purely on merit.

NEIL. Why else would I be in the team?

FATHER. No reason at all – it's just, well, who would've dreamt when you started lessons. It's only a couple of steps away from the National Championships, you know, Jean.

MOTHER (*a little away*). So you keep saying.

NEIL (*very close, voice over, facing tank*). The tunny can swim at 80 kilometres per hour, while its relative the swordfish has been known to reach 95 . . . the tunny has a streamlined body and a crescent-shaped tail . . . like a mermaid . . . it swims by beating its tail from side to side, hardly moving the front of its body at all . . . I, on the other hand, must rely on the pectoral fins . . . (*He turns to* MOTHER *and* FATHER.) Will you come and watch me, Mum?

MOTHER. Watch you, Neil?

NEIL. At the gala. There'll be hundreds of people there. Or would you be too ashamed?

FATHER (*uneasily*). Neil. . . .

NEIL. Hundreds of people. And just think, if I was to win my race I could get my photo in the local paper. Deformed leg and all. 'We always knew he had it in him,' says proud Mum.

MOTHER (*approaching*). Be quiet, Neil.

NEIL. We've just spent sixteen years trying not to let it out. . . .

MOTHER (*slapping* NEIL*'s face*). Shut up!

FATHER. Steady on, Jean, there's no need for that.

MOTHER (*quietly*). No need? You blame me for everything. (*Shouting.*) Everything!

Fade to the swimming pool. Fairly quiet. NEIL *and* MICHELLE *are reclining at the poolside.*

NEIL (*quiet*). I don't blame her for everything. . . . I don't blame her for anything at all. She pointed me in the right direction from a very early age.

MICHELLE (*considering*). I don't know whether I like your shoulders best, or your back. . . . (*She gently strokes his back.*) Jacko's got pimples all over his back, but yours is smooth and strong. . . .

NEIL. D'you know what she used to read to me as a kid, over and over again? *The Water Babies.*

MICHELLE. The what?

NEIL. *The Water Babies.* You know, Mrs Doasyouwouldbedoneby and all that.

MICHELLE (*laughs*). Mrs Who?

NEIL (*sitting up*). You must've heard of it.

MICHELLE (*laughs*). I haven't. What's it about?

Underwater music slowly fades up under NEIL*'s speech, and remains in the background.*

NEIL (*very close, voice over*). What's it about? To me it was about escape, freedom, living. . . . (*He laughs.*) I felt no guilt. That was Mother. She felt the guilt. It was medieval the way she drove home the morality of that story. Sin, repentance, self-improvement, as if by reading it often enough she could absolve us both from whatever sin had caused her son to be born with a deformed leg. (*He laughs.*) But there was no sin. Just a chance in a million. The doctor told her. The plain truth was she couldn't cope. (*Intense.*) I revolted her . . .

The music fades.

MICHELLE. What's it about, Neil? Neil?

NEIL (*roused from reverie*). It's a fairy story . . . about a grimy little chimney sweep called Tom who drowns and changes into a water baby . . . and a beautiful young girl called Ellie who does the same. . . .

MICHELLE. Oh, is that all?

NEIL (*vaguely*). That's all I can remember. . . .

A short pause.

MICHELLE. My Mum's dead.

NEIL. Yeh?

MICHELLE. She died when I was born.

NEIL. I think mine did too. Only she's still alive. . . . Shall we go for a swim?

MICHELLE. In a minute. (*She pauses.*) Have you had a girl friend before, Neil?

NEIL. Why, does it matter?

MICHELLE. No. Only you don't seem, well, you don't seem to know how to behave. When we're not swimming you, I don't know, you're, well, offish, cold, I don't know how to describe it. Only I do like you, Neil – I'm not just having you on. I don't care about your leg. But we can't spend all our lives swimming, can we?

NEIL. Why not?

MICHELLE (*laughs*). Why not? Well, because there's other things to –

NEIL *kisses her hard on the lips. At length she manages to push him away.*

MICHELLE (*breathless, slightly disconcerted*). What's that – making up for lost time?

NEIL. Isn't that what you meant?

MICHELLE. Maybe. No more here though.

NEIL. Why?

MICHELLE (*standing up*). It's not allowed.

NEIL. Michelle –

MICHELLE *laughs and runs away. She plunges into the water a little away.*

MICHELLE (*a little away, in water, laughs*). Come on in. You could do with a cold bath.

NEIL (*very close, voice over, excited*). She stretches out her arms as the mermaids do to all lost souls . . . for those who lie in the arms of the mermaids and sink with them beneath the waves are surely lost. . . . But who would stay safe on land or ship when he could sleep in such an embrace? (*Still voice over, crying out.*) Michelle!

MICHELLE (*laughs*). Well, come on then.

NEIL *plunges into the water. Underwater music slowly fades up. It becomes gradually louder during the scene.* MICHELLE *is in voice over.*

NEIL (*approaching, plaintive, slight distortion and echo*). Michelle . . . I need you, Michelle. . . .

MICHELLE (*voice over, laughs*). What now? You'll get Dad the sack.

NEIL. Tonight.

MICHELLE. Tonight? In the middle of the gala?

NEIL. After the gala.

MICHELLE *laughs.*

NEIL (*coming very close*). Don't laugh at me, Michelle, don't laugh at me.

MICHELLE. Neil, you're hurting my arm.

NEIL. Here. In the water. In the dark. When everyone else is gone.

MICHELLE (*pain and alarm*). Neil!

NEIL. Promise me, Michelle. It's the only thing I'll ever ask you . . . please . . . please . . . please . . .

MICHELLE (*sobs*). My arm. . . .

NEIL. Promise!

The music peaks, then we are in the swimming pool. MICHELLE *and* NEIL *are resting after their swim.*

MICHELLE (*reclining, sniffs, then quietly*). It might be nice . . . it's supposed to be good in the water.

NEIL (*seated on the ground, his voice is rather flat*). I'm sorry I hurt your arm.

MICHELLE (*laughs quietly*). Just us and the water and the moonlight. Like being in a tropical lagoon.

NEIL. I didn't mean to hurt you.

MICHELLE (*laughs*). They won't drain the pool, will they?

NEIL. No. Not on Saturdays.

MICHELLE. How will we get in though? Into the building.

NEIL. We won't have to. We'll be here already.

MICHELLE (*laughs*). What d'you mean, hide?

NEIL. There's plenty of places.

MICHELLE. But your parents won't go home without you.

NEIL. You tell them I'm coming home with you and your dad. When they've gone you find your dad and tell him you're coming home with us.

MICHELLE. Will that work? (*She pauses.*) Neil?

NEIL (*quiet but certain*). Of course it'll work. This is my day, Michelle. How can anything go wrong?

A short pause.

MICHELLE (*teasing*). You've got to beat Jacko first, don't forget.

The swimming gala. A crowd of a few hundred are present.

OFFICIAL (*a little away, into public address system*). In Lane 3, D. Stannard . . .

Ragged applause and whistles.

In Lane 4, M. Smith . . .

Ragged applause and whistles.

In Lane 5, N. Crosby . . .

Applause louder.

In Lane 6, J. Pender.

Loud raucous applause and whistles.

NEIL (*very close, voice over, at the poolside, waiting for the race to start*). Come on, for Christ's sake, let's start before I fall over. (*He pauses.*) I'll lose time on the dive. No thrust with this leg . . . Jacko's been practising his dive. He'll be two metres up before we start. Not that it matters.

OFFICIAL. On your marks . . . set . . .

The starting gun is fired. Six swimmers dive in and start swimming front crawl. The crowd cheers them on excitedly.

NEIL (*very close, voice over, ploughing through water*). Have your two metres, Jacko, the other ninety-eight are mine. (*He laughs.*) You have only those feeble human limbs of yours, thrashing wildly through the water like a drowning man. How can you compete with me, drawn along by a thousand sea horses with flying white manes, by the green-bearded Tritons, by the strength and will of the King himself who rules the world you'll never see . . .!

The excitement of the crowd rises in crescendo.

NEIL (*even more excited*). You're broken, Jacko, broken! (*He laughs wildly.*) Smashed like flotsam by the power of the sea and all that therein dwells . . .!

FATHER (*shouting in the crowd*). He's going to win it! Come on, Neil, come on, come on. . . . He's going to win it!

FATHER*'s voice is lost briefly as the cheering and shouting reaches its climax.*

(*Shrieking.*) He's won! He's won! Jean! Jean, he's won! (*He embraces* MOTHER *and laughs wildly.*)

The cheering slowly fades.

MOTHER (*voice over, very calm*). The first time it happened was when he was three. We took him on holiday to the seaside; he kept . . . he kept lying face down in the water. And every time we dragged him out there was a look on his face – indescribable – no . . . implacable . . . it was implacable. My husband refused to see it. He just used to laugh. 'That boy's got no fear', he would say, 'he'll be a champion swimmer one day, leg or no leg'.

In the background we hear the traditional victory music as the swimmers receive their medals.

FATHER (*a little away, excited*). He's getting his medal, Jean. Jean, stand up and see him get his medal.

MOTHER (*continuing in voice over*). We stopped going to the seaside. We stopped going anywhere there was water. That sounds ridiculous, doesn't it? It's very hard. Try it. It was me being hyper-sensitive about his leg, of course. . . .

As MOTHER *continues to speak in voice over, we slowly fade from the gala to a corridor at the deserted pool.*

Reading the *Water Babies* was Neil's idea. He found a copy in the library when he was seven and would read nothing else. He was like a drug addict. No matter how many times I took it away from him he always seemed to have a copy – I remember searching his room one day and finding ten copies hidden in different places. . . .

A door slowly opens a little way away in the corridor then quietly closes. NEIL *approaches, limping. His footsteps echo in the empty corridor.*

When he was ten we went on holiday to a cottage in Derbyshire. It was a beautiful spot, everything was going fine. I was almost relaxed. And then one very hot day Neil went missing. We searched and searched and at last . . . I found him. I was at the top of a hill, looking down across a meadow to a river – about 200 metres away – and there was Neil, sitting on the bank of the river staring into the water, with a little fair-haired girl from the local farm sitting beside him. . . .

NEIL (*calling softly*). Michelle . . .?

MOTHER. There was nothing I could do . . . suddenly he just grabbed her round the throat and pulled her with him into the water. I screamed and ran down the hill. (*She pauses.*) The little girl was swept away . . . Neil knocked out three of my teeth as I dragged him out. It wasn't right that Ellie should go without Tom, you see. . . .

We fade from the corridor to the deserted swimming pool. NEIL *approaches.*

NEIL (*calling quietly, his voice echoing*). Michelle . . .?

MOTHER. I was the only witness. I had a choice. (*She pauses.*) I chose not to tell the truth. Except to my husband, who chose not to believe me, but bought an aquarium to, as he put it, 'take Neil's mind off things'. . . .

The living-room. The fish tank bubbles.

FATHER (*facing the tank*). Neil'll be cross when he gets in . . . these ruddy swordtails have eaten their young.

The telephone starts ringing a little away. We fade back to the deserted swimming pool. The voices of JACKO *and the* BOYS *fade in and out in voice over. They are quiet, mocking and sinister with a slight echo, and seem to come from different parts of the pool.*

NEIL (*calling slightly impatiently*). Michelle . . .? Where are you, Michelle . . .?

JACKO (*voice over*). Where are you, Michelle . . .?

The boys titter.

FATHER (*speaking on the telephone*). There must be some mistake, Ken. She's not here . . . no, definitely not. We were told they were going home with you.

MICHELLE (*a little away, quiet*). I'm here, Neil. . . .

1ST BOY (*voice over*). I'm here, Neil. . . .

The boys titter.

NEIL (*relieved*). Didn't you hear me calling?

2ND BOY (*voice over*). Course we heard you.

The boys titter.

MICHELLE (*approaching, she sounds nervous*). I couldn't find my way. It's so dark – can't we put some lights on?

NEIL (*laughs*). What do we need lights for?

The boys titter.

NEIL (*moving away, barefoot*). Come on, let's swim. (*He laughs.*) Come on . . .

MICHELLE. All right – in a minute.

NEIL (*a little away*). What's the matter?

MICHELLE. Nothing's the matter. It's just . . . strange, being here at night. It's a bit creepy, that's all – there's no moon. I imagined there'd be a moon.

NEIL (*approaching*). Mermaids aren't frightened of the dark. They love the dark. They sing their sweetest songs in the dark. . . .

The boys titter.

You promised, Michelle. Don't fail me now. . . . (*Intense.*) You promised!

MICHELLE. I'm not undressed yet.

The boys titter.

(*Slightly nervous laugh.*) Go and warm the water up a bit while I . . .

JACKO (*voice over*). Come on, girl, get 'em down. . . .

The boys titter. NEIL *plunges into the water.*

NEIL (*very close with slight distortion and echo*). Cold . . . cold as the sea . . . cold and dark and clean and limitless . . . it only takes a second, Michelle. . . . Just a second to be rid of dirt and guilt and pain, to let ourselves be washed clean. Only trust me. . . .

He bursts to the surface a little away. Short pause.

MICHELLE (*in the water*). I'm ready. (*She pauses.*) I've always wondered how mermaids get it together. You'll have to show me, Neil. (*She laughs.*)

The laughter echoes, lightens and fades into the underwater music, which begins quietly but becomes gradually louder under the ensuing.

JACKO (*voice over, very close*). Yeh, show her, gimp . . . enjoy yourself. This is definitely your last stand. . . .

MICHELLE (*close, embracing* NEIL). Oh, Neil, hold me, I'm frightened.

NEIL (*close, urgent*). Michelle . . . Michelle. . . . (*Very close, voice over, intense.*) The nakedness of her body shines white above the black water. Her lips, her eyes, her ears are cold but her slender arching neck is warm beneath my fingers . . . she slips her arms around my waist and presses herself against me, oh so eager for the ultimate embrace. . . .

MICHELLE (*close, aroused*). Mmmm . . . that's the way, Neil . . . that's it . . . that's it . . . that's it . . .

NEIL (*very close, voice over, laughing with joy*). And as I squeeze her throat the golden hair falls at last around my face like a sweet, sweet shroud!

MICHELLE (*breathing fast*). Oh, Neil . . . Neil . . . Neil . . . (*Ecstacy changes suddenly to a strangled scream as* NEIL *squeezes her throat.*) Neil!!

The music becomes suddenly distorted and nightmarish. MICHELLE *chokes and gurgles as her mouth fills with water. She struggles and threshes about but* NEIL *is dragging her inexorably down with him under the surface. The water closes above them. Air bubbles rise rapidly. The music becomes quieter again and then gentler until by the end of* NEIL's *ensuing speech it is just as it was when he first heard it before meeting* MICHELLE.

NEIL (*very close, with slight distortion and echo. He laughs tenderly*). Why did you struggle, Michelle? Did you fear death? But this isn't death. I'm taking you back where you belong, that's all. . . . Down . . . down to the cliffs of coral and pavements of bright pearl . . . down to the emerald palace where the great King himself waits to welcome you home. . . . We'll be there soon, don't worry. . . . Just rest . . . rest, I won't let go of you. You're safe . . . rest and sleep until you're ready to swim forever. . . .

He moves gently away through the water, his voice echoing and fading.

Swim forever . . . swim forever. . . .

The music also fades out, leaving only a few bubbles rising, then these also stop. Pause, then we are in the deserted swimming pool.

JACKO. Been down there a long time, haven't they?

1ST BOY. Probably shagged out.

The boys laugh.

2ND BOY. Here they come now look – and they're still on the job.

The boys laugh, applaud and cat call. The welcome for the surfacing lovers peters out. Silence except for water quietly lapping.

JACKO (*close. Quiet. Shocked*). Christ . . . (*He pauses.*) Christ!

The water laps quietly. Fade out.

TEMPORARY SHELTER

by Rose Tremain

For Kay Patrick

Rose Tremain was born in 1943 and educated at the Francis Holland School, the Sorbonne and the University of East Anglia. Her first play for radio, *The Wisest Fool,* was broadcast in 1976 and *Temporary Shelter* is her tenth play for this medium. She also writes novels, television plays and short stories, and won the 1984 Dylan Thomas Short Story Award. She is a Fellow of the Royal Society of Literature and in 1983 was one of twenty young writers chosen as the Best of Young British Novelists. Her most recent novel, *The Swimming Pool Season,* was published by Hamish Hamilton in March 1985. Rose Tremain is married and lives in Norwich.

Temporary Shelter was first broadcast on Radio 4 on 5 March 1984. The cast was as follows:

LARRY	Roy Kinnear
MARJE	Fiona Walker
TRIST	Anthony Newlands
JEAN-LOUIS	Yves Aubert
ANNETTE	Grazyna Monvid

Director: Kay Patrick

Running time, as broadcast: 76 minutes.

Fade up TRIST.

TRIST. If you asked me to sum up, I would say that Larry and I were both travellers.

Pause.

We travelled from – and towards – different places and different understandings. We are very different men, and though we tried, I don't believe we ever really liked each other or ever could. But I'll never forget Larry, and though he may want to forget me, I don't think he ever will. Because we met at a point of change; a moment of self-revelation, you might almost say.

Pause.

We met in France, one June, on a municipal campsite to the west of Avignon. I arrived first and then I left again to wander about Provence on my own, going mainly from medieval church to medieval church, looking for 'direction' in alabaster Marys, ebony Christs. During that time, I spoke to no-one except shop assistants or café attendants. I was testing myself, to see if I could keep my own company and not die of tedium or heartbreak.

Pause.

Larry and Marje arrived while I was gone.

Pause. The sounds of early morning on the campsite are heard: dogs barking, cicadas beginning to buzz, movement and an occasional laugh or shout of the campers going to the wash houses, unzipping tents, making breakfast etc.

Marje told me that this was their first holiday for seven years. Larry kept up a lament for the ritzy hotels he couldn't afford. He didn't understand how best to live in a tent.

Hold campsite noises, dipped slightly.

MARJE. Aren't you going for your shower, Larry?

LARRY (*seeming not to concentrate*). What, Marje?

MARJE. I thought you were off for your shower.

LARRY. Yes, I am.

MARJE. The toilet paper's in the third from left blue wall pocket.

LARRY. Yes. Got it, Marje.

Pause.

MARJE. Off you go then, dear.

LARRY. Not the right moment, Marje.

MARJE. What?

LARRY. No hurry really, is there? It's not a very convenient moment.

MARJE. What d'you mean, it's not a 'convenient moment'?

LARRY. Nothing, dear. But I'll just hang on a jiffy.

MARJE. You know what you said yesterday: better to get to the showers before eight-thirty, otherwise you may have to queue.

LARRY (*in a tight whisper*). Look, Marje, I can't go past Jean-Louis' tent while he and Annette are so obviously . . . you know . . .

MARJE. Oh, good heavens, Larry! They're not going to *see* you. Now please hurry up, dear, and then I can start getting breakfast. And if you could call in at the shop on your way back and get a baguette.

LARRY (*still uneasy*). A what?

MARJE (*patient*). A baguette. That's what it's called, the loaf we like.

LARRY (*with disbelief*). A baguette?

MARJE. Yes. Now do go, Larry.

LARRY. Okay, Marje, okay. A bag-what?

MARJE. A *baguette*.

LARRY. I can't ask for that, Marje.

MARJE. Of course you can: 'une baguette, s'il vous plait'.

LARRY. How d'you know it's 'une' and not 'un'?

MARJE. I don't, dear. But I'm sure Madam Bidermann will understand. Larry, I'm trying to get up and you're in the way.

LARRY. Okay, Marje. I'm off. Here goes . . .

MARJE. It's not a high dive contest!

The campsite noises fade.

TRIST. It was of course typical – characteristic, you might say – of Larry to be embarrassed by the sexuality of his neighbours. He was the kind of man who has never been, nor wanted to be young.

Pause.

But they interested him, Jean-Louis and Annette. First of all, they were French, and Larry had never met any French people before except one, the proprietor of a restaurant in Bressingham St Mary, Norfolk. And secondly, Jean-Louis was a poet.

Pause.

Larry had never, *never* met a poet! And never may again. Amateur verse makers, yes, perhaps, but not poets. He told me that he had forgotten, until he ran into Jean-Louis, that poets existed.

Fade up the campsite noises. Dogs barking are now very noticeable.

MARJE (*sighs*). Oh dear, we did come for peace, Jean-Louis, didn't you?

JEAN-LOUIS (*light*). Oh yes.

MARJE. And we didn't expect dogs. I never gave them a thought. Not dogs.

JEAN-LOUIS. I don't think I really hear them.

MARJE. Well, I'm surprised. Perhaps it's to do with age. Bark, bark, bark! And I did want a bit of peace, for Larry's sake. He works so hard when we're in England.

JEAN-LOUIS. Does he?

MARJE. He works terribly hard. (*Pause. In a confidential whisper.*) And I know I can say this to you, Jean-Louise: I've been worried about him. He hasn't been himself at all, not just lately. He's started having these nightmares . . .

JEAN-LOUIS. The sunshine will help him, Marje.

MARJE. I hope it will. Do you think it will?

JEAN-LOUIS. Yes.

MARJE. Dreadful nightmares, he says.

JEAN-LOUIS: About what?

MARJE. Well, that's it, you see. He won't say what they're about. He bottles them up. And I often say, you might feel better if you talked about them, Larry. They might go away.

JEAN-LOUIS. Perhaps he would tell me, Marje?

MARJE. Oh no! He wouldn't. Larry hardly ever tells people things. I mean, he wouldn't like me talking to you about this. (*Catching sight of* LARRY *returning.*) So don't say a word, will you?

LARRY (*calls, triumphant*). Got the baguette, Marje!

MARJE. Oh, well done, dear. Coffee's on. It was 'une', wasn't it?

LARRY. Wouldn't know. Said 'une', anyway. Bonjour, Jean-Louis.

Had a good night, did you?

JEAN-LOUIS. Bonjour, Larry.

LARRY. Wouldn't go to the showers yet if I was you. Dreadful queues . . .

MARJE. You should have gone before eight-thirty, dear.

LARRY (*ignoring this*). Get the chairs, shall I, Marje?

MARJE. Yes please, dear. And bring the Nescafé, will you?

LARRY *unzips his tent and goes in.*

LARRY (*from inside the tent*). Where is the Nescafé, Marje?

MARJE. In the box marked 'Stores Essential', near the Horlicks.

LARRY. Okay. Got it.

JEAN-LOUIS (*to* MARJE). Well, I'm going to breakfast now.

MARJE. Oh yes. Well, bon appetit.

JEAN-LOUIS. Bon appetit, Marje.

JEAN-LOUIS *goes.*
LARRY *emerges from the tent, carrying folding chairs, which he erects with a snap.*

LARRY. Chairs, Marje.

MARJE. Larry, I wonder –

LARRY. Anything else, was there?

MARJE. It's going to be awfully hot today. I can feel it. It's going to be much hotter than yesterday I think . . .

LARRY. If you're going to say you think we ought to have another go at the awning, I'll remind you, Marje, that the idiotic tent rentalists have not supplied us with a centre strut for it. I mean, I'll certainly have a go at it, but with no centre strut . . .

MARJE. I was only going to say, I think it's bad for us to eat under a hot sun.

LARRY. Right. I'll have a go now, dear.

MARJE. I didn't mean now, Larry. I just thought, after breakfast, you might ask Jean-Louis to give you a hand . . .

LARRY. Marje, please get this into your head, will you: I do not ask people, especially foreigners, for a hand.

MARJE. Well, you couldn't put it up on your own, dear. You tried.

LARRY (*losing patience*). That Marje, is because the awning is defective. If we had been supplied with a centre strut, I would have had that awning up faster than your mother can say 'pigsty'.

Pause.

MARJE (*anxious*). You've been dreaming about them again, haven't you?

LARRY. About what?

MARJE. The pigs. That's what your nightmares are about, aren't they?

LARRY (*ignoring this*). Water boiling, is it, dear?

MARJE. Not quite. They are about the pigs, aren't they?

LARRY (*still ignoring this*). I don't know how Jean-Louis can drink that strong coffee Annette makes.

MARJE. If you'd talk about them, they'd probably go away.

The campsite noises fade.
Dawn: birdsong and a single church bell tolling six is heard.

TRIST. I'd be awake long before this. Sometimes, I'd imagine the campers zipped up in their tents, then slowly waking with the sun, setting out their tables and their seersucker table cloths and, in the case of some of the Belgians and the Dutch, plastic flowers!

Pause.

(*On the verge of laughter.*) Their rituals, so strictly observed, reminded them of their homes: everything in its place and clean.

Pause.

Larry called me a hillbilly once. And I looked like one by then. Beard wet with dew, clothes beginning to stink. I used to think, Peter wouldn't have approved. Heavens, no! 'Trist', he would have said, 'look at you, dear boy. You're beyond the *pale!*'

Pause.

Yet in the cafés, they were polite. By the time Marje had set out her table, I'd be ensconced in one, drying off, spreading out my map, feeling the blood beginning to go round . . .

Fade up the campsite.
MARJE *and* LARRY *are breakfasting. As are* JEAN-LOUIS *and* ANNETTE – *near enough to* MARJE *and* LARRY *to make conversation possible.*

LARRY (*calling to* JEAN-LOUIS). Jean-Louis, see that Dutchman, Jean-Louis? Can't control his shuttlecock.

JEAN-LOUIS (*not understanding*). *Comment*?

LARRY. That badminton freak. Just knocked his shuttlecock into Marje's baguette.

JEAN-LOUIS (*laughs*). You make us laugh, Larry!

LARRY. Do I? Figure of fun, am I? Well, I'm used to that; younger men taking the piss, if you'll pardon my French.

MARJE. Your Nescafé's getting cold, Larry.

LARRY (*restless*). I can't concentrate, Marje. I mean, it's just not peaceful on this campsite: Dutchmen impersonating Bjorn Borg . . .

MARJE. That's tennis, dear.

LARRY. I *know* that's tennis, Marjorie. Just figurative. On holiday, I should at least be allowed figures of speech. (*Addressing* JEAN-LOUIS.) Bet it's more peaceful than this in Paris, isn't it, JL?

ANNETTE. No, it's very noisy.

LARRY. Norwich is bloody noisy, isn't it, Marje?

MARJE. Oh, I wouldn't say that, Larry. Not compared to Paris.

LARRY. You've never been to Paris, girl.

MARJE. No. I know. I only meant to say –

LARRY (*to* JEAN-LOUIS *and* ANNETTE). We've never been to Paris. Hardly ever go to London, for that matter. Too expensive.

JEAN-LOUIS. Paris is expensive.

LARRY. Time was when we had a bit to spare.

MARJE. Do drink your coffee, Larry.

LARRY. But we've paid the penalty. You pay the penalty in Britain today if you stand up and go it alone.

MARJE (*nervous now*). Larry . . .

LARRY. Now to look at me, Jean-Louis, Annette, where would you say I lived?

MARJE. Please, Larry . . .

LARRY. No, hang on, Marje. Now, I'm not disturbing your *petit dejeuner,* am I?

JEAN-LOUIS. No, no . . .

LARRY. Good. Well, you listen to this. Where would you say I lived?

JEAN-LOUIS. What do you mean?

LARRY. What kind of house would you say I lived in? Have a guess.

ANNETTE. A modern house?

LARRY. You wouldn't call it modern, no. Would you, Marje?

MARJE. Larry, if you'd just drink your coffee . . .

LARRY. No, it's not modern, Annette. Have another try.

JEAN-LOUIS. A cottage?

LARRY. Not far off, is he, Marje? That's to say, we did once live in a cottage, or rather, it was a bit better than a cottage; it was more what you'd call a farmhouse.

JEAN-LOUIS. I see.

LARRY. No you don't JL! Because we don't live there anymore. We live in a pigsty!

There is a long baffled silence.

Surprised you, didn't it? It surprises everyone. It surprised me, I can tell you. I was proud of my house. Kids loved it, didn't they, Marje? It was a very solid house. Old, but solid. In quite a bad state when we bought it, but little by little, we improved it. No-one could have wished for a nicer home.

MARJE. Your coffee will be stone cold, Larry.

JEAN-LOUIS. What happened to your house, then, Larry?

LARRY. I can tell them what happened, can't I, Marje?

MARJE (*with pursed lips*). I'd much rather you didn't.

LARRY. Marje doesn't want me to tell you. She relives it, you see. Don't you, dear?

MARJE. I just don't want to talk about it now. Some other time, love. Tell them some other time.

LARRY. She says I can tell you some other time, and she's probably right, because we hardly know you, do we? I mean, what's a few days? Why don't you tell us a bit more about you, Jean-Louis? What on earth does a poet find to write about these days?

JEAN-LOUIS. Well . . .

ANNETTE (*quickly*). He writes from the heart.

LARRY. Left-wing, are you?

JEAN-LOUIS. Well . . .

LARRY. Like being a poet, do you?

JEAN-LOUIS. Yes.

LARRY. Can't imagine what you write about, though. There don't seem to be any English poets left, do there, Marje? Casualties of the 20th Century, I wouldn't wonder.

MARJE. I expect there are, Larry. We just haven't heard about them.

JEAN-LOUIS. Yes, there are. You have some fine poets.

LARRY. Do we, by jove? Hear that, Marje? Well, well . . .

MARJE. Are you going to eat some baguette, dear?

LARRY *ignores this and walks over to* JEAN-LOUIS *and* ANNETTE.

LARRY. Mind you, it's easy money, that, really. Just jotting down a few lines and getting paid for it! Not that you don't need to have talent, I admit, to jot them down properly, but it's an easy life, that, isn't it?

JEAN-LOUIS. No, it's not easy. Sometimes it's very hard.

LARRY. Slim volumes, you see. Now, I've always thought with all due respect, Jean-Louis, that slim volumes are extraordinarily over-priced. I mean, you pay almost as much for a slim volume as you do for a proper book, and what do you get? A few lines here and there and a lot of blank paper.

JEAN-LOUIS. You must understand that sometimes a few lines are important.

LARRY. Well, I'm not saying they're not important, to a few, but it's not what you'd call value for money, is it?

JEAN-LOUIS. You can't measure by money.

LARRY. Well, they do in Britain, mate! If you haven't got money, you're nothing. You have to fight tooth and nail to keep your head above water. Tooth and nail!

JEAN-LOUIS. You can choose not to fight.

LARRY. Not in Britain, you can't. If you don't fight, you sink, and your family sinks with you.

JEAN-LOUIS. Britain is like France, and France and Britain are getting more and more like America. It's no different, Larry. If you have capitalism, you have stress and fighting to stay ahead.

LARRY. Nothing wrong with capitalism, JL! Don't misunderstand me. It's the persecution of the little man I'm talking about. I'm living a century too late. I'm not allowed to get on. But don't tell me you can take away man's urge to get on. It's born in him.

JEAN-LOUIS. No, it's not born in him. He learns it. He learns to crave the things that money can buy and to compete.

LARRY. It's there, JL! I mean, even in Russia, where they keep trying to stamp it out –

JEAN-LOUIS. Intellectual freedom is quite another question, Larry.

MARJE. Listen, dear, I don't think at breakfast –

LARRY. Be quiet, Marje. Now, you tell me what you've got in Russia, Jean-Louis. And don't tell me you've got equality.

JEAN-LOUIS. Larry . . .

LARRY. I'll tell you what you've got. You've got concentration camps and nothing in the shops.

JEAN-LOUIS. Then if there's nothing in the shops, nobody is fighting for more and more money.

LARRY. Dignity, you see, Jean-Louis. It all comes down to *dignity*. Now, if I was a little cog in a dirty great socialist machine, where is my dignity? You can't find dignity being a cog. Don't tell me you can.

JEAN-LOUIS. But Larry –

LARRY. No. Hold on, hold on! You see, I know what it is to lose one's dignity. I know what it is to be trampled down by a socialist government hell-bent on exterminating individual enterprise. They pushed me into the muck! But I'm fighting. I'm fighting for Marje and the boys. I'm fighting for my dignity!

JEAN-LOUIS. Dignity can mean many different things . . .

LARRY. Not to me.

JEAN-LOUIS. What does it mean to you?

LARRY. Well, I do a lot of driving in my job. I'm a salesman now, you see. I never wanted to be a salesman, but at least it's a job, isn't it? I'm working, JL. And when I go round to my clients, I hold my head up. I put on a clean shirt and Marje irons my suit, and I can look my clients in the eye. I may live in a pigsty, but I'm the best salesman in the Anglia division, and that's dignity for you.

MARJE (*crossing to* LARRY). Larry, I think this kind of political chit-chat is very exhausting at breakfast time.

LARRY. It's not political, dear. We were talking about dignity.

MARJE. Yes, I know.

LARRY. Dignity's not political.

MARJE. Well, it sounds political to me, and I honestly think you should let Jean-Louis and Annette get on with their breakfast.

ANNETTE. No, it's okay, Marje.

MARJE. Well, that's very tolerant of you, Annette dear, but Larry's not very certain about any of these political things, are you Larry?

LARRY. Oh, for heaven's sake, Marje! Never been more certain. Never been more certain in my life!

MARJE (*ignoring this*). And it makes him worry, you see, Annette.

LARRY. Worrying never did anybody any harm. If I hadn't lain awake worrying, where would we be now?

MARJE. It's not a criticism, dear.

The campsite noises fade – on the urgent barking of a dog.

Fade up the music of a sung mass – a large church or cathedral. The music ends – a latin prayer is mumbled, low and distant. Footsteps echo in the church, then stop. The almost inaudible prayer continues under TRIST.

TRIST. I was getting nearer to the campsite – perhaps another two days' walking – when I stopped to hear the Mass. When Larry asked me to tell him what I'd seen and heard, I wasn't able to describe the

Mass to him, not for any lack of words in me, but because I understood the lack of understanding in him. I'm not a religious man. That isn't it. It's simply that, to describe an experience, you must first choose your audience.

Pause.

The joy I felt had to do with my invisibility in the church. On that morning of the Sung Mass I think I began to understand that yes, I had been right to give it up, just admit that I would never be more than adequate in my chosen profession and say, well, I chose it for a while, but now I must forget it absolutely and take another path.

Pause.

Certainties often come to me in foreign places.

Pause.

I'm not alone in this. Something exploded in Larry on the stifling hot night of the Municipal Ball. And he saw precisely what he had never been able to see, ever before.

Pause.

He was helped, of course, by Jean-Louis and Annette, and by Marje, and to some extent by what happened to me. But I think, all the while he was in France, he was trying to see things which, in his life as a salesman he only half-expected were there.

The choir go into a sung 'Te Deum', which begins to fade after several bars, and mixes with MARJE *singing rather badly 'Don't Cry For Me, Argentina'.*
MARJE *is dusting the tent.* LARRY *is settled on a sun-lounger. Louder cicadas should suggest buzzing heat.*

LARRY (*suddenly slapping his naked thigh*). Got it, Marje!

MARJE (*Startled*). What?

LARRY. 7522306!

MARJE. What on earth's that, dear?

LARRY. It's been bothering me ever since we arrived. I knew it had to mean something!

MARJE. Well, I wish you wouldn't burst out like that. It gave me a dreadful jump.

LARRY *swings his legs off the sun-lounger and sits. Elbows on knees.*

LARRY. I could do with a fag, Marje.

MARJE. You said you wouldn't, love. You said, if we came on holiday, you'd really try . . .

LARRY. What do you think I've been doing, Marje? Trying's not the word! I haven't had a cigarette for two days. Two *days*!

MARJE. Well, I think it would be a great shame to give in now.

LARRY. Easy for you.

MARJE. What, dear?

LARRY. Easy for you to say that.

MARJE. But if it's going to make you irritable . . .

LARRY (*getting up*). I am not irritable, Marje. (*He begins to pace about.*) It's merely . . . that I have not felt entirely free of worries, Marje. I have not felt as a man should feel on his first holiday for seven years . . .

MARJE. It's those dogs, Larry, isn't it?

LARRY (*ignoring this*). Not only my dreams. I've been puzzled by a lot of things . . .

MARJE. I never dreamt there'd be dogs.

LARRY. But I intend to solve them. I intend to find solutions.

MARJE. Solutions to what, dear?

LARRY. Are you going to stop dusting, Marjorie?

MARJE. I'm only keeping the tent clean.

LARRY. It's clean enough. Now take 7522306. I've solved that.

Pause. MARJE *stops dusting.*

MARJE (*tentative*). I don't really know what 7522506 is, Larry.

LARRY. 7522*306.*

MARJE. Well, 306 . . .

LARRY. The patron, you see, or the 'gardien' or whatever he calls himself; the bloke in the reception hut.

MARJE. What about him?

LARRY. You mean you didn't notice?

MARJE. Notice what?

LARRY. 7522306 – on his arm.

MARJE. What d'you mean, Larry?

LARRY. Tattooed on his arm – 7522306! Now I've been wondering and wondering why an elderly bloke like that, who's probably never heard the words 'Heavy Metal' . . .

MARJE (*calmly*). He must have been in a concentration camp.

LARRY (*amazed*). How did you guess, Marje?

MARJE. Well, all I know is that's what they did to Jews in concentration camps: they tattooed numbers onto them.

LARRY. Well, ten out of ten, Marje! But how could one have guessed? He doesn't look like a Jew.

MARJE. His name's Bidermann, Larry.

LARRY. How do you know?

MARJE. Because the woman who serves in the camp shop is Madame Bidermann, and that's her husband.

LARRY. Well! Well done you, Marje. Tell you got top marks in the Guides. (*Pause*.) He's a nervous bloke, though, isn't he. Expect he had a pretty terrible war.

MARJE. Poor man.

LARRY. Lucky to get out, I'd say. Lucky not to be buried alive in quicklime.

MARJE. Don't, Larry.

LARRY. Lucky not to be gassed.

MARJE. Larry . . .

LARRY. Mind you, now that I know what he is, it strikes me as extremely odd that he'd choose to run a campsite. I mean, you'd honestly think he'd want nothing more to do with a camp.

MARJE. It's not the same, Larry.

LARRY. I mean, you'd honestly think the very word, 'camp' . . .

MARJE. It's municipal site, dear. It doesn't belong to him.

LARRY. Unless it's revenge. He could have dreamt of it all these years – the day when he'd be master of a camp!

MARJE. Oh, don't be stupid, Larry.

LARRY. I mean, those dogs that yap all night – that could be a dog recording! He could be going round the camp with a tape recorder, waking everybody up.

MARJE. Larry, that is piffle!

LARRY. Drivel's the word you want, is it, Marje?

MARJE. Piffling drivel! Now listen, I think you ought to come out of the sun, dear.

LARRY. We *came* here for the sun, Marjorie! We came to get away from grey and damp.

MARJE. It's no good overdoing it.

LARRY. Well, you're *under*doing it!

MARJE. I'm taking it gradually.

LARRY. You're taking it so flaming gradually, Marje, the holiday'll be over and you'll still be white as a sheet.

MARJE. I know what I'm doing.

LARRY. We've only got seven more days.

The sound of sandalled footsteps on a country road: TRIST *walking with his knapsack. As he walks, he begins to whisper, with great emotional intensity, the Agincourt speech from* Henry V.

TRIST. 'This day is called the feast of Crispian.
He that outlives this day and comes safe home
Will stand a tip-toe when this day is nam'd
And rouse him at the name of Crispian.
He that shall live this day and see old age
Will yearly on the vigil feast his neighbours
And say, 'Tomorrow is Saint Crispian'.
Then he will strip his sleeve and show his scars
And say, 'These wounds I had on Crispin's day'.
Old men forget; yet all shall be forgot,
But he'll remember with advantages
What feats he did that day . . .'

(TRIST *tails off – then:*) Oh, rubbish! I never got it! Never *right.* Heard it somewhere in me, how it might be done. Thought I had it once. But I didn't. Had it inside me, but not out there. Useless.

TRIST *walks on.*

A moped passes him on the road, a young couple on it. laughing.

The campsite. It's midday. Very hot. LARRY *opens a bottle of wine with a loud pop and a sigh of satisfaction.*

LARRY. This is the stuff, Marje! Best thing about this country, if you ask me, the cheapo vino.

MARJE. There's more to France than wine, Larry.

LARRY (*pouring wine*). I'd trade a dozen cases of this for a medieval church – or rather, the other way round: a dozen medieval churches . . .

MARJE. There's a whole heritage, Larry . . .

LARRY. Course there is, dear, but you need *time* to appreciate all that. Why d'you think the package tour was invented? Because people are short of *time.*

MARJE. The time you've spent just sitting around, we could have done the wine caves and the giant bamboo forest and the Palais des Papes . . .

LARRY. If you want to go and look at a medieval church, you just feel free, Marje. Take the car. Right now I am going to enjoy my first drink of the day and I would very much like a cigarette. Now where did you put my fags, dear?

MARJE. I threw them away.

There is a stunned silence.

LARRY. *What*?

MARJE. It seemed stupid to keep them, when you were trying to give them up.

Long pause. LARRY *is flabbergasted and absolutely livid.*

LARRY. You don't understand a *thing,* do you?

MARJE (*nervous of his anger*). Don't Larry . . .

LARRY. You astound me, Marjorie. D'you know that?

MARJE. Smoking was so bad for you, dear. You were smoking so much . . .

LARRY. It's a waste of time explaining anything to you, Marjorie. Child of your mother, that's all you are.

MARJE. Larry . . .

LARRY. Child of your mother! Comfortable, ringside seat at other people's circuses! Sit in your shade there and sigh your little sighs and watch me work and sweat and make a fool of myself. You simply don't understand what it's like to be me!

MARJE (*defensive*). I've stood by you, Larry. I've seen my hopes disappear.

LARRY. *Your* hopes? What about *my* hopes? Eh? What about my sodding hopes?

MARJE. Don't shout, Larry.

LARRY. Sometimes, I feel ashamed of you, Marje. I'm out there day after day on the road, practising my rep's voice in the rearview mirror, and knowing, just *knowing* that if I don't meet my quota, if I don't bring home my commission . . . Well, I can tell you, Marjorie, I have to stop the car sometimes. I have to stop the car and have a fag, because the weight of that word, 'quota' . . . And I think of you and I think of the boys and what could happen . . .

MARJE (*quietly*). What about the boys, then?

LARRY. What d'you mean?

MARJE. I just don't know why we go on struggling to pay for this boarding school, Larry. I've really begun to believe –

LARRY. Principle, Marjorie! That's another thing you have never understood. Principle and dignity.

MARJE. They're only words, Larry.

LARRY. They are not words! They are the entire basis of my life, and if you haven't understood that by now –

MARJE (*calm*). I understand the words, Larry.

LARRY. They are not words. They are *not* words! Principle and dignity *are not words*!

Silence. Then MARJE *blows her nose.*

MARJE. If we took Jimmy and Paul away from that wretched school we might be able to afford a mortgage on a proper house . . .

LARRY. This is not the time or the place to discuss that. Now please tell me in which of the many idiotic wall pockets you have hidden my wallet. I shall then go and buy myself a packet of cigarettes.

MARJE (*ignoring* this). I don't see why you can't discuss it. You're the one who keeps coming out with everything. You're the one who told Jean-Louis about the pigsties.

LARRY. I am not discussing it, Marje. Now please inform me –

MARJE. And I've been thinking, since we got away from England, about the money we spend on school fees . . .

LARRY. The schools are a question I am not prepared to discuss, Marjorie.

MARJE. Why ever not?

LARRY. I'm not going into it.

MARJE. I don't see why you won't go into it. If you thought about it clearly, you'd see the sense of going into it. All the sacrifices we make to pay for that upper class school . . .

LARRY. Where's my wallet, dear?

MARJE (*ignoring this*). And when we go to see Jimmy and Paul, all they seem to care about it being Back Leg or Front Half or whatever the wretched rugger positions are, and neither of them has a clue how hard you work to keep them there.

LARRY. Marjorie –

MARJE. And it's not as if they can be at Crowbourne forever, is it, Larry? And I often think that school is telling them all the wrong things and when they leave and start being in the proper world, they'll be quite a bit confused.

LARRY (*sighs*). I thought I'd made it clear to you: I promised myself I'd give my boys a good start in life. I never had a good start, and look where I am. And if I can't give Paul and Jimmy a good start in life, where is my dignity, Marje? You just tell me that.

MARJE. I know that's how you feel, dear. But I think the time has come to re-evaluate, Larry.

LARRY. 'Re-evaluate'! Look, Marje, just let me go and buy some cigarettes.

MARJE (*ignoring this, bravely determined*). You see, I don't want to go back to the pigsties.

LARRY. They are not pigsties. They are converted pigsties.

MARJE. I simply won't go back there and watch the years pass.

LARRY. Marjorie, listen –

MARJE. I'll go to mother's. I'll go and stay there until you can see things clearly.

LARRY. I see things perfectly clearly.

MARJE. You don't, Larry. You fight all the time. You never let anyone advise you or help you.

LARRY. I don't need help, thank you.

MARJE. Jean-Louis says we all need help, but very few of us know how to ask for it. He says the first time we let ourselves ask for help –

LARRY. He's a poet. You cannot take at face value one single thing uttered by a poet.

MARJE (*ignoring this*). And he says that he and Annette go camping every year to try to renew themselves.

LARRY. 'Renew themselves'! Honestly, Marjorie . . .

MARJE. To try to look at their lives from a different point of view. I think different points of view are sometimes a good idea, Larry.

LARRY. Poetic nonsense!

MARJE. I don't think it is.

LARRY. And what's all this about going to your mother's? Don't tell me *you're* seeing anything clearly, girl, if you're planning to coop yourself up with that bloodless old woman!

MARJE (*firm, calm*). I'm not going back to the pigsties, Larry.

LARRY *swigs wine, ignores* MARJE*'s last statement.*

LARRY. She never believed in me, your mother. She never believed in the pigs. She never once went to *look* at the bloody pigs! It was *your* money getting fat in there, but she wasn't interested. She probably knew the crash was coming. She just sat and waited for it.

MARJE. Larry . . .

LARRY. And then put the blame on me.

MARJE. She had nothing to do with it.

LARRY. Don't tell me she couldn't have helped us out with the overdraft. Don't tell me that selfish old stick insect didn't have cash to spare! She could have saved our home, Marjorie, *your* home! But what did she do? Bugger all is what she did. Just sat pretty in her hideous, gigantic bungalow and never offered us a farthing. So don't you go running to her. If you go running back to your mother, when I've been working fourteen-hour days to take you on this holiday Okay, it's not the Ritz. Okay, it's an idiotic tent and you've got a five mile hike to the nearest toilet, but the wine's cheap . . . (*Running out of steam now.*) . . . and if you'd just come out into the sun a bit more . . .

Silence. MARJE *blows her nose again.*

I mean, that'd really be a dirty trick, to walk out on me. I don't believe you could do it, Marje. You couldn't do it, could you, girl?

MARJE. I don't want to go back to the pigsties, Larry. I'd rather spend my life in a tent.

LARRY. Nothing stopping you, dear! We could erect the old thing at the bottom of the field . . .

MARJE. It's on loan, Larry.

LARRY. Bit nippy in the winter, though. I mean, okay on a day like this. Even I can see the charm, but with an East Anglian frost on the ground . . .

MARJE (*tearful*). I don't know what to do.

LARRY. Oh my God, if you're going to cry, that's the last bloody straw!

MARJE (*still tearful*). I'm sorry, Larry . . .

LARRY. Oh my *Lord*. (*Then a sudden idea.*) Look, tell you what, Marje, 7522306 told me there's a ball on tonight up at the swimming pool complex. Live band. Haven't looked at my suit since we arrived, it's probably been carried off by ants by now for all I know. But why don't I get it out? Why don't I get my suit out now and hang it up, and I'll hang up one of your dresses, eh Marje?

MARJE (*blowing her nose*). I don't know, Larry. I don't think I feel much like a Ball.

LARRY *unzips the tent and wades in.*

LARRY (*from inside the tent*). A 'Bal des Roses', that's what 7522306 said. How can you resist a Bal des Roses, Marje?

MARJE. I don't know what a Bal des Roses is exactly dear.

LARRY. Got it! Got my suit, Marje!

He wades out again, holding his crumpled suit.

MARJE. It's awfully crumpled, Larry.

LARRY. It'll do a turn. Won't it? Won't it?

MARJE. I don't know, love.

LARRY (*dancing round, singing*). 'Dancing in the dark, till the tune ends, we're dancing in the dark!' Come on Marje, dance with me.

MARJE. I don't feel like dancing. And honestly, I haven't got a suitable dress for a ball.

LARRY. It's not a performance of *Cinderella,* Marje! You can wear any kind of dress.

MARJE (*tentative*). My blue flowered one?

LARRY. Yes, of course.

MARJE. It's awfully creased, your jacket.

LARRY. It'll hang out, won't it? I mean, I'd like to wear a suit, if we're going dancing. 7522306 said 'dress optional', but I've never been a one for an optional dress.

MARJE. Larry?

LARRY. What, dear?

MARJE. How do you always remember his number?

LARRY. Head for figures. Always had it. Now look, Marje, tell me where you hid the toilet roll, will you? Got the beginnings of that pain . . .

MARJE. Have you? Oh dear. Perhaps we should have camped nearer the toilets.

Silence.

TRIST. They had – Larry and Marje, and Jean-Louis and Annette – chosen the greenest bit of the site. Marje said that the oak trees reminded her of Norfolk; Annette said they reminded her of the the countryside round Dijon, where she was born.

Pause.

The oak trees were the only magnificent thing about the campsite. They had permanence on a piece of land where people came and lived and made their mess and then moved on, letting the ants eat up their leavings.

Pause.

I chose to camp near Larry and Marje, not because of their English number plate, but because of the oak trees. They reminded me of Peter's parents' house in Sussex, where we – during the time that Peter and I talked of ourselves as 'we' – had spent some Sundays.

Long pause.

Peter. I was trying to forget you. Forget it all. Do you remember that Mrs Edwards in the Manchester digs saying 'beats me how actors remember all those words', and I said – even then, I said – 'remembering isn't difficult, Mrs Edwards dear. The harder task is forgetting!

The campsite. Early evening.

Campers making quiet preparation for their supper. Dogs still barking now and then, cicadas fainter.

LARRY (*exaggerated whisper*). Marje, come here.

MARJE *is inside the tent, opening a can of soup.*

MARJE. Hang on a sec, dear.

LARRY. We've been invaded, Marje.

MARJE. What?

LARRY. Come and *look*.

MARJE *emerges from the tent.*

MARJE. What is it, Larry?

LARRY (*with finality*). Neighbours.

MARJE. Oh yes! Tiny little tent, isn't it? Looks as if it came from the Army Surplus.

LARRY. Spot on, Marje. Though I've never understood the word 'surplus' with regard to the British Army. You'd think our wilfully depleted Force de Frappe would be hanging onto everything it owns for dear life.

MARJE (*ignoring all this*). I wonder who's it is.

LARRY. Spoiling our view, anyway.

MARJE. No car. That's odd.

LARRY. Spoiling our uninterrupted view of those hills.

MARJE. Well, not really, dear.

LARRY. Oh my God, Marje . . .

MARJE. What?

LARRY. Someone's crawling out. Pretend we haven't noticed anything. Supper on, is it?

MARJE. He's coming over to us.

LARRY. Just turn away, dear. We want nothing to do with anyone looking like that.

MARJE. He's smiling, Larry.

Silence. TRIST *crosses the few yards of dry grass between his tent and* LARRY*'s.*

TRIST. I couldn't pass, seeing the English car without introducing myself . . .

LARRY (*feigning surprise*). Good heavens! We didn't see you, did we, Marje?

TRIST. My name's Trist. The French pronounce it 'triste', meaning sad.

LARRY. Oh. Trist, eh? Well . . .

MARJE (*friendly at once*). I'm Marje. Well, Marjorie, actually, but people only call me that when they don't like me, or if they're cross.

TRIST (*producing a bottle of wine*). Well, Marje, I've brought a small offering . . .

LARRY. Oh, good Lord, no, no. Got plenty of wine, haven't we, Marje?

TRIST *sets the wine down on* LARRY*'s camping table.*

TRIST. Selfishness.

LARRY. Sorry?

TRIST. I've been journeying – on my own. Lost all account of time and all memory of conversation. I wondered if you might spare me a moment or two – just to hear a voice, you understand, share my wine . . .

LARRY. Well, we've got supper on, haven't we, Marje?

MARJE. Oh, it's only soup.

LARRY. Why's it only soup?

MARJE (*discreet whisper*). For your upset tummy. (*To* TRIST.) Please do sit down. I'll get another chair. We brought three in case there was ever a guest.

LARRY. Soup's not enough, Marjorie.

TRIST. You're angry.

LARRY. What?

TRIST. The 'Marjorie' in your sentence . . .

LARRY (*rude*). *What*?

TRIST. Am I right?

LARRY. What on earth are you talking about?

TRIST. Marje just said that no one –

LARRY. Look, I'm sorry, mate, but we've got plenty of wine, and we've got to eat early because of the Bal, so this isn't a convenient moment.

MARJE. Larry . . .

TRIST. No, no. I understand. Dreadful intrusion. Please accept my apologies.

The sound of a Citroen 2CV bumping over grass. JEAN-LOUIS *calls.*

JEAN-LOUIS. Bonsoir Larry! Bonsoir Marje!

TRIST. I'll just slip away.

MARJE. Oh no, please don't go. I don't know what on earth Larry's thinking of, being so unwelcoming. Why don't you get us some glasses, Larry?

LARRY (*uptight*). Anything you say, dear.

LARRY *unzips the tent with an angry flourish and goes inside. We hear* JEAN-LOUIS' *car stop and doors open and slam.*

MARJE (*to* TRIST). Larry's not feeling very well today and that makes him grumpy. He's not usually like this.

TRIST. I'd be the last to intrude, Marje. So selfish . . .

MARJE. No, no. I'm delighted. We haven't met anyone else from England, and you begin to miss it after a while, don't you, the talk?

TRIST. The talk? Not an admission we want to make is it?

MARJE. Well, no man is an island, I mean I think that's absolutely true . . .

TRIST. Important to . . . *test,* though, from time to time, to see what can be done in isolation.

MARJE. Been very far, have you Mr Trist?

TRIST. Trist. Just Trist. It's short for Tristram, which I've come to detest. No, no, not the length and breadth of the country, but on my own for quite a while. And the wonders I've seen since I came to France! Did you know how unimaginably beautiful much of France is? A dry river is beautiful here, Marje. The wild flowers that push through the stones . . .

LARRY *emerges from the tent, carrying extra glasses.*

LARRY. You a poet too?

TRIST. Sorry?

LARRY. Talk like a poet. We're surrounded by them, Marje.

TRIST. No. Not a poet.

LARRY *passes the wine glasses to* MARJE.

LARRY. Glasses, Marje. (*Then to* TRIST.) What are you, then?

TRIST (*avoiding the question*). What's your name? I don't know your name.

LARRY. Larry Peacock. Some kind of artist are you?

TRIST. No. I'm . . . what you see.

LARRY. Oh, go on, mate, that's not good enough. Now we know Jean-Louis' a poet. He wasn't too proud to come out with that.

TRIST. I'm a vagabond, I suppose.

LARRY. Yes, well, got the uniform right. Don't you *do* anything, then?

MARJE. Don't pester, Larry.

LARRY. I'm not pestering. Just curious.

TRIST. Let me pour us some wine.

LARRY. And I abhor secrecy, you see. Secrecy of any kind. And I honestly feel, despite us all being from the UK, that we can't enjoy a drink with you unless your response to our questions is more forthcoming.

TRIST (*pouring wine*). What do you do, Larry?

LARRY. *Me*? Well, I'm not ashamed to admit what I do. I sell. I make no disguise of the fact that I sell. I'd even go so far as to say that I'm a bloody good salesman.

TRIST. What do you sell?

LARRY. Fertilisers.

MARJE. There's quite a good commission on fertilisers, isn't there, Larry?

LARRY. Not that good, dear. I'd do better in Heavy Plant. A man with my selling record should have been promoted to HP by now.

MARJE. I think Jean-Louis and Annette are coming over.

LARRY. It's not a fair game, my business. But then, what business it? The thing is, you've got to have a game. Everyone has to have a game. And I don't believe you haven't got a game.

MARJE. Here are Jean-Louis and Annette, Larry.

TRIST. Good, good. *Je m'appelle Trist. Pas 'Triste', n'est ce pas? Trist.*

JEAN-LOUIS. *Bonsoir. Jean-Louis Duval. Mon amie, Annette . . .*

ANNETTE. *Bonsoir Monsieur.*

LARRY. Look speak English, Jean-Louis.

ANNETTE. Okay.

LARRY. You sit here, Annette.

ANNETTE. Oh no. Don't get up.

LARRY. No, no. Sit here.

ANNETTE. Where shall you sit?

LARRY. I'll wander about.

MARJE. Don't wander about, Larry.

ANNETTE. Have this chair, Larry.

LARRY. No, no. You sit down.

JEAN-LOUIS. Sit here, Larry.

LARRY. I am not going to sit next to Mr Trist until he comes clean.

If there's anything makes me feel uncomfortable, it's a person not coming clean.

MARJE. You're being very rude, dear.

LARRY. It's not as if I haven't come clean, Trist.

MARJE. You haven't come clean, Larry.

LARRY. Yes, I have . . .

MARJE. You haven't mentioned the sties.

LARRY. For who's sake, Marjorie? Tell me that.

MARJE. It doesn't matter. I don't call that coming completely clean. So if Trist doesn't want to –

LARRY. Right! I'll tell him about the pigsties.

JEAN-LOUIS. Don't upset Marje, Larry.

LARRY. Marje is the one who said I was coming clean.

MARJE. I only said I don't think you should pester . . .

LARRY. I'm not pestering. I merely said I felt uncomfortable when a person is so obviously evasive about himself.

MARJE. Larry . . .

TRIST (*quietly*). I'm an actor. (*A moment's silence.*) I *was* an actor.

LARRY. Not an actor anymore, then?

TRIST. No.

LARRY. Gave it up, did you?

TRIST (*choked*). It gave me up.

Silence. Everyone is uncomfortable except LARRY. TRIST *gulps his wine.* LARRY *sits.*

LARRY. That's better, then! Now we know where we are!

TRIST. The stage was my life. (*Pause.*) Yet I don't often catch myself thinking about it. Not too often.

LARRY. You'll go back to it, won't you? Old actors never die.

MARJE. *Soldiers*, Larry.

LARRY. Don't be pedantic, dear. Could be actors. Take your Lord Olivier; he's had cancer . . .

TRIST. I should have faded away ten years ago. I've been rubbish for ten years. No truth in what I've done. No bloody truth.

LARRY (*recovering his humour*). Pass that bottle, will you, Trist?

ANNETTE. What was your favourite part, Trist?

TRIST. Favourite part? That's difficult.

ANNETTE. You don't have one favourite?

TRIST. I don't think so. But I loved Shakespeare. His words have a knack: they ask and you give. (*Pause.*) I've played Othello. The snag of Othello is body make-up. But I had Peter then. The gentlest hands in the business.

There is an awkward silence. LARRY *coughs.*
In the distance, a child's laugh is heard.

LARRY. You'd better get our soup on, Marje girl.

MARJE. No hurry, Larry.

LARRY. We want to eat before it's dark.

MARJE. No need. It's rather nice with our gas lamp.

LARRY. Moths, Marjorie.

MARJE. I like eating outside in the dark.

ANNETTE. I agree.

JEAN-LOUIS. I would like to have seen your Othello, Trist.

TRIST. Oh! Long ago and far away, Jean-Louis. I was too young for it. And it doesn't work with a white actor. Not anymore.

MARJE. I bet you miss being an actor, Trist.

TRIST. No, not exactly. The hardest thing is convincing myself it's all right not to belong. I *belonged* in the theatre, you see. It was like a club or a religion. I had my whole being through belonging, and I used to think, if I can't act anymore, I'll be adrift, nothing . . .

LARRY. Well, you *are* adrift, old man: rucksacks . . .

TRIST. No.

LARRY. You look adrift to me.

TRIST. Yes, I know. I look it. (*Pause.*) I didn't understand it myself for a long time – not till I came away from England – that it was all right not to belong anymore. I thought the leaving would be the end of me, but it wasn't. It was a bit like a beginning. Marje knows what I mean. Do you, Marje?

MARJE (*hesitant*). I'm not sure. I mean, I sometimes think I've never really belonged anywhere. I'm washing up, say, and I suddenly find myself thinking, I could go to China, I could go to Russia, I could become someone else.

LARRY. Wouldn't want to go to Russia, dear! Bugger all in the shops there.

MARJE. Oh, I don't mean literally, Larry! I just sometimes think I could be ever so different from what I am. I could sort of start again.

TRIST. That's good. Why not start again?

LARRY. And never mind me, I suppose?

TRIST. It's only that, when you have started again, it's no use wanting to be back where you were.

JEAN-LOUIS. It's difficult to end one part of a life.

LARRY. I wouldn't agree. I mean, anyone can just decide to wander about Europe like a hillbilly.

JEAN-LOUIS. No. You couldn't, Larry.

LARRY. Course I could. Anyone could. What's difficult about it? It's simply that I – unlike Trist presumably – have an extremely strong sense of responsibility. That may be a dirty word these days, but I put my family first.

JEAN-LOUIS. Yes. And you couldn't leave them.

LARRY. Wouldn't want to, would I?

JEAN-LOUIS. No. Nor your job.

LARRY. My job's important, Jean-Louis! You may find this hard to believe, being a slim volume man, but the fact that I am one of the best men in the Anglia Division and that I am owed a promotion to Heavy Plant is a source of pride to me, yes, *pride* to me. And four years ago, I had *nothing*!

MARJE. Larry . . .

LARRY. Cleaned out. Bankrupt!

MARJE. Larry, we were talking about Trist.

LARRY. I'm talking about me. Did you know, Jean-Louis, that to keep the bottom from falling out of my pigs, I mortgaged everything – house, land, everything we owned – to the bank, only to see the bottom *pushed* out by the men in Brussels monkeying about with farm price levels. If it hadn't been for the neanderthals in the EEC I'd still have my pigs, and my house. I wouldn't be living in a pigsty, and I wouldn't be holidaying in a sodding tent. I'd be in the Ritz!

JEAN-LOUIS. And that would make you feel proud, would it, to be in the Ritz?

LARRY. Course it would. Who wouldn't feel proud?

ANNETTE. I hate big hotels.

LARRY. Prefer a tent, do you, Annette?

ANNETTE (*without apology*). Yes.

MARJE. I know what Annette means . . .

LARRY. You've never been in the Ritz, Marjorie.

ANNETTE. We don't go to big hotels. I don't think we would even if we could afford them.

LARRY. Well, you may have to go one day. I mean, JL might get rich and famous on his blank spaces and start touring the capitals of the world, reading bits out.

JEAN-LOUIS. I won't be rich and famous. I write about the soul and this is unfashionable. Better to write about politique.

LARRY. Oh, sod *politique*!

JEAN-LOUIS. I write about change from within a man. Change from within a person will change society. Not parties. Not religions, I think. I ask that people open themselves up and see what is inside.

LARRY. Cirrhosis of the liver, hiatus hernias . . .!

LARRY *laughs and slaps his knee. No laughter from the others.*

JEAN-LOUIS. The question of belonging, as Trist has said, is important. So many of us are greedy for this belonging. We think to put on a mask, a badge is enough. We *become* the badge. We atrophy.

LARRY. Atrophy! Marje's mother could tell you a thing or two about atrophying!

JEAN-LOUIS (*ignoring* LARRY). I don't know . . . perhaps more people are understanding now that religions and parties cannot do what we hope of them. Not completely. Yet we want to believe that to offer ourselves to some organisation is enough. This is me, we say. But this is not true. This is not the whole me, the bit that follows some rule or other. No. So what must I do? I must stop relying on someone else's rules. I must find *new* ideas. New solutions.

LARRY. No, no, no, no, no, no, no! Don't know what you all think of that, but to me rules are highly significant. Take Scandinavia. Scarcely a rule in Scandinavia and what do they produce there? Porn and tennis players.

MARJE. I don't think that's relevant, Larry.

LARRY. Yes, it is. Rules are the guardians of civilisation as we know it.

TRIST. 'Civilisation as we know it' isn't at all wonderful, Larry.

LARRY (*ignoring this*). Take the theatre. You've got to follow the director's rules.

JEAN-LOUIS. That's all right, Larry. Joint endeavour is fine – sometimes marvellous. Only you must understand why you are there – for *you*.

LARRY. You're there to earn money. All this philosophical nickety-pickety doesn't help your bank balance one jot.

JEAN-LOUIS. Larry –

LARRY. And don't tell me the consequences of being without money. Don't you tell them to me!

JEAN-LOUIS (*patient*). I know, Larry. But supposing we taught ourselves to expect less, not more and more material things . . .?

TRIST. You're wrong, Larry. You don't merely follow the director's 'rules'.

LARRY. What? In a play? Course you do. Why else is he there, then? What's he paid for except to give orders?

TRIST. The director simply makes a shape.

LARRY. You've lost me there, Trist.

TRIST. He holds the shape of the whole production in his mind.

LARRY. But you've got to fit in with his shape, haven't you? Don't tell me he isn't the chief and you lot are the Indians.

TRIST. It's not like that.

MARJE. Of course it's not, Larry.

LARRY. What the heck do you know about the theatre, Marje? The nearest you ever got to it was *The Sound of Music.*

Fade up the sung 'Te Deum', in an echoey cathedral, as before. TRIST *is heard over the choir.*

TRIST. My invisibility in the church: so important to keep hold of, keep remembering that sense of . . . *relief* that I was, finally, off. No face in the lights, or the thousand eyes, moving in a mass like frogspawn, picking me over.

Pause.

Trist the actor died – his last sword fight! – in the cathedral Mass. And Trist the man began to breathe more easily . . .

Pause. The choir begins to fade.

Yet as soon as I began to listen to Larry, I knew that a feigned death, a mimed death is not enough, and that Larry, somehow, would not be satisfied until there had been a little blood spilt. Not a great deal. Just enough to make him understand.

Fade.

Campsite noises. Evening. Distant frogs, dogs barking now and then.

LARRY. Better get on with dinner, Marje.

MARJE (*in no hurry*). All right, dear.

TRIST. Dinner. (*Pause.*) I'd begun to wonder . . .

LARRY. Better get our lamp lit, dear. It's getting terribly dark.

MARJE (*rising*). What, Trist?

TRIST (*hesitant*). I'd begun to wonder . . . if we might not share a meal, all of us. Just tonight. What d'you say, Marje? Annette?

LARRY. We've only got soup, haven't we, Marje?

MARJE. I could open another tin.

ANNETTE. We have cold meats, olives, tomatoes . . .

TRIST. I know I should resist the temptation of sharing, but after being alone . . .

MARJE. I think sharing's very nice, don't you, Larry?

LARRY (*unenthusiastic*). Okay by me, dear.

TRIST. Annette?

ANNETTE. Yes. Fine.

TRIST. Thank you. All. (*Then rising.*) I'll go and fetch my contribution.

MARJE. I'll open another tin of soup.

LARRY. No hurry, dear. Just light the lamp.

TRIST (*as he goes, flamboyant*). I shall return!

TRIST *goes. We hear him walk off into the darkness.* MARJE *lights the gas lamp which hisses.* LARRY *opens the wine and pours it.*

LARRY. Have a drink on me, Jean-Louis.

JEAN-LOUIS. Thank you, Larry.

LARRY. Oddest one I've met in ages, eh?

JEAN-LOUIS. Sorry?

LARRY. Him. Trist. Know what I'd like to see him do.

JEAN-LOUIS. What?

LARRY. Act.

JEAN-LOUIS (*a moment's pause*). He doesn't act anymore.

LARRY. Bet you he never did! This stuff about Othello and mention of some gaiety girl called Peter! Bet you all that was years ago – if it ever happened at all.

JEAN-LOUIS. Why?

LARRY. I can smell it.

JEAN-LOUIS. Smell it?

LARRY. The unemployed. Failure. I can smell failure.

JEAN-LOUIS. No . . .

LARRY. I've been there, that's why I can smell it. I was a drowned man, JL. I was waking up at five in the morning and thinking, I'm a drowned man. (*Pause.* LARRY *sips wine.*) The job saved me. In the nick of time, I can tell you, or I'd have gone under. Junior Salesman, starting from scratch. No salary. Everything on a commission basis.

And I was competing with lads your age. But it saved me. That job saved me.

MARJE. The driving gives you headaches, though, Larry.

LARRY. Minor point, Marje.

JEAN-LOUIS. You do a lot of driving?

MARJE. He's always on the road.

LARRY. Extremely comfortable car, they let me have. I expect you noticed my car, didn't you. I'll show you my car tomorrow, if you like. We could go for a spin. Change from your little tin cereal packet, eh?

MARJE. It's only a Ford Cortina, Jean-Louis.

JEAN-LOUIS. I don't like cars very much.

LARRY. Don't like *cars*?

There is a sudden blare from a loud microphone: someone blows on it, then begins to test: 'Un, deux, trois, quatre, cinq . . . un, deux, trois, quatre, cinq . . .'

LARRY. Must be the Bal, Marje. Warming up!

MARJE. Oh I hope it doesn't rain, Larry. I can't see any stars, like we usually can.

LARRY. Never rains here, Marje.

MARJE. It must rain sometimes.

LARRY. Does it, Annette? Never rains at this time of year this far south.

ANNETTE. Not often.

LARRY. See, Marje?

TRIST *arrives back at the table with his contribution to the supper.*

MARJE. Oh, here's Trist.

TRIST (*brandishing bread etc.*). The Body and Blood of Christ, with a little Camembert thrown in!

LARRY. Odd meal, this is going to be, eh Marje?

MARJE. It'll be fine, dear.

LARRY. Better put the soup on then. They'll be starting the Bal soon by the sound of things, and I want to get in a bit of cabaret first!

MARJE. *Cabaret*?

LARRY. Yup! Trist.

MARJE. What, dear?

LARRY. Trist. He's going to be our cabaret.

MARJE (*amazed*). *Are* you, Trist?

TRIST. Of course not, Larry.

LARRY. Oh, you'll do it, Trist, won't you? Just a two-minute show. No more than a couple of minutes.

TRIST. Larry, I've told you –

LARRY. Two minutes.

TRIST. No.

LARRY. I know you've given it all up. I respect that. But you can't have forgotten it all. If you've been in the theatre for twenty years . . .

TRIST (*bleak*). I try to forget it.

LARRY. I mean, we'd all like that, Marje especially, if you did a piece for us.

TRIST. No, I can't, Larry.

LARRY. Well, not right now, mate. When you've had a bit more vino. When we've got the supper going . . .

MARJE. I'll go and do the soup Larry.

MARJE *goes into the tent.*

LARRY. Don't look so worried! I didn't mean now. When the moment takes you was all I meant. Jean-Louis and Annette would love it, wouldn't you?

JEAN-LOUIS. If Trist doesn't want to, Larry –

LARRY. Course he wants to! Mark of the great actor to procrastinate a bit, then turn into something first rate, eh Trist?

TRIST. I don't know.

JEAN-LOUIS. This wouldn't help Trist, Larry.

LARRY. Wouldn't harm him either. And it would make Marje's holiday. (*Then, confidential whisper.*) I mean, I was wrong when I said Marje had only seen *The Sound of Music.* She used to go on the W.I. Stratford trips at one time, before the crash came. She could quote you *Cleopatra* and bits of Hamlet's Mother, and to see you do a bit of a performance, I mean this would make up for all the things that have gone wrong on this holiday.

JEAN-LOUIS. What things?

LARRY. Oh, this and that. Dogs, shuttlecocks in her baguette – that kind of thing.

MARJE *emerges from the tent.*

MARJE. Soup's on, Larry. (*Then to* TRIST.) You don't have to do it for me, Trist.

TRIST (*sighs*). For you, Marje – patient Marje – I'll do something.

LARRY (*slaps his knee*). That's the spirit, Trist! Good for you to give my Marje a treat! Good for you! (*Pause.*) Now let's pretend this is an audition. We'll be the judges, like on your ice pairs dancing competition! 'Nine point seven from the French judges, and a massive nine point nine from the British duo!'

LARRY *slaps his knee again and guffaws. The others also laugh.*

TRIST (*anxious now*). I have to prepare a little . . .

LARRY. Yes of course you do! Course you have to prepare. Bring some more wine, Marje. We all need a top up.

MARJE. I think I'll take the soup off again, dear. It might boil over.

LARRY. Okay, Marje, okay. Just bring the wine.

ANNETTE (*to* JEAN-LOUIS). *Tu veux chercher du vin, cheri?*

JEAN-LOUIS. *Oui. D'accord.*

TRIST. I'll go and prepare . . .

LARRY. Well done! That's what I say: Well done!

JEAN-LOUIS, MARJE *and* TRIST *get up.*
TRIST *wanders off.* JEAN-LOUIS *and* MARJE *go to their tents.*
LARRY *sighs contentedly, turns to* ANNETTE.

Well, Annette, this is a lark, eh?

ANNETTE (*not understanding*). 'Lark'?

LARRY. Caper! Bit of fun! I mean, I'm beginning to enjoy myself.

ANNETTE. Good.

LARRY. You're a cool one, Annette. You don't say much, do you?

ANNETTE. I've forgotten English a lot.

LARRY. Shy, are you? (*Doesn't wait for a reply.*) It's okay to be shy, Annette, just as long as you're not selling anything. But in my trade, shyness will get you nowhere. Shyness is the kiss of bloody death!

ANNETTE. Do you like it?

LARRY. Shyness? Well, in women, young women like you, it can be most appealing . . .

ANNETTE. No. I mean your trade.

LARRY. Do I like my trade? Well, it's a trade. (*Sighs.*) Don't breathe a word, Annette. Don't you breathe a word to anyone, but sometimes – just on the odd day – I'd like to tell the Anglia Division, you go and stuff your fertilisers up your whatsits! But don't tell a soul, Annette. That's our little secret, yours and mine. Don't you go telling Marje I said that.

ANNETTE. No. I won't.

LARRY. And have some more wine. We've got to get into the right spirit for the show, eh?

MARJE *comes out of the tent with a bottle of wine.*

MARJE. Here's the more wine, Larry.

LARRY. That's it, girl! Happy, Marje?

MARJE. Yes, dear. I wonder what Trist's doing.

LARRY. Getting togged up. He's got to feel the part.

JEAN-LOUIS (*re-appearing with wine*). What part?

LARRY. Dunno. Bit old for Romeo, isn't he!

MARJE (*excited*). I'd like to know what he's going to do.

LARRY. Got your judging cards ready, Marje?

MARJE. Oh, I'll give him ten.

LARRY. You don't *know* that, Marje! You can't judge till you've seen his performance.

MARJE. Oh rubbish, dear. Anyway, here he comes.

LARRY (*drunken giggle*). Oh my giddy aunt! What's he wearing?

MARJE. He's got a cloak on.

LARRY. Army blanket, looks like.

MARJE. And a sword.

LARRY. What does he think he is!

MARJE. Ssh. Be quiet, Larry.

LARRY (*corpsed*). Oh my God!

To stop himself laughing, LARRY *begins to clap loudly, as if applauding an entrance.*

Good show, Trist!

The others clap. Then absolute silence except for distant campsite noises and now a church bell chiming a half hour. Slowly and with mighty intonation, TRIST *begins:*

TRIST. 'This day is called the feast of Crispian.
He that outlives this day and comes safe home
Will stand a tip-toe when this day is nam'd
And rouse him at the name of Crispian.
He that shall live this day and see old age
Will yearly on the vigil feast his neighbours
And say, 'Tomorrow is Saint Crispian.'
Then he will strip his sleeve and show his scars
And say, 'These wounds I had on Crispin's day.'
Old men forget: yet all shall be forgot,
But he'll remember with advantages
What feats he did that day.

TRIST *pauses. We expect him to stop, but he picks up:*

Then shall our names,
Familiar in his mouth as household words,
Harry the King, Bedford and Exeter,
Warwick and Talbot, Salisbury and Gloucester,
Be in their flowing cups freshly remember'd.

Another pause. From now on TRIST *begins to lose the kinglyness of the speech; his voice becomes gradually choked.*

This story shall the good man teach his son,
And Crispin Crispian shall ne'er go by,
From this day to the ending of the world,
But we in it shall be remembered;
We few, we happy few, we band of brothers,
For he today that sheds his blood with me
Shall be my brother; be he ne'er so vile,
This day shall gentle his condition,
And gentlemen in England now a-bed
Shall think themselves accursed they were not here,
And hold their manhoods cheap whiles any speaks
That fought with us upon Saint Crispin's day.'

Silence. TRIST *close to tears.*

LARRY (*to break silence, clapping*). Nine point eight, I'd say.

MARJE (*clapping*). Very good, Trist!

LARRY. Or nine point nine, eh? I'd say nine point nine, wouldn't you, Marje?

MARJE. I'll give him ten.

TRIST (*angry*). *Rubbish*! I was always rubbish! It took me twenty years to understand that I was rubbish, and I promised myself then, never again, not *one line*!

LARRY. Oh don't take on, mate. That was extremely moving. Very moving.

TRIST. It was rubbish!

MARJE. You mustn't say that, Trist. We all thought it was very good . . .

TRIST (*with rising irritation*). You don't understand!

MARJE. It was lovely acting.

LARRY. There you are, Trist! And my wife's a very good judge, I can tell you. I was absolutely at fault when I said the only theatrical experience she'd had was *The Sound of* –

TRIST. Shut up, Larry!

LARRY. What?

TRIST. You're just making me angry. I don't want to feel angry.

LARRY. Who's said anything out of turn? I gave you nine point nine . . .

TRIST. Shut *up*!

LARRY. Now look here, Trist . . .

TRIST (*very angry*). You shouldn't have pestered me.

LARRY. You agreed. You said you'd do it for Marje.

TRIST (*great burst of anger*). I've met dozens of people like you! Dozens! They never leave you alone. They always have to place you and number you and make you conform to *their* rules.

LARRY (*rising, defensive*). Now look here, Trist . . .

TRIST. *Thousands* of you! No wonder the world's dying of its own tedium. Numbers and categories and labels and petty little prisons – and I mean *prisons.* You lock everyone up in a cell, Larry, but you shouldn't bloody well meddle with other people's lives, because your own life is rubbish! I bet no one wants those poisons you peddle. I bet the land is dying – dying of *you*!

LARRY. Now look here, I honestly have no idea what I've done, friend, to get you so hot and bothered. I thought we were just going to have a nice evening, all together, sharing our food. I mean, all of that was your sodding idea.

MARJE. It's all right, Larry.

LARRY. It's not all right.

JEAN-LOUIS. Here's some wine, Trist.

TRIST. I'm not sitting with Larry. I don't want to be anywhere near him or near his suit.

LARRY. My suit? What's wrong with my *suit*?

MARJE. It is a bit crumpled, love . . .

LARRY. Shut up, Marje. Now just you tell me what is wrong with this suit.

TRIST. Your suit is your prison, Larry. Don't invite me in, that's all.

LARRY. Christ Almighty! He's gone bananas! This campsite is staked out with lunatics! What's that breadknife doing in your belt, anyway?

MARJE. That's a sword, Larry.

LARRY. That's a breadknife, Marjorie, and I wouldn't be at all surprised if he wasn't planning to use it!

MARJE. Don't be stupid, dear. Why don't you sit down?

LARRY. *Lie* down, don't you mean? Take all these insults like a Hush

Puppy! This is my holiday, Marjorie, my first holiday in seven years, and I will not take insults to my suit lying down.

TRIST. You never *listen,* do you? I don't suppose you've ever listened in all your life. You don't listen and you don't see. You're the deafest, blindest man I've met in all my life!

LARRY *pushes his way out from the table, knocking over and smashing a glass as he goes.*

LARRY. I'm not standing for this! I'm packing up and getting out of here.

MARJE. Larry . . .

LARRY. I'm moving on.

JEAN-LOUIS. Sit down, Larry.

LARRY. And don't you order me about! Don't *you* start meddling!

JEAN-LOUIS. There's no need to go, Larry.

LARRY. I've told you, Jean-Louis, just don't interfere.

JEAN-LOUIS. I'm not interefering. But why don't you stay and listen?

LARRY. To insults? Listen to insults?

JEAN-LOUIS. Not insults . . .

LARRY. I'm surprised at you, Jean-Louis. Honestly, I am. Never thought I'd make friends with a Frenchman, but I'd taken you for a friend. Now I can see I was spot on the first time; should have trusted my own good sense.

JEAN-LOUIS (*calm*). I am your friend, Larry. I'd like to help you.

LARRY. Help me! That's a good one! I'd say it was you that needed help. Rhymes and blank spaces never got anybody far. Help me, eh? Well, you can help me by getting out of my way, so that I can start packing.

MARJE. I don't want to go, Larry.

LARRY. You'll do as you're told, Marje.

MARJE. I'm not going.

LARRY. You're going, Marjorie.

MARJE. I don't want to.

LARRY. Suit yourself, dear. You just won't have anywhere to sleep, that's all. In five minutes that tent will be down.

MARJE. It's going to rain, Larry.

LARRY. No, it's not. it never rains.

MARJE. I can feel rain.

LARRY. Just get out of my way, Marje. I want everything out of that tent.

JEAN-LOUIS (*rising*). Why don't you sit down, just for a few minutes, Larry? Then you can go, if you still want to.

LARRY. I'm not sitting down to listen to pity! I never have and I never will.

JEAN-LOUIS. Not pity . . .

LARRY. Pity and offers of help – same thing.

JEAN-LOUIS. Why can't you accept help?

LARRY. Because I don't *need* it, that's why! Particularly from a poet, who knows nothing about the real world. You haven't got a clue what it's like to be me!

JEAN-LOUIS (*still calm*). I can try.

LARRY. You try then! You try spending every day of your sodding life in a Ford Cortina! You try driving a hundred miles a day, day after day, week after week. You try holding a family together without a proper salary. I tell you, mate, you know sod-all about the real world!

JEAN-LOUIS. Then why don't you tell me?

LARRY. You wouldn't understand. You wouldn't have a clue. So just let me get the tent down, will you?

MARJE. It's too late to drive to another campsite, Larry. They shut their gates, you know they do.

LARRY. We'll sleep in the car.

MARJE. I don't want to, Larry.

LARRY. We'll sleep in a ditch for all I care!

JEAN-LOUIS. It's stupid to go. The next place won't be any different.

LARRY. Yes, it will. Oh yes it will.

MARJE. Let's go tomorrow, Larry.

LARRY. We're going *now*, Marjorie! We're going right this minute. (*To* TRIST.) And I'm very sorry you don't like my suit, Trist. At least I can *afford* a suit! You won't catch a good salesman going about in tramp's clothing. And I say *good* salesman, because what are you all, if not salesmen? You look down on me. You pity me. 'He's just a salesman,' you say, 'he needs help.' But what are *you*? You tell me that? What are you? And you, Jean-Louis? You're salesmen!

JEAN-LOUIS. No, Larry.

LARRY. Oh yes you are. You're selling words, that's all! You're selling little pieces of punctuation and flaming blank spaces. There's no difference between us. I sell to live; you sell to live. And so does Trist. He sells a performance.

JEAN-LOUIS. Larry . . .

LARRY. Don't tell me I'm wrong.

JEAN-LOUIS. You are wrong. You're using the wrong words.

LARRY. Words, words, words, words, words, words, *words*! The whole world's gone mad inventing new words! You can't call a dustman a flaming dustman anymore, but that doesn't stop him *being* a dustman! And you and Trist, calling yourself actors or poets or whatnot; you've only got to look at what you do to see that you're salesmen!

MARJE. You've drunk too much, Larry. I'm going to put the soup on.

LARRY *ignores* MARJE. *She goes into the tent.*

LARRY. Take Trist. He's stopped selling his Othellos and his Hamlets and where is he? He's sleeping in ditches.

TRIST. You *create* a performance, Larry. Salesmen sell what other people have created. You could call theatre managements salesmen, or publishers even, but not the actors or the writers. That's rubbish.

LARRY. Call it rubbish. Call it what you like. It's the truth and nobody likes to hear the truth about themselves.

JEAN-LOUIS. Where's your truth, Larry?

LARRY. My truth? I know what I am, Jean-Louis. That's my truth. I'm not afraid to say what I am.

JEAN-LOUIS. Okay, you know what you are: you're a salesman.

LARRY. And I don't try to deny it. Not like some.

JEAN-LOUIS. But you're not just that, are you? You're not only that. People are more complex than the thing they *do*. So what else are you?

LARRY. I know what I am. Don't you worry about it.

JEAN-LOUIS. What are you? Tell us.

LARRY. I've told you. I know where I am. I've got my dignity and I –

JEAN-LOUIS. Where is it?

LARRY. Where is what?

JEAN-LOUIS. This dignity of yours.

LARRY. It's a waste of time talking to you. I've got to get on.

JEAN-LOUIS. No. (*And with anger rising now.*) I want to know where your dignity is. In this suit, is it? Is this it?

LARRY. You leave my suit alone.

JEAN-LOUIS. Not till you tell me. Is this it? Is it?

LARRY. Put it down.

JEAN-LOUIS (*shouting*). Is this your dignity?

LARRY. In a way, yes. Now put it down. Just give it to me!

JEAN-LOUIS. And when you take it off?

LARRY (*trying to snatch the suit*). Give it to me!

JEAN-LOUIS. What's underneath when you take it off?

LARRY (*hitting his chest*). This! *This*! A bloke on hard times! But my pride's okay, don't worry about that!

JEAN-LOUIS. Pride in what?

LARRY. Give my jacket back!

JEAN-LOUIS. Pride in *what*?

LARRY (*yelling*). Give it back! Give it back!

JEAN-LOUIS (*throwing the suit to* LARRY). Here you are. It's quite empty, you know!

Silence. LARRY *is suddenly confused and dejected. After a while:*

LARRY. You've spoilt my holiday. (*Silence.*) I wanted to give my wife a good time. And you've spoilt it. You don't care that my Marje hasn't had a holiday in seven years. You don't care that she's talking of leaving me. You didn't know she was talking of leaving me, did you? Now I may not be an intellectual. I don't have to be an intellectual to know that if Marje leaves me, I'm done for. All my flaming life, I've done my best, and the whole stinking stuck-up world spits on my best. What's underneath, everyone asks. On and on and on. What's going on under your suit, Larry? Why don't you show us what's underneath, so that we can spit on that, too. Well, I'll show you what's underneath . . .

LARRY *starts to take off his clothes.*

No better than you, Jean-Louis, or you, Trist, but no flaming worse! You spit on me if you like. I can take it! The whole world spits on the small man. Go on! Go on! And what about the rain Marje said she could feel? She's always right, Marjorie. All my life, she's been right and I've been wrong. So let's feel the bloody rain! Come on, rain, don't let Marje down! Don't let Marje be wrong for once in her sweet life!

LARRY *is now unzipping his trousers.*

MARJE (*emerging from the tent*). Larry, what are you doing?

LARRY. Can't you see for yourself? I'm offering myself!

MARJE. Put your trousers back on, Larry.

LARRY. I'm the one that everyone wants to spit on. They all want to have a go, even you, dear, with your talk of desertion and home to mother. So here I am, Marjorie! Now's your moment!

LARRY *is now naked.* MARJE *is near to tears.*

MARJE. Larry, don't do that. Put your knickers on, dear, please . . .

LARRY (*lying flat on the ground*). Come on rain! Here I am! Come on, you sodding rain!

MARJE (*in tears*). Put your clothes on, Larry.

LARRY. Leave me alone, Marjorie. I'm waiting for the rain. All it ever does in England: rain through the cracks in the roof, rains down all my walls with their pigshit stink. So rain now, you bastards! Spit on the little man!

MARJE. Stop it, Larry!

LARRY. Let go of me, Marjorie.

MARJE. Get up love, Please.

LARRY (*kicking his feet, like an angry child*). Come on, you sky! Rain for Marje and her mother! Rain for them!

MARJE (*unable to lift* LARRY). Jean-Louis, help me . . .

LARRY (*suddenly sitting up*). Don't you *dare*! Don't you dare ask for help. We don't need help from anyone, you understand? Not from *anyone*.

MARJE (*still tearful*). Larry, I've heated the soup. Please come and have some.

LARRY *gets up and begins tugging on his clothes.*

LARRY. No! We're off. You were wrong about the rain. You were wrong for once, weren't you? You were wrong, wrong, *wrong*! So we're going. *Now.* And you others just clear off, please. We've got packing to do.

JEAN-LOUIS. It won't be any different anywhere else.

LARRY. You just piss off.

JEAN-LOUIS. Okay, okay . . .

LARRY. And take your food. We don't want it.

JEAN-LOUIS, ANNETTE, *and* TRIST *begin to wander away.* LARRY *turns to* MARJE, *who is still weeping.*

LARRY. Now you find the dismantling instructions, please. I'll get everything out of the tent, and you find the dismantling brochure.

MARJE. I don't know how this happened. We were having a nice time . . .

LARRY. Okay, okay, I'll find it myself. In the wall pockets, is it?

MARJE. What, Larry?

LARRY. The dismantling instructions. Where are they?

MARJE. I don't know.

LARRY. Oh, lost, are they? Thrown away, are they, like every other thing of value? Okay, well any fool can dismantle a tent. You just start deflating the airbeds, and I'll pack up the rest of this junk, and I'll get the tent down.

MARJE. Oh, Larry . . .

LARRY. This is no time for crying, Marjorie. You've got to help me. How one's meant to know one sodding pole from another I'll never know!

LARRY *kicks out at the tent poles and part of the tent collapses.*

MARJE. It's falling, Larry!

LARRY. I know it's bloody falling! Look at it, stupid thing! When I hired that idiotic thing, I thought, okay, it's not the Ritz, okay, I'll never afford the Ritz, but I'll put that up in a bloody marvellous spot, with pines and wild flowers and no smell of pigshit, and feel the sun come through the plastic windows, and say to myself, I'm as good as the next bloke, bought my wife a holiday, bought us a bit of peace . . .

LARRY *is now choked and tired. His energy and anger have now drained away. He sits at the table.*

Oh God . . .

MARJE. It's all right, Larry. Here's the soup, dear.

LARRY. I don't really want it, Marje.

MARJE. I know.

LARRY. I'm cold, Marje.

MARJE. Yes. Have the soup, dear.

LARRY. I'll find a really nice place for the tent. You do see that we've got to be moving on?

MARJE. Eat the soup, Larry.

LARRY. I mean, we can't stand still, Marje. Not after what happened here tonight. I couldn't stay to be humiliated.

MARJE. I don't think it was like that, Larry.

LARRY. Like that?

MARJE. I don't think humiliation's what it was.

LARRY. I made a fool of myself. Just let myself go. I haven't a shred of dignity left, not with these people. I mean, they've seen it all, haven't they? Complete strangers and they've seen it all.

MARJE. I don't think they minded.

LARRY (*beginning to eat the soup*). Course they minded. Just feel sorry for me, making an idiot of myself. Broke all my own rules, lost control . . .

MARJE. Perhaps it's quite good for you.

LARRY. Good for me? What's good about it?

MARJE. Having a bit of a let-go. Just now and then.

LARRY. You're not leaving me, Marje, are you?

MARJE. Let's talk about it all some other time.

LARRY. No. I'd be sunk without you, Marje. Sunk . . . I know it. And you're right about the sties. We can't go on there. So we may have to look at the school situation. I mean, I'm willing, dear, because I do see that rugger doesn't equip a boy for life. Just as long as you don't desert us, Marje. Okay?

MARJE. I won't desert you.

ANNETTE *has wandered over quietly to* LARRY *and* MARJE.

ANNETTE. I'm sorry. I don't want to interrupt . . .

MARJE (*quiet*). Hello, Annette dear.

ANNETTE. I just wanted to tell you: Jean-Louis and me, we have been in all the campsites in the region. We know them. All are quite crowded now in the summer, and we think you are best here. This one is the best.

Silence. LARRY *eats the soup.*

I just wanted to tell you . . .

MARJE. Thank you, dear. (*Then tentative.*) I don't think we'll be going tonight, will we, Larry?

LARRY (*after a pause*). Tent's half down, Marje.

MARJE. I dare say we can put it up again.

ANNETTE. Oh yes. We can help, if you like . . .

Long pause.

LARRY (*to* ANNETTE). Didn't mean . . . what I said about Jean-Louis. (*Pause.*) He's a first-rate poet, I wouldn't wonder. Always envied anyone who could write and I . . . never want to underestimate a person, but I think I . . . well . . . with a lot of types of people I think I haven't had much practice.

A 50's style 5-piece band playing 'Dancing In The Dark'. It gradually fades.

TRIST. I moved on when Larry and Marje left. I began to go south and east into Italy. I also began a diary, that night of the Rose Ball, and the diary became a book, and the writer in me is eclipsing the actor rather nicely.

Pause.

Larry and Marje and Jean-Louis and Annette all went to the ball together, and came back at two in the morning, four unlikely friends, drunk together.

Pause.

I didn't go near the ball. I stayed behind, like Cinders, except that my Prince Charming has long ridden away.

Pause. He sighs.

I sometimes have these dreams about Larry. I don't know why on earth I should dream about him, except that the night of the ball was important for us both and I find myself wondering how he's got on since then.

Bring up 'Dancing in the Dark'.
Hold briefly. Then fade out.

Methuen's Modern Plays

Jean Anouilh	*Antigone*
	Becket
	The Lark
John Arden	*Serjeant Musgrave's Dance*
	The Workhouse Donkey
	Armstrong's Last Goodnight
John Arden and	*The Business of Good Government*
Margaretta D'Arcy	*The Royal Pardon*
	The Hero Rises Up
	The Island of the Mighty
	Vandaleur's Folly
Wolfgang Bauer	*Shakespeare the Sadist*
Rainer Werner Fassbinder	*Bremen Coffee*
Peter Handke	*My Foot My Tutor*
Frank Xaver Kroetz	*Stallerhof*
Brendan Behan	*The Quare Fellow*
	The Hostage
	Richard's Cork Leg
Edward Bond	*A-A-America!* and *Stone*
	Saved
	Narrow Road to the Deep North
	The Pope's Wedding
	Lear
	The Sea
	Bingo
	The Fool and *We Come to the River*
	Theatre Poems and Songs
	The Bundle
	The Woman
	The Worlds with *The Activists Papers*
	Restoration and *The Cat*
	Summer and *Fables*
Bertolt Brecht	*Mother Courage and Her Children*
	The Caucasian Chalk Circle
	The Good Person of Szechwan
	The Life of Galileo

	The Threepenny Opera
	Saint Joan of the Stockyards
	The Resistible Rise of Arturo Ui
	The Mother
	Mr Puntila and His Man Matti
	The Measures Taken and other Lebrstücke
	The Days of the Commune
	The Messingkauf Dialogues
	Man Equals Man and *The Elephant Calf*
	The Rise and Fall of the City of Mahagonny and *The Seven Deadly sins*
	Baal
	A Respectable Wedding and other one-act plays
	Drums in the Night
	In the Jungle of Cities
	Fear and Misery of the Third Reich and *Senora Carrar's Rifles*
Brecht Weill Lane	*Happy End*
Howard Brenton	*The Churchill Play*
	Weapons of Happiness
	Epsom Downs
	The Romans in Britain
	Plays for the Poor Theatre
	Magnificence
	Revenge
	Hitler Dances
Howard Brenton and David Hare	*Brassneck*
Mikhail Bulgakov	*The White Guard*
Noël Coward	*Hay Fever*
Shelagh Delaney	*A Taste of Honey*
	The Lion in Love
David Edgar	*Destiny*
	Mary Barnes

Michael Frayn	*Clouds*
	Alphabetical Order and Donkey's Years
	Make and Break
	Noises Off
	Benefactors
Max Frisch	*The Fire Raisers*
	Andorra
	Triptych
Jean Giraudoux	*The Trojan War Will Not Take Place*
Simon Gray	*Butley*
	Otherwise Engaged and other plays
	Dog Days
	The Rear Column and other plays
	Close of Play and Pig in a Poke
	Stage Struck
	Quartermaine's Terms
Peter Handke	*Offending the Audience* and *Self-Accusation*
	Kaspar
Kaufman & Hart	*The Ride Across Lake Constance*
	They Are Dying Out
	Once in a Lifetime, You Can't Take It With You and *The Man Who Came To Dinner*
Barrie Keeffe	*Gimme Shelter (Gem, Gotcha, Getaway)*
	Barbarians (Killing Time, Abide With Me, In the City)
	A Mad World, My Masters
Arthur Kopit	*Indians*
	Wings
John McGrath	*The Cheviot, the Stag and the Black, Black Oil*
David Mamet	*Glengarry Glen Ross*
David Mercer	*After Haggerty*
	The Bankrupt and other plays
	Cousin Vladimir and *Shooting the Chandelier*
	Duck Song
	Huggy Bear and other plays

	The Monster of Karlovy Vary and *Then and Now*
	No Limits To Love
Arthur Miller	*The American Clock*
Percy Mtwa, Mbongeni Ngema, Barney Simon	*Woza Albert*
Peter Nichols	*Passion Play*
	Poppy
Joe Orton	*Loot*
	What the Butler Saw
	Funeral Games and *The Good and Faithful Servant*
	Entertaining Mr Sloane
	Up Against It
Harold Pinter	*The Birthday Party*
	The Room and *The Dumb Waiter*
	The Caretaker
	A Slight Ache and other plays
	The Collection and *The Lover*
	The Homecoming
	Tea Party and other plays
	Landscape and *Silence*
	Old Times
	No Man's Land
	Betrayal
	The Hothouse
	Other Places (A Kind of Alaska, Victoria Station, Family Voices)
Luigi Pirandello	*Henry IV*
	Six Characters in Search of an Author
Stephen Poliakoff	*Hitting Town* and *City Sugar*
David Rudkin	*The Sons of Light*
	The Triumph of Death
Jean-Paul Sartre	*Crime Passionnel*
Wole Soyinka	*Madmen and Specialists*
	The Jero Plays
	Death and the King's Horseman
C.P. Taylor	*And a Nightingale Sang . . .*

	Good
Peter Whelan	*The Accrington Pals*
Nigel Williams	*Line 'Em*
	Class Enemy
Charles Wood	*Veterans*
Theatre Workshop	*Oh What a Lovely War!*
Various authors	*Best Radio Plays of 1978* (Don Haworth: *Episode on a Thursday Evening:* Tom Mallin: *Halt! Who Goes There?;* Jennifer Phillips: *Daughters of Men;* Fay Weldon: *Polaris;* Jill Hyem: *Remember Me;* Richard Harris: *Is It Something I Said?)*
	Best Radio Plays of 1979 (Shirley Gee: *Typhoid Mary;* Carey Harrison: *I Never Killed My German;* Barrie Keeffe: *Heaven Scent;* John Kirkmorris: *Coxcombe;* John Peacock: *Attard in Retirement;* Olwen Wymark: *The Child)*
	Best Radio Plays of 1982 (Rhys Adrian: *Watching the Plays Together;* John Arden: *The Old Man Sleeps Alone;* Harry Barton: *Hoopoe Day;* Donald Chapman: *Invisible Writing;* Tom Stoppard: *The Dog It Was That Died;* William Trevor: *Autumn Sunshine)*

The Master Playwrights

Collections of plays by the best-known modern playwrights in value-for-money paperbacks.

John Arden	PLAYS: ONE *Serjeant Musgrave's Dance, The Workhouse Donkey, Armstrong's Last Goodnight*
Brendan Behan	THE COMPLETE PLAYS *The Hostage, The Quare Fellow, Richard's Cork Leg, Moving Out, A Garden Party, The Big House*
Edward Bond	PLAYS: ONE *Saved, Early Morning, The Pope's Wedding* PLAYS: TWO *Lear, The Sea, Narrow Road to the Deep North, Black Mass, Passion*
Noël Coward	PLAYS: ONE *Hay Fever, The Vortex, Fallen Angels, Easy Virtue* PLAYS: TWO *Private Lives, Bitter Sweet, The Marquise, Post-Mortem* PLAYS: THREE *Design for Living, Cavalcade, Conversation Piece,* and *Hands Across the Sea, Still Life* and *Fumed Oak* from *Tonight at 8.30* PLAYS: FOUR *Blithe Spirit, This Happy Breed, Present Laughter* and *Ways and Means, The Astonished Heart* and *Red Peppers* from *Tonight at 8.30* PLAYS: FIVE *Relative Values, Look After Lulu, Waiting in the Wings, Suite in Three Keys*
John Galsworthy	FIVE PLAYS *Strife, The Eldest Son, The Skin Game, Justice, Loyalties*

Henrik Ibsen	*Translated and introduced by Michael Meyer* PLAYS: ONE *Ghosts, The Wild Duck, The Master Builder* PLAYS: TWO *A Doll's House, An Enemy of the People, Hedda Gabler* *PLAYS: THREE* *Rosmersholm, Little Eyolf, The Lady from the Sea* PLAYS: FOUR *John Gabriel Borkman, The Pillars of Society, When We Dead Awaken*
Molière	FIVE PLAYS *The Misanthrope, Tartuffe, The School for Wives, The Miser, The Hypochondriac*
Clifford Odets	SIX PLAYS *Waiting for Lefty, Awake and Sing! Till the Day I Die, Paradise Lost, Golden Boy, Rocket to the Moon (introduced by Harold Clurman)*
Joe Orton	THE COMPLETE PLAYS *Entertaining Mr Sloane, Loot, What the Butler Saw, The Ruffian on the Stair, The Erpingham Camp, Funeral Games, The Good and Faithful Servant*
Harold Pinter	PLAYS: ONE *The Birthday Party, The Room, The Dumb Waiter, A Slight Ache, A Night Out* PLAYS: TWO *The Caretaker, Night School, The Dwarfs, The Collection, The Lover, five revue sketches* PLAYS: THREE *The Homecoming, Tea Party, The Basement, Landscape, Silence, six revue sketches* PLAYS: FOUR *Old Times, No Man's Land, Betrayal, Monologue, Family Voices*

Terrence Rattigan	PLAYS: ONE *French Without Tears, The Winslow Boy, The Browning Version, Harlequinade*
Strindberg	*Introduced and translated by Michael Meyer* PLAYS: ONE *The Father, Miss Julie, The Ghost Sonata* PLAYS: TWO *The Dance of Death, A Dream Play, The Stronger*
J.M. Synge	THE COMPLETE PLAYS *In the Shadow of the Glen, Riders to the Sea, The Tinker's Wedding. The Well of the Saints, The Playboy of the Western World, Deirdre of the Sorrows*
Oscar Wilde	THREE PLAYS *Lady Windermere's Fan, An Ideal Husband, The Importance of Being Earnest*
P.G. Wodehouse	FOUR PLAYS *The Play's the Thing, Good Morning, Bill, Leave it to Psmith, Come On, Jeeves*

	ANATOL *(translated by Frank Marcus)*
Synge	THE PLAYBOY OF THE WESTERN WORLD *(introduced by T.R. Henn)*
Tolstoy	THE FRUITS OF ENLIGHTENMENT *(translated and introduced by Michael Frayn)*
Wedekind	SPRING AWAKENING *(translated by Edward Bond; introduced by Edward and Elisabeth Bond)*
Wilde	THE IMPORTANCE OF BEING EARNEST *(introduced by Adeline Hartcup)* LADY WINDERMERE'S FAN *(introduced by Hesketh Pearson)*